YOUNG PEOPLE'S UNDERSTANDINGS OF MEN'S VIOLENCE AGAINST WOMEN

For my children

Young People's Understandings of Men's Violence Against Women

NANCY LOMBARD
Glasgow Caledonian University, UK

ASHGATE

Published by
Ashgate Publishing Limited
Wey Court East
Union Road
Farnham
Surrey, GU9 7PT
England

Ashgate Publishing Company
110 Cherry Street
Suite 3-1
Burlington, VT 05401-3818
USA

www.ashgate.com

British Library Cataloguing in Publication Data
A catalogue record for this book is available from the British Library.

The Library of Congress has cataloged the printed edition as follows:
Lombard, Nancy, 1977–
Young people's understandings of men's violence against women / by Nancy Lombard.
pages cm
Includes bibliographical references and index.
ISBN 978-1-4724-1991-0 (hardback)—ISBN 978-1-4724-1992-7 (ebook)—ISBN 978-1-4724-1993-4 (epub) 1. Women—Violence against. 2. Violence in men. I. Title.
HV6250.4.W65L66 2015
362.82'92—dc23

2014042386

ISBN 9781472419910 (hbk)
ISBN 9781472419927 (ebk – PDF)
ISBN 9781472419934 (ebk – ePUB)

Printed in the United Kingdom by Henry Ling Limited, at the Dorset Press, Dorchester, DT1 1HD

Contents

Acknowledgements

Writing these acknowledgements is something I have really been looking forward to. It confirms that the process is (almost) over and provides an opportunity to reflect upon the journey and all those that have helped me along the way. This book arises from my doctoral thesis and the many talks and discussions I have given about the findings. Firstly, I would like to thank all the young people who took part in this research. Without their input, enthusiasm and time this book would not have been possible.

I would like to say a big thank you to Linda McKie for giving me the original 'life-changing' opportunity of the PhD and for always believing that I could do it. I am grateful to the many wonderful colleagues I have met since moving back into academia who I now count as good friends, Dave Gadd, Liz Jagger, John Stewart, Jeni Harden, Louise Dobbie, Rachel Russell, Alice MacLean, Lani Russell, Angela O'Hagan, Susan Batchelor, Lesley McMillan, Sarah Morton, Oona Brooks, Clare McFeely, Melanie McCarry, Andrew Paterson, Evan Stark and Anne Flitcraft.

Nel Whiting deserves a special mention for her unrelenting enthusiasm when mine was seriously waning and for providing that initial platform at Scottish Women's Aid to disseminate my findings. Thanks also to those who work in the VAW sector (Lesley Orr, Ellie Hutchinson, Jenny Kemp, Laura Thomson, Mhairi McGowan and Marsha Scott) for providing opportunities, training ideas and inspiration. Also, to the women and children at North Kensington Women's Aid and Burnley Women's Aid, your lives, determination and resilience inspired me to try and make a difference.

Thanks also to my friends (in particular, Karen, Claire, Jim, Alison, Ali, Christine and Gill) who have been my rocks over the years, providing shoulders, laughter and fizzy wine. Thank you also to my Roy. His absolute conviction and belief in me has meant more than he will ever know. There is a feminist saying that behind every successful woman is a man who tried to stop her. Well behind me is a good, loving, gentle and beautiful man who has supported me every step of the way – he really is a star.

I would also like to say a big thank you to all my family who weren't always sure what it was that I was doing but knew it was taking a long time, Dad, Dave, Jenny and the rest of you. Also, to my mum, for always looking after me, encouraging my education, those countless phone calls and for helping me in ways only my mum can. In part, much of my interest in this area arose because of the family my mum grew up in. A family which produced four very strong-minded, inspiring women who each dealt with abuse in very different ways. So, Grandma Mary, Aunty Frances, Aunty Pat and mum, this continues to be my journey for you.

And finally, this book is for my children, for whom I continue in my quest to change the world: Dylan, Milo, Autumn Mary and Baby Bombard.

Chapter 1
Violence

> Violence against women is not the result of random, individual acts of misconduct, but rather is deeply rooted in structural relationships of inequality between women and men.
>
> United Nations 2006

This book examines how young(er) people, aged 11 and 12, define, construct and understand violence, specifically *men's violence against women* (incorporating physical, emotional, sexual, psychological and economic abuses) and including *domestic violence and abuse.* Men's violence against women is both a socially constructed and endorsed social problem. As such, the solutions to challenging and preventing it lie within those same systems of constructed power and gendered inequity. The research upon which this book is based enabled young people to explore their own understandings of violence against women and in doing so how this relates to their constructions of normative gendered roles.

Gender and violence pervade and shape young people's social relations and understandings very powerfully, already informing both their own understandings and, at times, their own actions (McCarry 2010; Barter 2014; Gadd 2014; Gadd et al. 2014). By using the broad term of *men's violence against women,* the gendered dynamics inherent within the concept of 'violence' are made explicit. A short discussion of domestic violence and abuse is undertaken in this introductory chapter to explain why it was necessary to include the terms within the research, whilst also highlighting the need to broaden the scope to include all forms of violence against women.

Purpose of the Book

There are two aims of this book. The first is to confront and challenge the 'everyday' occurrence and acceptability of the social problem of men's violence against women (Stanko 1985). It is an issue that impacts upon everyone, not only the lives of adults or those who are judged old enough to talk about it. As young people have generally not been given the power to define violence, here they are afforded the ability to 'name' violence (Kelly 1988) as they understand it. Enabling young people to engage with the discursive issues of men's violence against women and explore their own perceptions can be one way to look beyond the 'public' or powerful appropriation of the concept. Part of their construction involved drawing upon their own experiential knowledge and everyday understandings, which may be at odds with dominant discourses or officially recognised definitions. Specifically this book will examine how young people aged 11 and 12 name and define men's violence against women and interpret how they explain and account for its occurrence.

The second aim is to challenge the perception that 11- and 12-year-olds are too young to 'know' about violence or to offer opinions on it. This is achieved in two ways, by finding ways to talk to younger people about men's violence and through confronting preconceptions of younger people's existing knowledge, capabilities and understanding thereby demonstrating that this is an area that young people can happily and confidently participate in using appropriate research methods.

Defining and Naming Violence

There are differing debates around the actual defining of violence, men's violence and domestic violence, demonstrating how such definitions have concurrently both shaped people's understanding and been indicative of the advancement of the feminist project (Lombard and Whiting 2015). Violence can take many forms; it can be legally sanctioned or condemned with various intentions or motives: power, political, accident, repercussion and retaliation. Violence can involve a myriad of behaviours and a multitude of consequences, physical injuries, emotional abuses, personal and sexual violations or material deprivations. That certain acts of men's violence are still considered 'understandable', 'defensible' and 'honourable' demonstrates that particular discourses still endorse some expressions of men's violence (Gill 2013; Lombard 2013b, 2014). The historical legacy of the UK and other western countries, evidenced through religious, legal and social and political examples, accepted, endorsed and legalised men's right to control and physically chastise their partner and children (Clark 1992; Lentz 1999). For example, in law children may still be chastised using 'reasonable force' (Children (Scotland) Bill 1995). It is argued here, that young people's views are significant because they are living in a time and a culture where many aspects of men's violence against women are outwardly condemned and are subject to consequence.

There have been numerous studies that have looked at 'interpersonal' violence, seeking to label men and women as equal combatants (Gelles 1983, 1987, 1993, 1997; Straus et al. 1980), undertaking 'mutual acts of aggression' (Fergusson et al. 2005: 1,116) and endorsing women as being as violent as men (see Steinmetz 1977–1978). Continuous research contradicts this gender symmetric view of violence, as well as disputing the role of women as equal aggressors (Gadd et al. 2002; Johnson 2005; McFeely 2013; Stark 2007).

Men's Violence Against Women: Gendered Violence

The term 'men's violence' is used in this book. Hearn (1998) and others (see Kimmel 1987) have argued for the need to focus upon *men* and not *maleness*. To do so renders such violence innate and therefore the options for change are limited. It is important however that in appropriating the term *men's* violence we do not detract from the behaviour and actions of *boys*.

Gender is integral to 'the way we speak, conceptualise and challenge violence' (Stanko 2006: 551) whether it is violence that is experienced, perpetrated or witnessed. Gender is significant because men's violence is so often treated as gender neutral through terms such as 'spousal abuse', 'date rape', 'sexual harassment', 'marital rape', 'battery' and 'child sexual abuse' (Hague and Malos 1998). Skinner et al. (2005) maintain the use of 'gender violence' is a more inclusive term than (men's) violence against women as the definition does not restrict itself to women but engages with the theoretical connection between violence and gender relations thus including gay and lesbian people as well as children and young people. The term 'gender violence' also incorporates a wider definition of abuses and violations including prostitution and trafficking as well as violence where women are the perpetrators (Skinner et al. 2005: 3).

A gendered analysis of men's violence views it as a manifestation of 'male' power that is replicated and endorsed through individual experiences and wider structural inequalities (Dobash and Dobash 1979, 1994; Radford and Kelly 1996; Rowland and Klein 1990). This gendered system of power is termed patriarchy, or patriarchal relations (Hearn 1998, 1999; Lovenduski and Randall 1993; Rowland and Klein 1990) and is propagated through embedded social (and gendered) practices and institutions. It is important to acknowledge the importance of Connell's term patriarchal relations that compensates for many of the shortcomings of the initial concept of patriarchy. Here the two concepts interchangeably, whilst embracing the elaborated dynamics of Connell's term. In viewing patriarchy as a series of relations we are more able to conceptualise its cross-cultural, dynamic and relational status and thus encapsulate its spatial and temporal diversity. This system perpetuates, legitimates and sustains the powerful position of men, as both a group and as individuals.

Gender is the most significant risk factor for domestic abuse (Dobash and Dobash 2004; Johnson 1995, 2005; Stark 2007) meaning that women are more likely to experience violence from their intimate (or ex) partners than men are. This indicates is that the intimate violence is taking place within wider structures of gender inequality. Gender is important in any analysis of violence because men and women use violence in different ways and have different motivations for doing so (Hester 2009).

Gender has been identified as a key component in previous studies looking at young people's views of men's violence (Burton et al. 1998; Burman and

Cartmel 2006; Dublin Women's Aid 1999; Kelly et al. 1991; McCarry 2003, 2007, 2010), alongside wider studies looking at societal attitudes. For example, Kenway and Fitzclarence (1997) found that men's violence against women was legitimated as an accepted part of normative gender roles; it is part of how men are and what they do. This book proposes that young people's position in childhood, impacts upon how they construct and understand men's violence against women and that they draw upon gender to explain certain forms of violence. However, to do this, these constructions of gender are also dependent upon the temporal and spatial positioning of the young people in relation to the violence.

'Naming' Violence

Kelly (1988) developed the concept of the 'continuum of violence' which discouraged the generation of a hierarchy for forms of violence and abuse. As a theoretical framework, it also succeeded in merging the gendered spheres by illuminating the notion that men's normative behaviour and women's oppression crossed these spatial boundaries. Kelly sought to highlight that these examples of men's behaviour, however commonplace for both men and women, were not normal or acceptable and needed to be named and challenged as wrong. In doing so, the continuum facilitated the labelling of apparently normal behaviour as part of men's ability and choice to control, conceptualising commonalities experienced by many women and girls in their day to day lives by 'enabl[ing] women to make sense of their own experiences by showing how 'typical' and 'aberrant' male behaviour shade into one another' (Kelly 1988: 75).

Kelly's definition is highly relevant to my research in that it contextualises violence and abuse as something that is not always experienced or acknowledged as violent at the time. The temporal aspect of this definition is relevant also because of the age of the participants and their own constructions of time and age:

> In the development of the feminist movement, women have seized the power of naming. This is a revolutionary power because in naming (describing) what is done to us (and inevitably to children and men as well), we are also naming what must change. The act of naming creates a new world view. The power of naming resides in the fact that we name what we see from the basis of our own experience within and outside patriarchal culture simultaneously. (Ward 1984: 212)

The feminist project of 'naming', 'involves making visible what was invisible, defining as unacceptable what was acceptable and insisting what was naturalised is problematic' (Kelly 1988: 139). It enables women to name, understand and challenge what has happened (or is happening) to them, by moving the private into the public domain and shifting the boundaries of acceptable and unacceptable behaviour.

This research endorses the feminist arguments of naming, of knowledge and of power (Dobash and Dobash 1979; Kelly 1988; Stanley and Wise 1993), by locating the young people within a framework that recognises and respects their own language, understandings and situated knowledge. Indeed, it is through lived experiences of childhood that young people explore their own understandings and constructions of violence, with such experiences also informing their knowledge of normative gender roles (Renold 2005). Dobash and Dobash maintain such knowledge is critical in understanding the 'everyday' nature of male violence:

> [l]ocating violence in the midst of daily life demands a focus on the mundane, the ordinary rather than the extraordinary, the conflicts of interest embedded in daily life, and the rationales and justifications of perpetrators as well as the reactions and responses of victims. (Dobash and Dobash 1992: 142)

As such, Kelly's continuum is useful as a tool in this research, to name and locate men's violence, by generating a means to situate it within everyday life. The concept also incorporates the temporal and spatial characteristics of men's violence, in that the violence may occur over time, or is located a long time in the past, or can impinge upon present and future lives. For example, Kelly (1988: 23) claims the experience and/or naming of violence is not always an immediate or present one, rather it can be 'experienced by the woman or girl at the time or later, as a threat, invasion or assault'. This is relevant in enabling young people themselves, to have a role in the naming of behaviour that they may understand as problematic, or not recognised by others, particularly those in authority.

However, Hearn (1999: 131) argues against laying the task of 'naming' solely at the door of women. He maintains that they may have normalised the events and therefore find it difficult to challenge this or to link it to public discourses of violence that do not reflect their own experiences. Instead Hearn argues for the involvement of men in this process to compel them to recognise their own actions and consequences as violent and abusive. The involvement of all men (and boys) is necessary for this reason and is one step in the direction of countering the huge personal, interpersonal and social costs of violence that continue to be borne by women and their supporters. This journey has begun with the promotion of non-violent masculinities and the continued contribution of men in the movement (for example, the White Ribbon Campaign and the UN Women campaign He For She). As such it should also be the responsibility of men (and boys) to also recognise their behaviour as unacceptable. Encouraging men to challenge their own and others' behaviour, highlights the potential dynamism of men's role in changing the patriarchal relations of society. As Connell (1995, 2000) has claimed, the structures of patriarchy thrive on women's resistance and men's acceptance.

The Magnitude of the Problem

The United Nations states that there are three areas where men's violence against women manifests itself: within the family, within the community and that perpetrated by the state.

> Violence against women is remains pervasive worldwide. It is the most atrocious manifestation of the systematic discrimination and inequality women continue to face, in law and in their everyday lives, around the word. It occurs in every region, country and culture, regardless of income, class, race, or ethnicity. (United Nations (UN) secretary-general Kofi Annan 2005)

Unlike men who are most likely to be victims of stranger assaults and violence, women and children are attacked, beaten, raped and killed by their family and partners (Department of Health 2000; World Health Organisation 2005) with the patterns and types of violence illustrating the persuasive inequalities between men and women (Bond and Philips 2000). Globally, nationally and locally, men's violence against women is endemic within all societies:

> At least one out of every three women has been beaten, coerced into sex, or otherwise abused in her lifetime … Usually the abuser is a member of her own family or someone known to her. (Amnesty International 2004)

Women are identified as the 'most heavily abused group' being more likely to experience interpersonal violence, especially violence of a sexualised nature including rape and sexual assault (Walby and Allen 2004; World Health Organization 2005; Watts and Zimmerman 2002). Murder statistics indicate that on average two women a week are killed by a current or former partner in the UK (Flood-Page et al. 2003; Scottish Government Statistical Bulletin 2013).

In 2014, the Europe wide study by the European Union Agency for Fundamental Rights found that one in three women have experienced abuse in their lifetime; one in ten within the past 12 months. Findings from the British Crime Survey (Walby and Allen 2004) reveal that almost one in two (45 per cent) women has experienced some form of domestic violence, sexual assault or stalking illustrating again that gender is a 'significant risk factor' in victimisation. The England and Wales Crimes Survey (EWCS) reported that 1.2 million women had experienced domestic violence in 2011–2012 (Dar 2013). In 2012–2013, the police in Scotland attended a domestic incident every nine minutes, accounting for 15 per cent of all violent crime in Scotland. In this same period 60,080 domestic incidents were recorded with 60 per cent of incidents involving a repeat offender. There were 11 domestic abuse related homicides, 313 attempted murders and serious assaults and 248 sexual offences recorded (Scottish Government Statistical Bulletin 2013).

The gendered trends of this violence and the systematic power inequalities that it (re)produces illustrates the global and national scale at which women and girls suffer abuse at the hands of men known to them. However, official data cannot provide a full analysis of the true extent of men's violence against women, as it is both under reported and under recorded (Kelly et al. 2006) as well as being so 'deeply embedded' in cultures that it is almost 'invisible' (UNICEF 1997: 41):

> Whilst clear categories and definitions are important for statistical and research purposes, we must never forget that these are abstract analytic concepts developed for a specific purpose – to count the extent of violence. They do not reflect experiential reality, which is always more complex. (Kelly 2000, Domestic Violence: Enough is Enough conference, London, October)

Websdale et al. (1998) also argue that the magnitude of such violence cannot simply be documented through the use of official or hidden figures alone, but needs to be viewed in conjunction with women's social, economic and political subjugation. This relationship can be achieved through the application of sociological theory and understanding to the phenomena of men's violence against women.

Much of the violence remains hidden or unreported because of a reluctance to report for fear of being disbelieved, or being doubly victimised by the criminal justice system and also because of a lack of faith in the low rates of conviction (Lees 1993; McMillan 2013). Statistics also remain partial because of the process by which they are collated and the methods by which categories of violence are determined and defined. Discrepancies also arise from the use of conflicting definitions, methodologies, measurements and contexts (Johnson, 1998; Walby and Myhill 2001; Dar 2013). Some forms of abuse that women may experience are not labelled as 'violence' by legal codes or frameworks and thus are not classified as crimes. Indeed, as Greenan (2004: 18) astutely asserts, some areas of women's experience remain invisible in any attempt at 'counting'. Even when instances of violence reach the definitive realms of the criminal justice system, they may then be 'no crimed' (see Lees 1997)[1] or the charges downgraded. Global agencies such as Amnesty International have attempted to counter localised and judicial discrepancies by declaring that all violence against women should be seen as a violation of their human rights leading to the creation of new international standards and practice, such as the definition of rape as a war crime and a crime against humanity in the statutes of international crime tribunals (Amnesty International 2004), with such violence consistently viewed as the most universal human rights violation (Bond and Philips 2000).

Locating Men's Violence Against Women: Domestic Abuse

Domestic violence has been recognised as the most prevalent form of violence against women (Orr 2007) in its various guises and perpetrations:

> domestic violence has both received far more attention and has been more defined as a gendered crime in recent government guidance and legislation than any other kind of men's violences'. (Hearn et al. 2002: 211)

Thus it is often crucial to separate domestic violence from other forms of violence so as not to, as Kelly suggests, engender a contradiction:

> There is, however, a contradiction at the heart of treating domestic violence as a crime 'like any other', because it isn't. The fact that it takes place in private, between parties who have/had an intimate relationship, and may be connected to each other in complicated ways … makes a difference. (Kelly 2000)

Some government departments, agencies and voluntary groups use the terms men's violence against women and domestic violence concurrently, while others specify the use of one or the other. In common with psychosocial models (see Bacchi 1999), it is questionable whether it is useful to construct violence against women as a subset of general societal violence. Whilst the issues are not wholly separate and there are elements of all forms of violence and abuse that overlap with others, domestic violence has received particular attention both theoretically and through policy and practice in Scotland (where this research is based).

Indeed Stanko (2006: 546) insists that familiarity between perpetrator and victim *disables a language of criminal harm.* It is important here to acknowledge domestic violence as a form of men's violence that has been traditionally and theoretically positioned within the private sphere, historically and socially

---

1 This describes the process whereby the incident is reported but does not proceed to court.

located as 'a women's place' thus associating it with restricted forms of gendered social practice.

McKie (2005) has argued that the term domestic violence has *significant shortcomings as an analytical concept.* It is a degendered concept that emphasises the physicality of violent acts, rather than identifying emotional and financial abuses as well as its cumulative and repetitive nature. It also alludes to the space of the violence as being within the domestic sphere of the home, aligning women with the domestic and glossing over the intimate relationship between offender and victim.[2] In doing so, the lesser value placed upon the private sphere and the gendered alignment of a woman's place are emphasised. The home is also referred to as a safe haven away from the everyday violences of public life. The significance of space and place were explored throughout this research. In using the term 'spatiality' I am arguing against space as simply a physical entity or boundary (such as the home or the street) and instead focusing upon social and spatial practices and the use of space (see Harvey 1993). As such, space and place are identified as socio-cultural constructions rather than physical locations.

Yet focusing upon domestic violence, as a specific form of men's violence against women, has proved of critical importance in generating awareness and political activity and it was for this reason that the young people are asked specifically about their knowledge of the terms domestic violence and domestic abuse. It is also crucial to note how more recent theoretical developments have both grappled with the shortcomings of the terms 'domestic abuse' and 'domestic violence' whilst also consolidating the significance of the gendered definition most notably Stark's (2007) theory of coercive control (Stark 2007) and Johnson's paradigm (2005, 2008) of intimate terrorism. Stark defines coercive control as:

> a strategic course of self-interested behaviour designed to secure and expand gender-based privileged by establishing a regime of domination in personal life … useful to subdivide its tactical dynamics into those used to hurt and intimidate victims and those designed to isolate and control them. (2013: 21)

He maintains it is a liberty crime that prevents women from exercising their social, economic and political rights and responsibilities. Women are unequal in violence because they are unequal in society, in terms of the resources and opportunities they can access; therefore recognising the broader social context in which the violence takes place is crucial (Stark 2007). Johnson and Kelly

---

2 This research recognises the use of the feminist term 'survivor' to describe women's strength and agency in dealing with male violence and abuse but uses the word 'victim' here as it was the term most commonly used and understood by the young people.

(2008) support this view maintaining that the meaning of violence differs greatly depending upon the gender of the perpetrator and that because heterosexual relationships are rooted in patriarchy they further validate men's power. Johnson's term 'intimate terrorism' describes a pattern of coercive control by one partner over another. Physical violence is one of the ways perpetrators gain control within this pattern.

> Thus, although situational couple violence is nearly gender symmetric and not strongly related to gender attitudes, intimate terrorism (domestic violence) is almost entirely male perpetrated and is strongly related to gender attitudes … men's violence produces more frequent and more severe injuries, thereby producing a fear (or even terror) that is quite rare when women are violent toward their male partners. (Johnson 2005: 1,128–29)

'Official' Definitions

Definitions and constructions of violence against women are culturally, historically and spatially specific (Hester et al. 2004). The research was conducted in Glasgow, the city in which both the research participants and I live. Scotland has recognised the social problem of domestic abuse within the continuum of violence against women as a form of gender based violence. In so doing it explicitly acknowledges domestic abuse as an issue which disproportionately affects women and is overwhelmingly perpetrated by men and is associated with long-held cultural assumptions about the roles of men and women in society (Gadd et al. 2002; Lombard 2013a; McFeely et al. 2013).

The social and political context of Scotland is of note as it is the only country in the UK to recognise and facilitate a gender-based definition – see National Strategy to Address Domestic Abuse in Scotland (Scottish Executive 2000) and Preventing Violence Against Women: Action Across the Scottish Executive (Scottish Executive 2001) – thereby acknowledging the 'broader gender inequalities which women face' (Scottish Executive 2000).

> Domestic abuse (as gender based abuse) can be perpetrated by partners or ex-partners and can include physical abuse (assault and physical attack involving a range of behaviour), sexual abuse (acts which degrade and humiliate women and are perpetrated against their will, including rape) and mental and emotional abuse (such as threats, verbal abuse, racial abuse, withholding money and other types of controlling behaviour such as isolation from family and friends) … Domestic abuse is associated with broader gender inequality and should be understood in its historical context, whereby societies have given greater status, wealth, influence, control and power to men. It is part of a range of behaviours

> constituting male abuse of power, and is linked to other forms of male violence. (Scottish Executive 2000: 5)

The adoption of the term 'abuse' in 2000 was intended to better reflect the range of behaviours enacted by perpetrators to control their partners. It highlights that such abuse need not be physical and includes emotional, psychological and financial tactics all of which are used to create compliance in a partner. In Scotland, domestic abuse is set within a wider framework which acknowledges the influence of gender on men and women's lives: the decisions they may make, the status accorded them and the relationship between them. It is important to link together women's experience of abuse through public and private spheres in order to illustrate the extensive nature of men's violence and the different types of abusive behaviours (Kelly and Radford 1996).

The Westminster government updated their definition of domestic violence in 2013. The main differences are their lack of gendered definition and the inclusion of those aged 16 and over within the parameters of it:

> Any incident or pattern of incidents of controlling, coercive or threatening behaviour, violence or abuse between those aged 16 or over who are or have been intimate partners or family members regardless of gender or sexuality. This can encompass, but is not limited to, the following types of abuse:
>
> - psychological
> - physical
> - sexual
> - financial
> - emotional
>
> Controlling behaviour is: a range of acts designed to make a person subordinate and/or dependent by isolating them from sources of support, exploiting their resources and capacities for personal gain, depriving them of the means needed for independence, resistance and escape and regulating their everyday behaviour.
>
> Coercive behaviour is: an act or a pattern of acts of assault, threats, humiliation and intimidation or other abuse that is used to harm, punish, or frighten their victim.*
>
> * This definition, which is not a legal definition, includes so called 'honour' based violence, female genital mutilation (FGM) and forced marriage, and is clear that victims are not confined to one gender or ethnic group. (Home Office 2013)

This book, where appropriate, uses the term domestic violence (whilst also asking the young people about domestic abuse in case this is a term with which they are more familiar). The decision to do so reflects the author's perspective that the term violence is has more common currency among wider legal and social definitions; the desire to enable the young people to link domestic with other forms of violence and to encourage reflection of other forms of violence.

Both Government definitions (Scotland and Westminster) now include coercive control, drawing attention to the *pattern* of behaviour rather than focusing upon specific *incidents* of violence as constitutive of such abuse.

Why Does it Matter What Young People Think?

The case for young people's involvement is made here using the feminist defined arguments that maintains access to naming engenders the creation of knowledge and power (Dobash et al. 1979; Kelly 1988; Stanley and Wise 1993; Williamson 2000) while locating the young people within a framework that epistemologically prioritises their language, understanding and knowledge. This research aims to find out younger people's attitudes to violence against women including how they conceptualise and understand such violence. Stanko (2003a: 11) asserts that the meaning of violence is embedded within its context. Young people therefore, will understand and interpret the discussions and examples of violence through their own subjective lens of identity, gender, age, lived experience and personal relationships. Part of the rationale is to enable the feminist inspired project of 'naming' violence to be appropriated by the young people.

Kelly's influential work on 'naming' violence and her concept of a continuum of violence (to illustrate how the temporal and spatial elements of her work are relevant but often overlooked) are drawn upon in this book. In previous studies and theoretical explanations of men's violence against women the focus has been on the spatial elements of the violence (the sometimes blurred boundaries between public and private spaces) and the gendered nature of power inequities. In bringing in the concept of childhood it is asserted that more emphasis needs to be placed upon the concepts of temporality and spatiality within childhood in order to challenge dominant, static concepts of violence.

Thrift (1983, 2001) has maintained that time and space are central to theorising social action resulting in more recent moves to develop temporality and spatiality as critical theoretical and sociological constructs (see also Giddens 1979; Urry 1996; Valentine 2007). The concept of 'temporality' is defined as 'the time *in* things, events and processes which is unidirectional and irreversible' (Adam 2000: 136, original emphasis). It is applied here to bring together 'age' (as a socially constructed phenomenon) with 'time' (as a dynamic concept).

I use both to demonstrate how young people construct their own understandings around their present knowledge and their anticipations of the future. Time and temporality are crucial concepts in framing childhood but they have been neglected in existing work on violence.

There is no previous research that looks specifically at what 11- and 12-year-olds think about men's violence against women. The work that does exist focuses upon those over the age of 14 (Burton et al. 1998) and more generally on those aged 16 and older (see Burman and Cartmel 2006; Dublin Women's Aid 1999; Kelly et al. 1991; McCarry 2003, 2009, 2010). As a result, understandings of violence have not been theoretically situated within the paradigm of childhood. Whilst feminist theories (Hearn 1998; Hester 2006; Johnson 1995; Kelly 1999; Radford and Hester 2006; Stark 2007) have highlighted violence as gendered, dynamic and transitory, they have not capitalised upon exploring violence as a temporal and spatial phenomenon; concepts which are integral to the paradigm of childhood.

Theories of childhood have ignored younger people's understandings of violence, unless the young people have been personally involved; for example, violence in residential care homes (Barter et al. 2004) and territorial violence among young gang members (Kintrea et al. 2008). There has, however, been an abundance of work on young people's constructions of gender (Brown 2007; O' Donnell and Sharpe 2000; Renold 2000, 2005; Sharpe 1994); relevant here because of the gendered nature of violence (see Burman et al. 2001; Stanko 2006) and young people's constructions of it in their wider understanding of violence.

Research focusing upon young people and 'violent' spaces has examined specific locations such as public spaces (Kintrea et al. 2008) institutions, such as nurseries (Brown 2007) schools (Willis 1977; Mac an Ghaill 1994, 1996), prisons (Batchelor 2007) and the family (Mullender 2004). Space is often defined by adults, rather than by young people, and succeeds in labelling young people as 'bad' ('hoodies', ASBOs, gangs) or as in need of protection. By creating this dichotomy, the binary of 'inside' and 'outside' space has also been reinforced. In doing so the emphasis has been upon the space where the violence occurs rather than the representation of that space by the young people themselves. It is critical to address not just violent spaces but also the concepts of spatiality, distance, location and proximity so as not to simply strengthen gendered dichotomies of violence.

The research on which this book is based, sought to involve younger people, aged 11 and 12 to find out how they constructed and understood men's violence against women. Although legally classed as 'children' because they are under the age of 16, using the term 'young people' alludes to their competencies and responsibilities as participants in this research. The age of the young people in this book was a significant factor for five main reasons:

- Men's violence against women is not limited to certain age groups. Violence is happening in people's lives and in homes where young people and young children live. Ignoring the opinions or refusing to engage with those who are 'too young' or just 'not old enough' does not mean that this violence will cease to exist.
- Young(er) people (those under the age of 14) have previously been overlooked or ignored by attitudes to violence research and are also absent from much of the theoretical literature on violence. James (2005) argues often this is because they are judged by researchers and/or gatekeepers as not old *enough*, thereby questioning the capabilities, understanding and knowledge of young people under a certain age.
- It was thought that by focusing upon young people in the final year of primary school and approaching a period of transition (e.g. the move to secondary school) that they would be presumed by their gatekeepers to be 'older', and therefore more able to engage with the research, making access easier than with even younger age groups.
- As the young people are still within education they can be considered 'educable' in terms of any prevention or awareness raising work that may result from the findings.
- It has been argued that the younger the person, the more receptive they are to new or different ideas (Hendry 1996). Women's Aid has also supported this view through their campaigns for preventive education primary schools.

The Structure of the Book

Chapter 2 draws upon sociological childhood theories to create a framework to explain how young people 'intersect' time and space and gender to construct and make sense of violence, as a fluid and transitory concept. To further illustrate the significance of 'time', 'temporality' and 'space' in young people's own constructions, Adam's (2002) theory of temporality is intersected with existing accounts of the concept of time 'in' and 'of' childhood (see James and Prout 1997; Prout 1990; James et al. 1998). This is overlapped with developing notions of space and spatiality used mainly by cultural geographers (see Bell et al. 1994; Valentine 2007) to illuminate how young people use space to understand violence through notions of distance and proximity – both in physical, emotional and metaphorical terms.

Chapter 3 explores the philosophical underpinnings to the research study. The main aim of this chapter is to provide theoretical and ethical evidence to support the argument that young people can engage constructively on the subject of men's violence. The pivotal work of James and Prout (1997) is critically examined to explain why it was important to challenge assumptions of capability, knowledge and understanding among those previously thought too young to participate in certain research topics. The second half of the chapter explores the process of undertaking the research with its aim being to provide a clear understanding of the rationale behind the choice and implementation of methods and analysis. It details the day-to-day management of the work; an aspect that is sadly lacking in many research projects. The laborious nature of gaining access; negotiating different schools, teachers and participants; conducting fieldwork in differing environments (collating the field notes, questionnaires and transcripts) with competing expectations and outcomes is considered. Time is spent reflecting upon the pilot study and illustrating the changes made in light of this. The chapter concludes with a discussion of how the data was analysed and coded using thematic analysis, honest reflection and critical reflexivity.

Chapter 4 looks at young people's constructions of, and negotiations with, gender. It examines how young people construct their own and others' gender identities focusing specifically upon the themes of embodiment, performance and institutional regimes. Chapter 5 explores the ways in which young people construct violence and how they understand it. The key theme here is the idea of 'real' (defined) violence and how young people sought to naturalise violence perpetrated by men in terms of innate biological traits of anger, physicality and 'toughness'. The concept of a constellation of violence is introduced to illustrate how young people make sense of such violence, detailing the factors that have to be in place to enable them to define actions as violent: gender (men); age (adult); space (outside); actions (physical violence); and consequence (injury and official sanctions). When (abstract) examples followed this linear route they were more likely to judge them as violent. Chapter 6 charts examples of violent behaviour that were likely to be experienced by the young people themselves, 'named' violence. It is explored how such behaviours were less likely to be labelled as violence, particularly if they involved girls as 'victims' (of male peers' actions) and where there was no official consequence (such as the intervention of a teacher). The chapter also focuses upon young people's discussions of the terms domestic violence and abuse and their tendency to minimise and degender its occurrence unless police intervention validated the actions which I argue is in keeping with their constellation of violence. This chapter concludes with the assertion that the proximity of the violence to the young people directly impacts upon how they define (or how they are resistant to name) the violence.

Chapter 7 examines the justifications of men's violence provided by the young people. The themes of gender inequality, male power, normative gender roles and heterosexuality were pertinent in young people's understandings of men's violence against women. It is by anticipating and normalising these frameworks of male power as acceptable that young people construct adult relationships in terms of power, regulation and control and blaming women when things go wrong. It becomes clear through the analysis that young people repeatedly access adulthood to understand certain forms of gender identity and construct adult heterosexuality as a rigid and narrow framework, using heterosexuality as a lens through which to examine men's violence against women.

In Chapter 8, 'A Change is Gonna Come?', I explore the pivotal relationship of violence, gender, time and space through the understandings and voiced knowledge of young people. It draws together the key themes and ideas locating a number of them within existing theoretical frameworks. The original contribution made by intersecting space, gender and age to analyse young people's understanding of men's violence against women is highlighted. The book concludes by drawing together the key themes and illuminating aspects for future policy initiatives.

Chapter 2
Childhood

Young People and Violence

Young people's position in childhood can impact upon how they define, name and understand violence. Yet age, as a conceptual tool (with which to construct or conceive of men's violence against women) has been largely overlooked. When age has been generated as a specific variable, it has been appropriated in terms of the linear stages of 'victimisation': children (under 18) as victims of child abuse (Roberts and Taylor 1993; Wolfner and Gelles 1993) or living within a domestic abuse household (Hester et al. 2000; Mullender 2004) and older women (over 55) as 'victims' (Scott et al. 2004, 2008; Lombard and Scott 2013). What young people think about violence is an under-researched area – with the focus more specifically upon wider (adult) society, particularly in relation to how the issue is perceived and regulated by statutory and non-statutory agencies, such as the police (Dunhill 1989; Grace 1995; Hague 1999); legal institutions and the courts (Barron 1990; Buzawa and Buzawa 1996; Edwards 1981, 1986, 1991; Radford et al. 1996b), social work (Radford and Hester 2006) and health services (García-Moreno 2002; Mildorf 2007).

More recent feminist research and activism have maintained that to challenge and prevent men's violence against women, changing attitudes and behaviour is key, with young people identified as the main 'target' (see Flood 2009a, 2009b; Hester and Westmarland 2005; McCarry 2003, 2009, 2010). Existing feminist research that has examined young people's attitudes to men's violence however, has been less about their *own* constructions of violence and more about how they understand *adult* men's violence as being characteristic of normative *adult* masculinity (see, for example, Burman et al. 2006; Burton et al. 1998; Chung 2005).

For example, McCarry's study (2003), looking at young people aged 15 to 18 in Glasgow secondary schools substantiated existing research that found young people had a high tolerance of men's violence against women, and that they found ways to legitimate it (see also Burton et al. 1998; Mullender et al. 2002). McCarry stated that the young people in her study framed domestic abuse in terms of physical actions (unless it was perpetrated by women), thereby naturalising the associations of men, masculinity and the perpetration of physical violence (see also Connell 2005; Messerschmidt 2000; Stoudt 2006; Totten 2003).

Whilst such research has been critical in informing the need for pragmatic policy intervention, seeking to develop awareness-raising and educational strategies (see Burman et al. 2006; Burton et al. 1998; Dublin Women's Aid 1999; Kelly et al. 1991; McCarry 2003), it has failed to recognise the conceptual framework of childhood as having a critical role in informing constructions of younger age groups.

The lack of research on young people's *present* experiences of men's violence against women has recently been rectified by international studies, with Leach and Humphreys (2007) looking at boys' violence in schools in Africa (with a view to promoting awareness around HIV and AIDS). There have also been wider discussions around the phenomena of (US defined) 'dating' violence, analysing the lived experiences of young people aged 14 and over in relationships (see Allen 2003; Barter and McCarry 2013; Chung 2005; Holland et al. 2004). Barter and McCarry's work (2013), funded by the NSPCC, looked specifically at young people's own experiences of violence and abuse within their intimate relationships. They found that whilst boys experienced some violence, girls' own experiences were of more multiple forms, which were more frequent, severe, and detrimental in their impact. Their study replicated findings from America and Australia, where young women frequently spoke of their persistent experiences of coercive male power (Allen 2003; Chung 2005), although Allen's work offered more examples of young women's own mediations of this power.

This research in this book was premised upon the understanding that 'violence is preventable. The more we gather knowledge about it, the better off we are to contribute to its minimization in society' (Stanko et al. 2003: 11). Part of this 'gathering of knowledge' needs to include the views of younger people who have previously been overlooked.

> Any work with young people about domestic violence must start at a very young age, in all primary schools, because, by the age of 13, attitudes that condone gender violence are already entrenched, particularly among boys. This work needs to focus on gender stereotypes, on mutual respect in intimate relationships, and on challenging the condoning of gendered violence, within a broader context of work on respect, safety and conflict resolution. (Women's Aid's Consultation Response 2003)

To explore these issues and to overcome presumptions about knowledge and capability, younger people (aged 11 and 12) are placed at the centre of this research, located within the social paradigm of 'childhood'.

Childhood

To construct a theoretical framework that explores the multiplicity of young people's constructions of violence, we first need to engage with the paradigm of childhood. James and Prout (1997) and James et al. (1998) theorise childhood as both a social institution and as being defined by the actions of individual children. For Jenks, childhood is:

> [a] social status delineated by boundaries that vary through time and from society to society but which are incorporated within the social structure and thus manifested through and formative of certain typical forms of conduct. Childhood then always relates to a particular cultural setting. (1996: 7)

As such, it is important not to imply that the definitions and experiences of young people are timeless and universal or that age defines experience and knowledge. Rather the assumption here is that the concepts of childhood and age vary across time, space and cultures (see also Brannen et al. 1996; Christensen and James 2000). James and Prout (1997) agree, asserting that childhood is a social construction 'constituted at a particular moment in time and point in space' (1997: 29). In their influential text, James and Prout (1997: 216–17) focus upon time 'in' and 'of' childhood. Time 'in' childhood looks at time as a means of structuring everyday lives, and time 'of' childhood is constituted by the social construction of the ageing process – the 'periodization of the life course'. It is this process of conceptualising the life course (by the young people themselves) that is most pertinent here – but is an approach that others have shied away from, for fear of prioritising adulthood, or the move into adulthood as being more important.

It is necessary to overcome the alignment of age 'with linear time consciousness' (Davies 1989: 185) in order to avoid the construction of childhood as a lesser phenomenon, related to development and progression, which implies that the adult world is complete, in 'statis' and desirable (Brannen and O'Brien 1996; Grieve and Hughes 1990).

Children and Age: Legalities and Perceptions of 'Capability'

The social constructionist paradigm of childhood emphasises the differing ways that young people have been categorised, defined and institutionalised by those with the power to do so: adults (Hendrick 1990: 36). Hendrick charts the temporal and spatial changes to the construction of childhood over the past 200 years, demonstrating how they correspond (and respond) to socio-economic and political challenges of the time:

> Each new construction may be observed in approximate chronological order as: the Romantic child, the Evangelical child, the factory child, the delinquent child, the schooled child, the psycho-medical child, and the welfare child of the era just prior to the first world war. Between 1914 and the late 1950s, further developments produced what might more accurately be described as two 'reconstructions', such they depended so much on their nineteenth century heritage, namely, the child of psychological jurisdiction – meaning child guidance clinics, psycho-analysis, educational psychology, and Bowlbyism; and secondly, the family child (which included the 'public' child, usually children in care). (Hendrick 1990: 36–7)

Hendrick (ibid.) goes on to argue that the perception of childhood in the last 40 years has been harder to distinguish. This is in part due to a paradigm shift in how young people are constructed in their roles in society, policy and research. There has been a jarring between the restrictions of nostalgic tradition and common sense discourses, with a focus upon young people's independent position in civil society and the need for their rights to be recognised.

In the 1960s and '70s precedence was given to a child development model in both practical (often medicalised) research and theoretical definitions of young people, defining biological and social development as synonymous (see, for example, Piaget 1953, 1955, 1977) positioning children and young people as not fully complete and 'lesser' than adults (e.g. ado*les*cence) or human 'becomings' (Qvortrop 1994: 4). It was this reluctance, or inability, to see children as social agents that fostered the development of child centred paradigms and methodology, defined collectively as the sociology of childhood (see James et al. 1998). Many 'child centred' methods have developed to enable young people to become active participants in the research process. Fraser et al. (2004: 23) describes the two conflicting definitions of the term 'child centred'. The first is when the researcher relates to the child in terms of their developmental stage. That is, the methods are consciously infantilised so as to pander to the child's apparent lack of social and intellectual development. The second definition, and one that is embraced by theorists within the new social studies of childhood, is finding appropriate methodologies that engage young people enabling them to negotiate and participate with the research process (Alderson 2000; Barker and Weller 2003; Thomas and O'Kane 1998). Empowering children and young people by giving them a voice is crucial in child centred research but listening to their voices is the key (Prout 2001).

The research in this book is situated within the current legislative climate that has elevated the position of children and young people. At an international level, the United Nations Convention on the Rights of the Child (1989) set down a directive encapsulating the discourse of citizenship for the world's children: the child as an active citizen with rights and responsibilities. These included

> Article 3: In all actions concerning children … *the best interests of the child* shall be a primary consideration.
>
> Article 12: State Parties shall assure to the child who *is capable of forming his or her views the right to express those views* freely in all matters affecting the child, *the views of the child being given due weight in accordance with the age and maturity of the child.*
>
> Article 13: The child shall have the *right to freedom of expression*; this right shall include freedom to seek, receive and impart information and ideas of all kinds.
>
> Article 19: State Parties shall take all appropriate legislative, administrative, social and educational measures to protect the child from all forms of physical or mental violence, injury or abuse, neglect or negligent treatment, maltreatment or exploitation, including sexual abuse, while in the care of parent(s), legal guardian(s) or any other person who has care of the child. (United Nations Convention on the Rights of the Child 1989, my emphasis)

The discourse of citizenship set out above was further ratified in Scotland with the Children's Act (Scotland) 1995, moving away from parental rights towards parental responsibilities and stating that 'a child twelve years of age or more shall be presumed to be of sufficient age and maturity to form a view' (Children's Act (Scotland) 1995: Part 1.6.b). However, much of the legislation focused upon particular rights at certain ages. The establishment of the Children's Parliament and the creation of the post of Scotland's Commissioner for Children and Young People sought to make children's issues and views a higher priority, encourage active citizenship and consultation in policy making. This commitment to listening to the voices of children and young people is expressed in the Child Strategy Statement from the Scottish Executive (2000):

> Children form one fifth of Scotland's population but may have only limited opportunity to consider or comment on policies which impact on them. Whereas most adults are silent by choice, many children are not in a position to have an influence on matters which greatly affect them. In the vast majority of instances, adults in the wider community act effectively in the interests of children. However it remains the case that children have decisions made about, for and against their interests *without their views being taken* or needs properly considered. (Borland et al. 2001: 7–8, my emphasis)

This socio-legal shift in the conceptualisation of children as citizens corresponds with their changing role in research paradigms. However, it needs to be acknowledged that certain ages award young people with specific legal rights or responsibilities (and power); for example, joining the army (16), getting married (16 in Scotland; 18 in England), driving a car (17) and legal sexual intercourse (16). There are also areas where decisions are made subjectively based upon an adult's *perception* of a young person's understanding (e.g. Gillick competency)[1] and the age of criminal responsibility (ten in England and Wales, eight in Scotland) highlighting the potential power and subjectivity involved in classifying age and competency. This subjectivity was exemplified by some of the gatekeepers' responses to this research. While their role was ostensibly one of protection and responsibility for the welfare of the children in their care (loco-parentis),[2] this 'paternalism' differed between institutions and individuals. This succeeded in creating a chasm between statutory obligations and subjective opinions that were based upon young people's perceived lack of knowledge due to their chronological age.

> Although some children may have their own experience on which to form opinions, domestic violence in particular and violence against women in general are subjects which are *not explored in any depth until secondary school*... therefore you might have difficulty in finding a primary school *willing or able* to help you with this research. (Head teacher, Glasgow primary school 47, consent letter return, my emphasis)

This quote also assumes that children and young people are only able to talk from their own experience rather than expressing opinions about wider issues (see Rix 2004; Thomas and O'Kane 2000; Thorne 1987). Whilst some of the young people involved in this research may be living with violence or abuse, others may not. All of the young people, however, live in a society where men's violence against women is prevalent. There exists a discourse of innocence pertaining that there are those who are 'too young' to know and talk about certain topics or issues.

> Having only been a head teacher here for a short while, I feel I do not know the pupils or parents well enough to participate in such a *sensitive* subject. (Head teacher, Glasgow primary school 83, consent letter return, my emphasis)

---

1 Based upon the Gillick ruling: parental rights were recognised by the law only as long as they were needed for the protection of the child and such rights yielded to the child's right to make his own decision when he reached sufficient understanding and intelligence to be capable of making up his own mind (*Gillick* v *West Norfolk and Wisbech Area Health Authority* (1986), cited in Newell 1989: 101).

2 Mason (2004: 46) maintains that gatekeepers have no legal right to prevent young people from participating. However, they do hold legal responsibilities for the child's wellbeing and protection and they were in control of the places to which I needed access.

Such arguments are used to reinforce the powerless position of young people in our society, which in turn propagates the myths of the unspeakability and privacy of men's violence against women. The sensitivity of research is a subjective consideration (Sieber 1993: 18) and we need to question whether it is the violence itself that is 'sensitive', the young people talking about it, or the potential for revelation. I believed it was a combination of all of these factors, as well as the explicit gendered dimension used in the framing of the research question. Taking an explicitly gendered position meant that gatekeepers (in this research) may object to linking young people directly with gender, sex and sexuality, because of the continued discursive constructions of children as asexual beings (see Renold 2005) and as requiring protection from sexual threats or predators. Thus the notion of innocence is a provocative but ultimately a socially constructed (and socially endorsed) concept to encourage 'protectionist' measures and the promotion of schools as desexualised spaces (for example Section 28). Within this discourse of childhood as a linear progression, there exists a discursive dichotomy between the child as a representation of original innocence (a concept derived from the French philosopher Rousseau) and the child as the inheritor of 'original sin', a theory that was widely propagated in the eighteenth century (see Hendrick 1990: 37). This dichotomous relationship still exists today and is perpetuated greatly within the media: the innocent child in danger of being corrupted, juxtaposed with the demonised child.

Adult anxiety around young people and the 'protection of innocence' has resulted in either a dearth of research on younger people, sex and/or sexuality (see Farquar 1990), or else researchers modifying their proposals to preclude elements of overt references to sex or sexuality (McCarry 2003; Renold 2005). Williamson and Goodenough question a researcher's right (read adult) to keep information from children:

> Our intention may be to protect children from unwanted or 'inappropriate' knowledge but in doing so we limit their opportunities to engage fully ... we are denying them information which they believe they can handle, which they might be angry at being denied, and could potentially be putting children at more 'harm' by keeping information from them. (2005: 407)

Research has shown that young people can talk about (adult defined) 'sensitive' issues, whilst highlighting the significance of their own life and social experiences over their chronological age (see Barnard and Barlow 2003; Cree et al. 2002; and Highet 2003). By not giving younger people the space or means by which to talk about, challenge or resist men's violence against women, we are colluding in the perpetration of the issue as a 'private' problem and assuming that children are 'too young' to engage. It is for this reason, that the ages of the young people in this research – 11 and 12 (and at primary school) – is significant for and as a means to challenge the preconceptions which relate their age to their capabilities with '[a] major obstacle in conducting research with children concerns infantilising them, perceiving and treating them as immature and, in doing so, producing evidence to reinforce notions of their incompetence' (Alderson 2002: 243).

Temporality: Age and Life Stage

The theoretical framework of temporality is pertinent because of its relationship to the young people's own age (or life stage). It is also relevant as a means to understand violence through different 'timescapes' (Adam 1995, 2002) and enables the theorisation of young people's own temporal constructs of 'young' (me) and 'old' (them). Some of the sociological work that has utilised the concept of temporality does so by mapping one perspective directly on top of the other, for example looking at one's past in order to make sense of one's future, such as life history stories (for example, Bateson 1990). Adam's theory takes this one step further, by looking forwards as well as backwards to make sense of life now, 'there is no single time, only a multitude of times which interpenetrate and permeate our daily lives' (Adam 1995: 12). Adam (see Adam 2000: 136–7) addresses four key aspects of the multi-dimensionality of time, which she uses as the foundation to elaborate her theory of 'timescapes': time frames (the past, used to conceptualise duration), temporality (the present, the time 'in' things), tempo (the future, the processes of change) and timing (within the moment):

> In the timescape perspective these diverse ways of taking account of time are brought together and theorized as a coherent whole ... timescape is conceived as the temporal equivalent of landscape, recognising all the temporal features of socio-economic events and processes ... a timescape analysis is not concerned to establish what time is but what we do with it and how time enters our system of values. (Adam 2000: 137)

For the purposes of this book, Adam's concept of temporality is the most relevant as it conceptualises the present as also being transitional. Childhood theorists have begun to reconceptualise age as a temporal framework of interconnected and constructed life stages. Brannen (2005) maintains that young people use their present knowledge to make sense of their past (see also Adam 2002), whilst James (2005) confers that young people's memories are a discourse of identity which is fundamental to their present identities. Treacher (2006: 100) asserts that the complex relationship between time and temporality is a shared point of identity between children and adults; looking forwards and backwards to make sense of now. Indeed, for children, '[b]eing engaged in the present and looking forward to adulthood influence their fantasises and feelings about the future'.

Time is not only a temporal dimension but also a means to convey distance and proximity within the life course of individuals. Introducing the framework of temporality, challenges the idea of a scheduled progression (Griffin 1993) from childhood to adulthood, further endorsing the concept of 'transitions'. This is a critical framework to help understand the intersections of time, space and gender in young people's accounts. Time has been used to understand violence but linearly i.e. in terms of the distance of time to help frame events as violence (see Kelly 1988). It has not been appropriated using temporality as a means to overlay the different timescapes (in and of childhood, adulthood) in order to conceive of what is violent and how time impacts upon that construction.

Here childhood is conceived of as both a social structure and a temporal and spatial lens, through which to contextualise young people's own trajectories of their past, present and future selves. It is not enough to view childhood as a separate identity, rather it needs to be theorised as a temporal and transitory phenomenon. Yet it is important to note the difference between transition and transitory. Thus the preposition that childhood is a period of transition *into* adulthood is *not* being endorsed; rather in recognising childhood as 'transitory', the impact that the 'anticipation' or 'expectation' of adulthood has on the young people themselves, is incorporated into the definition.

Existing research on transitions has tended to look at the transition from education to paid employment, particularly among working class young people (Schoon et al. 2001; Thomson et al. 2003; Willis 1977). Such work analyses the prospect of a specific change in context, from one location (school) to another (work) and from one specific point in life to another. In their study, Brannen and Nilsen (2002: 514) sought to develop a theoretical framework to examine young people's time orientations, examining how young people spoke about their futures. In doing so, they identified the concept of social transitions as undergoing a process of 'destandardisation' not only in terms of the prescribed order of its phases, but also in terms of the 'linearity of its progress' linking back to Adam's timescape theory. On a similar topic, Gordon and Lahelma (2004) explored the contradictions inherent in 18-year-olds' anticipations of the transition into adulthood, with many wanting the independence of adulthood, but girls in particular wanting to postpone being 'locked' into the lives of adult women:

> Young women often want to stay apart not only from past childhood but also from their future adulthood (relating to) how they observe the lives of adult women, and how they see possibilities and limitations in their own imagined futures as women. (Gordon and Lahelma 2004: 84)

They maintain that these transitions focus upon the individualistic rather than social trajectories, a contradiction also identified by Thomson et al. (2003). Whilst these studies may encapsulate the anticipation of the future, they fail to take these imagined futures as a means of understanding the present lived lives.

This book aims to integrate the structures of society – aligning with Giddens theory of structuration (see 1979, 1984) – and the individual practices contained within, all of which are reflected in assumptions of temporality, spatiality and gender. By drawing upon the work of Adam (1995, 2000), the present time and the space of childhood are emphasised – in terms of their impact upon constructions of violence. Indeed by theorising childhood as transitional, the 'timescape' of childhood (in bringing together the past, present and future) is significant in understanding how young people construct and understand men's violence against women.

As already detailed, Kelly's definition contextualises violence and abuse as something that is not always experienced or acknowledged as violent 'at the time'. The dynamic aspect of this definition is relevant here for two reasons. Firstly, it is a significant means by which to note the historical context of violence; that is how the way violence is defined and named changes over time (and can be exemplified through, for example, the creation of new policies in Scotland) and secondly, because of the age of the participants and their own constructions of time, age and childhood.

Childhood and Gender

This period in young people's life course has been identified as a significant time for the development of gender identities, often because of the association with puberty and the distinction of differing social experience (Burke and Weir 1978). Gender is understood ontologically as both a social structure of norms and institution and as a discursively constituted lens though which we see the world, where language and actions provide meaning. For the purpose of this book, gender refers to the socially constructed roles, behaviours, positions, responsibilities and expectations that are ascribed to men (and boys) and women (and girls), differentially informing ideas of how they are meant to behave and act.

Initially, the understanding of the formation of gender identity was centred wholly upon the family, through the socialisation of accepted and appropriate gender roles (Merton 1968; Parsons 1959; Stainton Rogers and Stainton Rogers 1992). Traditional sociological theories focused upon the cultural explanations of gender within the paradigm of the socialisation thesis. Socialisation, or the sex role theory, developed from functionalism in the 1940s. Divisions and differences between males and females were viewed as natural and necessary for the sexual division of labour and were achieved through primary (within the family) and secondary (wider society) socialisation. Sex role theory, according to Parker (1996: 142):

> [c]entred primarily around functionalist notions of the nuclear family and the 'instrumental' and 'expressive' roles portrayed therein, this paradigm accepts that sexual differentiation is a socially constructed phenomenon occurring via an individual internalisation of familial and wider societal expectations in terms of ascribed sex roles.

Socialisation theory is now widely criticised for creating children and young people as passive recipients of one- way socialisation (from parent to child), whilst ignoring the significance of wider influences (Connell 2001; Holstein-Beck 1995; Thorne 1993).

The sex role theory, however, enabled the move from understanding gender as a 'biological imperative' (Kimmel 1990: 95) to a social construction, a concept that was further developed in Ann Oakley's definitive sociological text *Sex, Gender and Society*. Although Oakley's assertions provided a sociological insight into the division of sex and gender, and more crucially the social construction of unequal gender roles, it did not seek to challenge the 'naturalness' of the body or its reciprocal relation with gender:

> The *constancy* of sex must be admitted, but so also must the variability of gender. (Oakley 1972: 16, my emphasis)

Thus, the sex (body) of a person was fixed and taken for granted as an essentialist entity with the actions that constituted one's gender illuminated as culturally and socially constructed. By accepting and perpetuating the dichotomy between 'male' and 'female', Oakley's original thesis[3] failed to challenge the socially produced categories of masculinity and femininity. Connell (1987) argued strongly for a deconstruction of this notion:

> Challenge … the assumption that the biological make-up of our bodies is the 'basis', 'foundation', 'framework', or 'mould' of the social relations of gender. (67)

Such a challenge provided a foundational argument for those seeking to advocate that the body should be analysed as a social construction and not a taken for granted blank canvas onto which one's constructions of gender were painted.

3 In her later work, Oakley asserted that biology (sex), like gender, was a social construction (1994: 25).

By focusing upon the differences of gender, but not the relations between genders (Kimmel 2004: 96), the socialisation framework denies concurrently individual agency and the importance of social structure in the organisation of gender (Connell 1993). This aligns gender as a set of attributes rather than as a social and structural relation (Kimmell 2004: 97) as well as ignoring the mediation of other social factors such as class, sexualities, 'race' and ethnicity. Consequently sex role theory did not allow for any conceptualisation of power, rather it sought to naturalise any understanding of it,

> Socialisation is not simply about the acquisition of roles, but rather it is about the acquisition of power by one group over another group. (Brittan 1989: 45)

Kimmel maintains that power is not a consequence of gender difference rather it is power that produces the gender differences in the first place (2004: 99). He uses Hannah Arendt's description of power to illustrate his argument:

> Power corresponds to the human ability not just to act but to act in concert. Power is never the property of an individual; it belongs to a group and remains in existence only as long as the group keeps together. When we say of somebody that he is 'in power' we actually refer to his being empowered by a certain number of people to act in their name. The moment the group, from which the power originated to begin with … disappears, 'his power' also vanishes. (Arendt, cited in Kimmel 2004: 101)

A key argument in this book is that to analyse young people's understandings of violence it is crucial to understand how they construct gender. Young people's discussions and interpretations of gender and power are interpreted through a social constructionist framework, through the layers of individual identity; social interactions, ideologically and structurally.

The social constructionist paradigm developed from the limitations and criticisms of the sex role theory. Within this paradigm are situated different and competing feminist theorists, pro feminist writers and proponents of masculinity theory that define social constructionism within either materialist or discursive paradigms. Common to all is an agreement that gender is a socially produced, continuously contested category that is perpetuated and negotiated at both ideological and institutional levels. The concept of power is integral to social constructionist analysis in general, and feminism in particular.

Kimmel (2004: 10) uses the term gender to encapsulate both masculinity and femininity whilst emphasising the need to explore the differences between and among men and women. The gendered ascriptions of masculinity and femininity are not fixed by biology, but learned and contested processes that change over time and culture. It is crucial to pluralise these identities and to talk of masculinities and femininities to illuminate the implicit and explicit differences, fluidity and power relations that exist between them.

It was through the discursive framework of social constructionism that the concept and position of 'men' and 'masculinity' began to be questioned and challenged, in the same way that feminists and childhood theorists had sought to deconstruct the categories of 'woman' and 'child'. Prior to this men had been accepted as gender-neutral subjects; the bench mark on which all 'others' were measured. Deconstructing 'men' and 'masculinity/ies' has been an important step forward in the theorisation of violence (Segal 1997; Hearn 1998, 2001; Connell 1993, 2000).

Understanding and illuminating discursive constructions of gender are also relevant here in understanding how young people maintain, resist and accept their gender identities and expectations, which is discussed further in Chapter 4.

Queer theorists have championed the work of Foucault to illuminate how gendered and sexual identities are created and constructed through discursive and social processes. Language ascribes these processes with meaning. It is through these processes that inequality, and power, is created and maintained. Judith Butler's writings were the forerunner of queer theory, which deconstructed and destabilised the concepts of gender and sexuality. Her theories have problematised the notion of gender identities (masculinity and femininity) because they are derived from and remain upon the same binary as biological models of sex (male and female). For Butler, as long as biological sex is viewed as a core indicator of an essential self, an embodiment on which to base gender identity, then heterosexuality will continue to be envisaged as a natural progression, with opposition constructed as normative. Thus for Butler it is imperative to theorise sex as a social construction and to view all gender identity as performative.

Therefore, in order to deconstruct existing limiting dichotomies that restrict gender to conceptualisation of binary opposites, a theory that embraces the structure and agency of both gender construction and women's oppression is necessary. The need to see the agency within the young people's constructions and decision-making is an imperative part of this process. The young people recognised their own gender performances and as such could change these performances depending upon the audience, the situation and their own intentions. For agency to be dismissed as an impossibility (see Walker 1995) the potential for change cannot be grasped and the link to children's active engagement with the research process simply appears obtuse.

Paechter (2006) argues that one of the problems with gender is the limit of language and definition with which to theorise it. Indeed, our understanding of gender and gender identity is hindered and:

> exacerbated by our inability to define either masculinity or femininity except in relation to each other and to men and women. (254)

She goes on to argue:

> This is because masculinity and femininity are not just constructed in relation to each other; their relation is dualistic. A dualistic relation is one in which the subordinate term is negated, rather than the two sides being in equal balance. (256)

In order to overcome these discursive restrictions of gender, Paechter maintains that people should be defined by their sex: man, woman, or intersex, and that the term masculinities and femininities be used to describe but one aspect of their identity. Although the original ideas about the restriction of language are pertinent, Paechter ironically lapses into essentialism to challenge the dichotomies. This has been but one effort in queer attempts to create new categories through which to describe gender. Halberstam (1998) adopted the phrase, 'female masculinity' to challenge the presumption that masculinity belonged entirely to men to create new masculinities for women as it was this identity that was most privileged. The main crux of it being that masculinity is valorised in our society and femininity is not and positioned in opposition to it. However, Hester (1992) sought to demonstrate that sex and gender can be used interchangeably because it is not the biological differences but the social meanings attached to the categories which gives them their meaning. I was interested to explore how young people constructed and presented their varied and multi-faceted gender identities and how, if at all, this would align with heteronormative/heterogendered practices (Ingraham 1994) or challenge the frameworks of compulsory heterosexuality (Rich 1980).

Intersections of Gender and Age

Described by some as a 'fashionable term' (Bradley 2007: 190), or as simply a new word for interrelationships, originally the term 'intersectionality' was used to illustrate the 'intersections' of various identities – generally in relation to oppression (see Hill Collins 1990, 2000) or burden (Kanyoro 2001). I adopt the term here to explore the interrelationships specifically in relation to age and gender and to convey the process whereby existing and multiple identities are mapped onto one another (McCall 2005; Valentine 2007). It is not the intention to focus specifically upon other intersectional identities of self, such as class, ethnicity, sexuality or (dis)ability but where they are introduced as relevant either by the young people themselves or present as pertinent themes, they are discussed. Intersectionality is also a means by which to overlay the material and discursive concepts of time and space, which are already widely drawn upon within the sociology of childhood (Prout and James 1990) and align them with the key concepts of violence and gender.

In this sense, intersectionality is used as a conceptual bridge to link the lived (and present) gendered experiences of the young people with their projected gendered futures and also to convey the concurrency of structure and agency in young people's constructions. It enables us to envisage social life as a process and also apply the referential framework of heterosexuality by which gender is understood. In doing this I am making two claims. Firstly, that the incorporation of time and space is critical to moving away from the binary concepts which inform gender. Enabling all interaction to be framed by temporal and spatial relations opens up a fluidity – gender across time and the life course. Secondly, that the temporal projections of their own lived and anticipated experiences are intersected with their understandings of space (using the constructs of distance and proximity) which they subscribe to as a means to comprehend violence. The spatial dimension of their accounts incorporates not only physical locality but also their own personal sense of location and self.

Transitions: Bringing Together Childhood and Gender

In this book, the concept of childhood is located within the past, present *and* the future in order to encapsulate the temporality and dynamism of the concept. Young people use their lens of childhood to position their own lives – now – and as a means to anticipate their future 'adulthood' – what Nowotny (1994) refers to as their 'extended present' – which in turn informs their understanding of men's violence against women. Here we can also look at how young people's present knowledge contributes to their expectation 'in' and 'of' adulthood, especially in terms of violence and also gender identity. These discussions of childhood and time are replicated in discussions of gender and heterosexual identities – but less overt attention has been given to the inherent critique needed, of how young people's gender identities are in the process of 'development' with fully fledged adult gender as the ultimate 'fixed' goal. To illustrate temporality and transition, we can draw upon the example of socially constructed gender identity, specifically the focus upon adult masculinity and heterosexuality as the 'end' point in gender construction.

The concept of 'transitions' has also been highlighted as a pertinent period in the lives of young men, when their development of gender identity is still ongoing (see O'Donnell and Sharpe 2000). Whilst this is relevant for intervention and awareness-raising work, it also assumes that at some point their identities will become more fixed, constructing adulthood as an end point.

However, gender is not a process of becoming (in the same way that childhood is not), but age refracts how gender is experienced, anticipated and reproduced by the young people themselves. The dimension of age and, in particular, their lived experience of childhood thus impacts upon how they experience gender now and how they anticipate it in the future. Temporality therefore is a useful conceptual framework with which to understand heterosexuality (and gender identities) because it too is fluid and in a constant state of movement and flux, rather than a static, constant entity. As such, it is also a useful tool to help destabilise the rigidity of the heterosexual framework. Therefore it is critical to engage with the transitory nature of gender, as an ongoing process rather than in terms of a precursor to adulthood identity. By introducing the dynamic concept of 'transitions', there is more fluidity in how young people are able to construct and define their own gendered identities, rather than adhering to adultist (heterosexualised) frameworks. This means there is a need to develop a more fluid framework, rather than limiting young people to the dichotomy of singular masculinity and feminine identities, which are also fixed, by the dichotomy of 'child' and 'adult'. As Giddens (1994: 80) has pointed out, 'identity is the creation of constancy over time, that very bringing of the past into conjunction with an anticipated future'. Therefore, in summary, a theoretical framework needs to incorporate the following:

- Childhood to be conceived of as transitory.
- Theorisations of violence should incorporate not only gendered definitions but also temporal and spatial understandings. How does young people's position in the lifecourse, and their conceptualisation of this (past, present and future), alongside distance or proximity impact their understanding of violence?
- Theorisations of gender and violence that do not reinforce young people as static or adulthood as an 'end point' in gender construction and heterosexuality identity.

Chapter 3
Research Methodology

Introduction

This chapter explains the beginnings of the research journey: the rationale behind the methodology (ways of thinking about the research) and also the decision to use qualitative methods. It is maintained that qualitative methods enable the drawing together of the subjective position of young people by grounding their knowledge in their everyday realities. This was encouraged by generating participatory methods that the young people could actively engage with. It is demonstrated that, by uniting the epistemological and research philosophies of feminism and the sociology of childhood, a reflexive and empowered research process can be created.

Researching Violence

Ray (2000) argues that whilst violence is an enduring aspect of social life it has received very little attention within academic sociology other than in terms of 'domestic' violence and 'violent crime'. He maintains that the concept of violence is more likely to be understood within the overarching category of power. This is indicative of the contribution made by feminists to the areas, who locate violence against women within the wider social structures and frameworks of (men's) power. Theoretical and practical research in the arena of violence has been developed and sustained by the contribution of feminists, masculinity theorists and pro feminist writers. Its prevalence is more prolific within the specialisms of feminist and gender studies than the academic discipline of sociology as a whole (Walby 2013).

McKie (2006: 4) endorses this claim in her discussion of the patterning of sociological work on violence. Studies of violence within the family and intimate relationships are generally conducted under the umbrella of women's or gender studies drawing upon feminist and pro feminist theories whereas studies of violence on a national scale such as genocide and war utilise grand meta theories thus locating themselves within the sanctity of reputable 'old school' sociology. Thus McKie (ibid) notes that the prevalence of violence in everyday lives and its gendered nature and experience still remain an 'absent presence' in much 'male stream' work.

Smart (2004: 1,048) has drawn parallels between this division and the gender order (and thus the public and private spheres) with 'those of a feminine persuasion … doing the equivalent of the essential but hardly visible small-scale housework'. Therefore, it is important when undertaking such 'housework' that its parallels and implications for the wider public sphere be noted. C.W. Mills (1959) said a combination of structural and interpretive approaches was the only way forward for the academic discipline of sociology and was imperative for the cultivation of the sociological imagination. This is achieved for example by McKie and Lombard (2005) who explored the role of (micro) families in creating and reinforcing collective identity and memory which were identified as factors in the perpetuation of sectarian and ethnic (macro) violence. It was crucial therefore when undertaking this work to locate the personal, interpretive approach alongside the political structural institutions.

Qualitative Methods

Holliday (2002) describes qualitative research as being based upon the philosophy that social reality is not constructed by 'facts' but is socially constructed, and as such subjectively interpreted through an exploration of people's understandings of the world around them. The philosophical underpinnings of both feminist research and constructions of childhood are based upon social constructionist models of knowledge, and this is the main reason qualitative methods were chosen.

There have been countless arguments about the merits of using either qualitative or quantitative methods of research. Quantitative methods have tended to be aligned with positivism, statistics and social facts (Robson 2002; Silverman 2000) and qualitative methods with interpretation, subjectivity and in-depth understandings (Mason 2004), resulting in a chasm between social science methods. As such, qualitative and quantitative methods occupy the binary equivalent of masculinity and femininity. However, I am by no means dichotomising qualitative and quantitative methods as explicitly *feminist* and *masculinist*. To do so would be to reinforce the very gendered boundaries that I am attempting to mitigate (see Letherby 2002, 2004; Oakley 1998, 2004). However, many feminists have aligned themselves with the latter, in the belief that feminist methodology needs to prioritise experience, knowledge and subjectivity (Stanley and Wise 1993).

Qualitative methods have also been described as the only 'suitable' methods for research with or about children (Ghate, 2002) ensuring they are given 'a more direct voice' (Hazel 1995b: 16). Whilst this has been disproven (see Scott 2000; Sweeting and West 2003), qualitative methods do allow researchers the opportunity to capitalise on the unique qualities of children and young people as researcher participants (Ghate 2002). It enables young people to have a more active role in the research question because their own experiences, behaviours and actions are contextualised to assist in their everyday understanding and knowledge of violence. In choosing to use qualitative methods, I make explicit that it is the richness and meaning of the data that is relevant, rather than the replication of it. The subjectivity inherent in the use of qualitative methods is acknowledged from the start and is viewed as a positive aspect of it.

Methodology: A Feminist Method?

Research methods are chosen in relation to what you want to find out and how you want to go about doing that (Bergin et al. 2003). There has been much debate as to whether there constitutes a distinctive feminist method. Hammersley (1992) controversially denied the possibility of its existence, arguing that 'a separate methodological paradigm based on distinctive political and philosophical assumptions ... to motivate a unique form of research practice' was both impossible and non-desirable.

Feminist researchers use many of the same methods as traditional social research (for example, interviews and focus groups), yet it is the methodological and epistemological values that underpin feminist research, which differentiates it from these (see Bograd 1988; Kelly 1988; Kelly et al. 1994; Letherby 2004; Oakley 1994; Stanley and Wise 1993). The exact nature of these values differs from feminist to feminist. As Kelly (1988: 6) points out, it is not the methods which make the research feminist but 'the questions we have asked, the way we locate ourselves in our questions, and the purpose of our work'. The aspects highlighted by Kelly here are further drawn out through the transparency of the development of the methods, questions and techniques.

Mills (1959) maintained that sociology's aim to inform and provide a new form of consciousness could only be achieved through the possession of a 'sociological imagination'. The epistemological grounding shared by Mills and feminist researchers alike, extends to a fusion of the political and personal, that is the development of correlations between the 'intimate realities of ourselves' with 'larger social realities' (Mills 1959: 15). Stanley and Wise (1993: 205) assert 'that feminist social science research must begin with the recognition that "the personal", lived experience underlies all behaviours and actions'.

There are many crossovers in the epistemological and methodological values of feminist research and research where children and young people are the participants. This illustrates what Oakley (1994) has termed their shared status as social minority groups, alongside shared characteristics and philosophical underpinnings that bind them:

> Their status as social minority groups, their relative lack of rights and moral construction as non-adult [and their] ideological restriction to the domestic sphere [resulting in] temporal and spatial restriction. (16–17)

It is the acceptance and perpetuation of such characteristics that resulted in women and children being ignored, marginalised, or treated as 'objects' or unreliable 'subjects' within research. I have identified, from the existing feminist literature, the ways of thinking about research and the research process that contribute to my own feminist methodology. They are identified here as prioritising gender and women's experience; the empowerment of women through the research process and consciousness raising; lived experience as a form of knowledge (Stanley and Wise 1993, 1993); and the importance of reflexivity (Letherby 2004).

Feminist research is not restricted to being solely about 'women', otherwise it would exist as an 'add on' to existing (malestream) sociological theories (Oakley 1994) and fail to challenge the 'idea of the male as norm' (Layland 1990: 129). This research is specifically concerned with the ideas and understandings of young people, both girls and boys. As Kelly has argued, the gender of the participants does not make the research any less feminist:

> Much of our research has not been exclusively 'on' or 'with' women, since it has involved men and focused on institutions. The issues we have researched, however are 'feminist issues' – primarily domestic violence and child sexual abuse. We have throughout attempted to 'do' our research as feminists and to ask feminist questions. (Kelly et al. 1994: 32)

Therefore, this research incorporates the 'feminist issue' (Kelly et al. 1994: 32) of men's violence against women from the perspective of young people, girls and boys.

According to MacKinnon (1989), what defines research as feminist is the practice of 'consciousness raising'.[1] For Stanley and Wise (1993) 'consciousness raising' describes the process whereby:

---

1 I ended the discussion groups on the subject of domestic violence and domestic abuse. Because I had questioned the young people on their understanding of these terms, they often asked about their meaning when the sessions had finished. This was my opportunity to explain about the gendered nature of domestic violence and relate the term back to the vignette examples. This was my own personal commitment to consciousness raising on men's violence against women, although my explanations did not go unquestioned, thus my feminist perspective was not accepted as 'fact' or as constituting superior knowledge.

> A previously untapped store of knowledge about what it is to be a woman, what the social world looks like to women, how it is constructed and negotiated by women. This knowledge is made available through feminist insistence on the importance of the personal. (120)

They go on to argue that instead of dichotomising consciousness into true and false, there is a need to interpret it as continuous dialectic, with feminist consciousness pertaining to different ways of understanding, interpreting and constructing experiences and interactions. This feeds into the position that there is not one feminist identity and consequently no one way to be a feminist.

There are different feminist strands (radical, liberal, black, Marxist, postmodern), as well as constant dialogues within these positions about competing ideas, theories, research and practice. There have been many disagreements over whether feminism can continue to operate with a single concern (see Jackson 1999), given the multiple forms of identity that women have and the intersections of oppressions that they experience (see Heywood and Drake 1997).

Third wave or postmodernist feminists argue that there is no one explanation for women's subordination. Dicker and Piepmeier (2003: 14) argue that third-wave feminism is less a shift between feminists of the 1970s and feminists of today; rather it is an identity and a theory (or a range of theories) that is located culturally within 'in a world shaped by technology, global capitalism, multiple models of sexuality, changing national demographics and declining economic viability'. Whilst I broadly define my own position as radical feminism (in that I believe women's oppression originates from the inequities of power between men and women, and that men's violence against women is a manifestation and consequence of this power),[2] there are elements of third-wave feminism that are relevant to the approach taken here. For example, there needs to be a wider recognition that young people cannot be judged to be a homogenous group in the same way that women cannot, in terms of their identities and the oppressions they experience (see work on children in the majority world, for example, Groves 2003; Punch 2002, 2007, 2008).

Unlike positivist research, feminist research does not allege to be value free, rather it embraces the 'value' base and the subjectivity of knowledge, identifying knowledge production as being grounded in individual and collective experiences (Miller and Bell 2002: 54). Lived experience is understood as a form of knowledge (Stanley and Wise 1993; Brah and Phoenix 2004). Although Stanley and Wise (1993) only make reference to the social knowledge

---

2 There are other theoretical positions and analyses (psychological, sociological, family violence) but they do not acknowledge the gendered, social and political consequences of men's violence which feminist theories argue are central.

of women, this position is transferable to the concept of empowering children and young people.

It is critical to reiterate that the claims to personal knowledge are not the same as personal experience. Although it is likely that some/many of the young people involved in this research may have experienced forms of men's violence, their own personal narratives are not the focus. A caveat has to be made here to emphasise that young people are not 'experts' in men's violence against women per se, but are acknowledged as being 'experts in their own lives' (Langsted 1994: 42) and as such are 'experts' in expressing *their own opinions*. Highlighting the subjectivity inherent in my own and the young people's personal knowledge hopefully reinforces the correlation between the methodological approaches of feminist research and the sociology of childhood.

In addition to locating the participants within the research process, feminist researchers need to make it clear where we situate ourselves and also explain that position in terms of making reference to the claims of (interpretive) authority and power. As a means of contextualising the subjective interpretation of knowledge, Kelly (1988) contends that the problems and experiences of the researcher should be included within the research process. This continual cycle of reflexivity is an important part of the feminist methodology. Thus in advocating self-awareness we are always reasserting the subjectivity of our research. Letherby (2004: 176) argues this is a key issue in feminist research, describing it as: 'the relationship between doing and knowing: how the way we undertake research (the process) relates to the knowledge we present at the end (the product)'. Therefore, as Glucksman (1994) has insisted, we need to recognise the different kinds, and claims to knowledge that we have in terms of our position to the topic. Having previous experience of working within the refuge movement, and as a government researcher, I have considerable 'located' knowledge. Politically, I also have a personal agenda in terms of conscious raising and working towards change.

The Researcher, Young People and Power

As a feminist undertaking research, I believe in the importance of situating yourself: recognising your own personal interests and subjectivities in order to be reflexive in your work. I am a white woman from a large working-class industrial town in the north of England, living in Glasgow, in a relationship, working as an academic and the mother of three (almost four) children. I have been active in the field of violence against women for 19 years, having previously volunteered and worked in Women's Aid refuges and conducted research for the then Scottish Executive on male domestic abuse.

When working at the refuges I had daily contact with women and their children who were fleeing domestic violence. At first I was idealistic in my views and expectations of both the system and the women, wanting them to escape and live new lives. However, the daily realities for the women: financial difficulties, the emotional bonds and a lack of provision meant that many of them returned to abusive relationships. I needed to respect the choices they made and having children of my own encouraged me to reassess my expectations and presumptions about many of the women at the refuge and the realities of their daily lives.

Also, for me, the relentless and evolving population of the refuge began to normalise the issue of men's violence against women. Although each individual woman and her children personified the issue, the normalisation came from listening to the same narratives told and retold, different women with the same stories to tell and to move on from. Although the refuge was a transitional place, the abusive men remained a perpetual constant.

In charting my autobiographical path (Letherby 2004; Oakley 1998) I generated many thoughts about why I became interested in this field. Often women become involved in the area of working against men's violence because of direct experience, but I had always assumed that I was not one of them, as I didn't have any personal history. However, when I sat down and thought about it, I was shocked, not only by the list of abuses I had experienced, but by my minimisation of them – to the extent I did not (initially) class them as abuse. To prevent identification and to protect others, I have listed the abuses (by known and unknown men) very generally. My own recalled experiences of abuse included:

- Physical abuse
- Experiences of coerced sex
- Flashing and indecent exposure
- Sexual assaults
- Physical assaults
- Verbal sexual abuse.

Being aware of my own normalisation of personal experiences of violence made me acutely sensitive to the young people's narratives of their own experiences and conceptualisations of men's violence against women, and the professional and practical skills I have acquired (counselling, women's refuges, child protection, children's panel system) were also helpful in enabling me to identify and deal with the experiences of others.

My position, however, is no more valid than the participants in this study. Yet I do claim to have a wider frame of situated knowledge with which to position the young people's constructions, as well as access to resources and networks so I can act as a conduit to enable young people's voices to be heard. These serve as examples of when I was 'productively using my power' (Skeggs 1994) to provide information or to further knowledge. This reflexive approach is also widely advocated in research with children and young people (Morrow 2001; O'Kane 2000; Thomas et al. 1999) demonstrating various ways for the researcher to recognise their own subjectivity but also to critically analyse their position as the person in 'power'.

It is crucial to recognise that challenging power by disguising it is not reflexive research. Specifically in research with children, power has simplistically been aligned with physicality, such as height differences (Farquar 1990; Mandell 1991) or in life experience; 'studying the child within ourselves' (Oakley 1994: 28). Yet doing this fosters an acceptance of developmental discourses, leading to the position that only like can interview like (see Harding 1987; Stanley and Wise 1993, 1993) as well as homogenising all groups. Therefore, what is important is not to make yourself more like the people you are working with, but to reflexively acknowledge these discrepancies and power differentials from the start. Whilst openly acknowledging that I was an adult, I did try and disassociate myself from the role of a teacher because of the authority aligned with this role in the school environment. I attempted to minimise power differentials through symbolic means; in terms of using first names, dressing casually, using informal language, not reacting to their swearing and reassuring them that I was not a figure of authority testing their knowledge.

Yet, I was not naïve enough however to believe I removed all power from the process. It was me who ultimately had control over the research process: the design, implementation, analysis, writing up and dissemination (Mauthner 1997; Mauthner et al. 1998; Letherby 2004). Although the young people had a role in choosing the topics they were structured within a framework that I had mainly dictated. I also managed the time and chose when to move discussions forwards. I had control over the group, its contents, structure and timing. There were moments when I thought I was giving young people choices, yet upon reflection I realised that I was still demonstrating power in giving them instructions ('sit where you want'). I used the opportunity of disseminating the findings back to the young people to demonstrate my gratitude, giving them access to the research they have been part of and as a means for them to recognise the role that they had in the creation of the research, hopefully demonstrating their empowerment (through their choices, their participation, their own critical reflections) in the process. The power, and workings of power, promoted and constrained by the education system and the individual schools meant that at times the gatekeepers held the power: to commit to the research, dictate when, where and with whom the research took place, as well as having the authority to stop my research at any point.

I found that the 'spadework' of preparation – in terms of thinking and arranging the practicalities was a much more laborious task than the fieldwork process. However, it was a process that was continuously overlooked in research articles and monographs, when often I would crave a step-by-step approach to organising and conducting the research. The next section provides this in detail.

The Research Process

The main aim here is to deliver a step-by-step explanation of what I did and why, to provide a reflexive and critical account of the research process.

Research in Schools

Previous research investigating the attitudes of young people towards violence against women accessed participants from a range of sites: secondary schools and colleges, work places and youth groups. Although there are club activities that involve young people under the age of 14, they are not accessible to all and I chose to approach primary schools. Conducting research within schools, particularly primary schools, is not without its detractors. Morrow (2001: 212) claims that because children are the 'objects of schooling it is possible to argue that they are similarly the objects of the research'. Mayall (1994: 7) has argued for more research to be carried out with children in their homes as 'it is the arena where kids have more scope than in other settings as parents want them all to be individual'. Whilst this may overcome some of the negative aspects of school based research, such as accommodating time tables, making space and issues of conformity, it would be naïve of me to think all young people would feel safe and comfortable within their own homes. As Mullender (2002) reminds us, home is the most dangerous place for children to be.

Research in schools can provide consistent fieldwork conditions and good response rates as well as being cost effective (Sweeting and West 2003) whilst also ensuring 'a readily accessible population' (James et al. 1998). Yet some researchers have described participants in schools as 'captive' (Morrow 2001; Rae and Fournier 1986) with little choice as to whether to take part or not. The physical space of the research encounter is not just important in terms of practicalities, but also in terms of how such a space frames the methods, the researcher and the participants. Due to the practicalities of the individualised nature of completing the exploratory questionnaire (and the involvement of the whole class at once) there was little option but for this to take place in the classroom reinforcing, for some, an expectation to provide the 'right' answer (for the 'teacher'). The discussion sessions took place among friendship groups in more privatised spaces: libraries, 'sick' rooms, staff offices or empty classrooms – but still in rooms that had (positive and negative) connotations for the young people (see Hazel 1995b).

Conducting research in schools had a significant impact upon issues such as ethics and access. Young people aged 11 and 12, and those much younger (see, for example, Clark and Moss 2001) are increasingly more involved with research projects because of the growing interest and impact of the sociology of childhood. Yet because of the combination of the age of the young people, the subject matter of men's violence against women and their location within primary schools, the ethics were considerably more precarious. The next section details an account of the structured procedures that it was necessary to negotiate but also the attempts made at including the young people in a process that continually sought to exclude them.

Children, Young People and Ethics

Ethics comprise of guidelines and practices that seek to prevent harm, protect participants, ensure privacy, informed consent and confidentiality and provide policies for action around disclosure thus, 'safeguard[ing] the rights and feelings of those who are being researched' (Liebling and Stanko 2001: 424). Preparing and demonstrating adherence to these guidelines was necessary to ensure the young people had (and knew they had) their own rights respected as well as demonstrating to 'gatekeepers' my own personal and professional commitment. When researching a topic such as violence and abusive behaviour, there is potential for the young people to disclose violence that is happening in their own lives. As part of my ethical practice gatekeepers were assured that I would work within the child protection guidelines set out by the school and local authority, and the issue of disclosure was raised with the head teachers at all participating schools,[3] as well as with all of the young people (see below). Highlighting the clear ethical procedures of the research was also imperative to gaining ethics committee approval from the university.

Ethics has been a central theme throughout this research both practically and conceptually situated within shifting frameworks of power dynamics. It is important to recognise that ethics are based on your own and others' values. Edwards et al. (2002: 1) question objective definitions of ethics, which they term the 'tick box approach to ethical standards', which implies that all ethical issues can be determined and solved before the research and fieldwork begins. The framework of ethics in this research draws upon an alliance with 'a feminist

3 Some researchers have expressed their unwillingness or inability to react to disclosure (for eample, Hazel 1995b). Having 19 years of practical experience within this field and a sound knowledge of child protection issues, I felt competent in dealing with possible instances of disclosure from young people.

informed social value ethical model' (ibid. 2002: 19) that prioritises personal experience, context and the nurture of relationships with participants. This is not an uncritical position and is one which was approached as reflexively as the research process itself. By aligning the two principles feminist methodology and the rights of the young people, my own motivations and assumptions became clear, in turn, generating a critically reflexive and ethical approach to my method.

Negotiating Access

Access was a key part of the ethics. It had to be demonstrated that strong ethical consideration had been given to the issues of prevention of harm and protection in order to gain access to the young people. Indirect negotiations began with the writing of my research proposal. Being aware of the potential requests to see this from each layer of bureaucracy meant that the proposal had to be clearly written with specific aims and objectives and a strong, thoughtful ethics section. The proposal was passed by the University Higher Degrees Committee and the University Ethics Committee. This academic approval added weight to my application when writing to the gatekeepers – council education departments, head teachers and parents.

Following advice from an educational researcher, a wide research field was generated by writing to all four of Glasgow's councils to increase the chances of success[4] readily anticipating the delays, refusals and frustrations inherent in any research process (Butler and Williamson 1994; Hornsby-Smith 1993).

I approached 99 schools and received a total of 20 replies, of which six were positive responses. The schools that had chosen not to take part, and had not provided a written reason as to why, were re-contacted and the amalgamation of their (oral and written) reasons ranged from:

- Time constraints of teachers, individual classes and other commitments
- Already involved in research (on a number of other topics)
- A belief that Primary Seven children were too young to take part in a study of this nature (see earlier)

4 I decided to discount all fee-paying schools in the area. Although theoretically there may have been fewer gatekeepers to contend with (as such schools are outside of local authority control) it would be more difficult to disseminate policy implications among the differing systems. In addition to this, I had been advised that several people who had approached these schools in conjunction with violence against women initiatives or studies had been refused access. Although I cannot confirm that this would have remained the case, I thought it best to concentrate upon the schools within the remit of the local education authorities.

- Thinking that those children who had not directly experienced 'domestic violence' would not know anything about it and so such research was not necessary at this juncture.[5]

For the first meeting with the head teachers I took along a draft copy of the exploratory questionnaire, parental consent letters, information sheets and consent forms for the young people and my Disclosure Scotland form. I had requested that I be able to meet with the young people at the end of the meeting, which all agreed to.

Informed Consent

There are very few ethical guidelines that relate specifically to social science research with children in general and obtaining consent in particular. The guidelines that do exist are generic and encompass all social science research.[6] As a result researchers have different ideas and beliefs about consent procedures because there are no definitive legal guidelines. At each stage of the access negotiations, there was a need for somebody to give consent for the research to progress because of the age of the young people. Therefore, the decision to participate could not begin with the young people themselves, each gatekeeper (in this case the council, the school and then the parent/guardian) has to agree first.

Councils and schools can have competing agendas regarding the research: time (how long the research will take, fitting it into the lesson schedule); resources (providing a separate room for discussions and additional work for children who are not taking part); as well as the implications of the research findings and the welfare of the children. Parents will usually only be concerned with the latter. In this research, only two parents (out of 91 households) actively refused to give their child consent to take part and what was interesting was the number of parents who left the decision to their child, stating this specifically on the reply slip. This action suggested that these parents (and those who had discussed the research with their child before signing the form) saw their child as being able to make their own choice about participating in research that was about them.

It was imperative for the young people to participate in the consent process within the school environment as they had not been involved in the negotiations

---

5 It is significant to note that the gatekeepers most likely to grant access will be those with an interest or affinity with the subject matter of men's violence against women.

6 For example, the British Sociological Association (BSA); Economic and Social Research Council (ESRC); and the Social Research Association (SRA).

of access to date;[7] firstly for their actual involvement as participants and secondly to further inform their consent. Their own consent was even more significant when framed by the compulsory nature of school activities (Morrow and Richardson 1996: 101). The working definition of informed consent used was taken from the Social Research Association's Guidelines (2003: 28): 'ensuring that research subjects understand what is being done to them, the limits of their participation and an awareness of any potential risks they may incur'.

The issue of informed consent will always remain an irresolvable tension with some people (of all ages) never wholly understanding what they have consented to, by basing their consent not on information but on trust (Barnard et al. 2003). Verbal and written information was incorporated to empower the young people so they would trust me, the researcher, as well as the research they were involved in. This would enable them to be active participants (Alderson 2004) both in the research and through their own informed choice to take part.

After being introduced to the children I talked about the research and handed out information sheets that explained it further. This also contained my contact details for if they wanted to discuss the research further or ask questions. The information sheets took longer than anticipated to design. I attempted to strike a balance between being short enough to sustain interest but long enough to convey the relevant information, whilst also being 'readable' but not patronising.

During the initial session the young people asked questions about their involvement and what the research would be used for, all of which were clearly answered. It was then explained that as they were under 16 years of age their parents also had to agree to them taking part. They were shown a copy of the letter they were taking home for their parents and carers to sign. This was done to demystify the sealed envelope and to involve them in the consent process rather than placing the importance of the consent entirely with the adult. To reinforce their participation further, they were shown the consent form they would be asked to sign. It was stressed that as it was them taking part it was important that they were happy to do so. It was also made clear that consent would be a continual and renegotiated process so they could change their minds about participating at any time even if they had already signed the consent form and said yes. By giving the young people choice, information and knowledge about the research process (both verbally and with written information sheets) their consent was as informed as possible. They were encouraged to ask questions

7 Following the access process, I realised that when working with young people in a school, there would always be an obstacle/barrier between you and them, whether that be the education authority, the head teacher of their school or their parents and guardians – who were all involved in the decisions before the young people even knew about it.

whenever they wanted to and also assured that they did not have to answer anything that they did not want to. Their informed consent also extended to the written material they gave me. Upon its completion they were asked to mark it with a tick or a cross depending on whether they minded me reproducing it so other people would see it (for example, at future conferences and in further research papers).

It was during this initial meeting that the issue of confidentiality and disclosure was raised with all of the young people. This was repeated each time we met. I said:

> During these sessions, what you write and talk about is confidential, which means that nobody will be able to identify that it is you personally who has said something. However, if you say something, or tell me something, which I think might mean that you or someone else is in danger or at risk of being hurt, I will have to tell somebody else. I will not do this without telling you and talking to you about it first.

I was aware that in saying this, some young people may be prevented from speaking out, while still being at risk of experiencing forms of abuse or violence. An information sheet with telephone numbers and websites was prepared to help and/or empower anybody who was seeking further information. The areas of confidentiality and disclosure are interlinked with the discretion of where the boundaries start and finish, being subject to ethical debate and a degree of researcher subjectivity. There is much literature that addresses the issue of disclosure (Alderson 1995; Barnard et al. 2003; Cree et al. 2002) and those that detail opposing views; the researcher's duty to protect (Boyden and Ennew 1997) and the autonomy of the young person (Thomas and O'Kane 1998). Some researchers have even gone so far as to maintain that 'complete confidentiality can never be guaranteed to child research subjects' (Mahon et al. 1996: 151). These positions are not mutually exclusive as the young person is autonomous in choosing to disclose, and in acting in their best interests you are enabling them to access or receive help. In terms of confidentiality, all of the young people, teachers, schools and places and people mentioned were afforded pseudonyms to protect their own and others' identity. The young people were also reminded at the beginning of each session that what was talked about should not be discussed outside of the groups.

Methods

Before designing the research material, a number of people were consulted for help, information and suggestions on how to collate the research tools. Whilst

I did not want to dwell on the age of the participants I had to be aware of it in terms of their language skills, their level of understanding and ways of making the material engaging and accessible. To enable the young people to have space in which to explore and express their opinions, the methods needed to be flexible in order to accommodate possible developments and changes within the direction of the project. When devising methods, Christensen and James (2000: 7) advocate the adoption of 'practices which resonate with children's own concerns and routines'. To find out what these were an exploratory questionnaire was devised. All of the methods were piloted first – the pilot study is discussed after this section on methods.

Exploratory Questionnaire

The idea of an exploratory questionnaire provided an opportunity to involve the young people more directly and use some of their answers and ideas as the stimulus for the collection of further data (Boyden and Ennew 1997; Cree 2003). It was also a chance to explore what the young people already knew about the topic and explore their preliminary attitudes. Unlike earlier studies on young people's attitudes (for example, Burton et al. 1998) the 'results' of the questionnaire were not collated statistically and used to demonstrate how many people thought one thing, or how answers differed by school, class or ethnic background. Rather, it was the themes, gendered assumptions and the answers to the open ended questions that highlighted their understanding and constructions of violence that I was most interested in, as well as having access to the language and ideas of the young people, with which to construct the design of the next stage in the research process – the discussion group topics and the vignettes.

The exploratory questionnaire consisted of seven pages, comprising 21 questions, which the young people completed in an average of 20 to 30 minutes. An important aspect of the questionnaire was its focus upon young people (as opposed to adults). The opening pages of the first section therefore asked about their interests, aspirations and responsibilities at home. The third page comprised of statements that sought to challenge (or reveal) gendered stereotypes, which the young people had to rate as *okay*, *not okay* and *not sure*. The inclusion of questions about gender was relevant because of previous research findings detailing the prevalence of restrictive and normative gendered roles and expectations (see McCarry 2003). The final statements focused upon violence to lead them in to the latter half of the questionnaire, which dealt solely with violence and abuse. Many of the questions retained young people as the focal point, but questions pertaining to adults were introduced to see if distinctions were made in relation to the acceptability (or otherwise) of issues among those who were older.

The next section asked specific questions about teasing, abuse and violence: firstly, from the perspective of the first person, then to that of young people and finally culminating with the adults. Each question asked if it was okay or not okay to do these things with enough space provided for the young people to write why this was so. The aim of this section was to replicate some of the myths surrounding violence (such as it is okay to hit a woman if she has had an affair) and extricate what the young people thought about this.

The final section of the questionnaire asked for the young people to take on the role of a news reporter and report upon a violent incident. They were given the choice of either writing a report, drawing a picture to represent the incident or both. It was important to give them a choice of medium so as not to patronise them by asking them to draw a picture simply because they were children (Farquar 1990; Barker and Weller 2003). There was also a wariness of assuming 'that drawing enables children to communicate their thought any more than does conversational language' (Backett-Milburn and McKie 1999: 387).

It was important however to have an alternative element to the questionnaire, where the young people were able to express themselves in a different way rather than simply responding to a question asked of them. Boyden and Ennew (1997: 118) maintain:

> Drawing places children at the centre of the research process as an acting subject. This means that what is expressed is a reflection of a child's own feelings and experiences, capturing more aspects than a researcher might have imagined and freeing the child from the researcher's preconceived frameworks.

Because the drawings represented the participants' own cultural interpretations, they were asked to write a sentence or two to describe what was happening in the picture. This consultation involved a further degree of participation, enabling the young people to note what was significant to them. I agree with Boyden and Ennew (1997) that the child is 'freed' from 'adultist' interpretation, but propose caution when claiming that their words or pictures were always a reflection of their own feelings and experiences. My initial idea was to collate the pictures and use them as stimulus for discussion in the follow-up sessions.[8] On reflection, and following the pilot session, this was decided against, as young people commented more on the standard of the drawings and less on what they thought the picture represented.

8 To ensure informed consent, I had asked the young people to mark their newspaper reports with a tick or a cross to inform me whether I could use them with other schools or replicate them within my own work.

Discussion Group Sessions

Previous research conducted with young people has utilised the 'focus group' method. The rationale for doing so has been a combination of the following factors: to facilitate and access opinions; to explore how views are formed (Bloor et al. 2001); the (ethical) safety of the group environment and enabling the representation and empowerment of the participants. These are all elements of the research process that as a researcher I too wished to harness. Kitzinger and Barbour (1999) maintain that any group discussion can be labelled a focus group as long as the researcher is actively encouraging of and attentive to the group interaction. However, there is a greater distinction between the two than this simple renaming allows for. It was important for the discussion session to be just that: a discussion, without labelling it as something else. The term 'focus group' had the connotation of 'focusing' upon one topic and I felt it was necessary that the participants should not feel restricted in doing so. Also, much of the group session would involve reflecting upon previous answers and opinions, as well as discussing three vignettes.[9] The multiplicity of the sessions therefore, was not reflected in the term 'focus group'. The sessions were called 'discussion groups' to avoid any confusion.

Discussion groups were a method to further explore the thoughts and opinions expressed in the exploratory questionnaire as well as other issues relating to violence against women and girls. Using discussion groups with small numbers of young people (between three and five people), enabled the greatest amount of participation, whilst also making, in practical terms of the discussions and transcribing, more manageable. The sessions took place among friends, ensuring a safe and trusted environment (Morrow 2001: 207), to enable the young people to have a space to explore their own and others' attitudes more reflexively and to question, agree and challenge the responses of others. The group discussion method has previously been used with young children (see Mauthner 1997; Mayall 2000; Highet 2003) a method that they were uninhibited by and very enthusiastic about. Young people can also express opinions without having to draw upon personal experience (Highet 2003), which they may feel obligated to do during individual interviews.

The original intention was to facilitate self-selected friendship groups but discussion of this method was met with reservation by all of the head teachers in the schools taking part. Their concern was about children being left out of the groupings. This was a valid point (and one I had overlooked), as previous research that had incorporated self-selection had usually taken place in youth clubs (for example, Highet 2003), a place where young people tend to go with

9 I recognise the tensions inherent in the fact that I devised the vignettes (although they were based upon some of the issues raised by the young people themselves).

friends. The reservations of the teachers, coupled with my own memories of PE lessons (the same children were always left until last when it came to peer selection of teams) modified the group selection process. Instead, the groupings were decided upon using responses from the exploratory questionnaire, where young people were asked to list three friends in their class.[10]

Developing the Material for the Discussion Groups

After the completion of all four batches of exploratory questionnaires, I sifted through them for an initial analysis. At this stage I was more worried about whether the young people would talk to me, than what we would talk about, resulting in my initial ideas focusing more upon activities and prompts than on the themes identified. However, by rigidly defining the sessions, I had fallen into the trap of hiding my own insecurities as an adult researcher behind such structured activities (Harden et al. 2000; Backett-Milburn 2004). So I took a step back and started again.

There was an incredible amount of data and information resulting from their initial ideas, opinions and responses, so each of the aims of the research was written on a separate piece of paper, which in turn informed and structured the sessions. At the beginning of each discussion group session, the research was verbally described again. I then explained how some of the ideas they had expressed in the exploratory questionnaire would be the basis for the discussion here. What follows is a brief synopsis of how the discussion topics were developed.

A main theme that had come out of the exploratory questionnaire was the gendered expectations and stereotypes that young people attributed to boys and girls and men and women. Whilst of course there were exceptions, many of the young people thought that boys and girls should do different jobs in the home (whereas in reality the young people did similar chores). This highlighted a difference between abstract beliefs and lived realities. There were also restrictive answers given to questions that asked about gender behaviour and equal opportunities, as well as highly gendered responses to the questions on emotional and physical violence (which is discussed further below).

A discussion of what I would call 'gender' (but labelled as 'talking about boys and girls') was a perfect ice-breaker for the group sessions and would be less confrontational (for all) than violence. It was also a means of seeing how young people contextualised violence when talking about gender (or boys and girls), rather than talking about violence first which may have narrowed their focus onto a simple gendered dichotomy. Much research on gender with

10 Although this worked well I had not anticipated how time consuming a process this would be.

younger people has used (participant) observation rather than asking young people what they think, thereby imposing adultist frameworks upon young people's perceptions and views (Thorne 1987; Brown 2007; Tisdall et al. 2009). My initial intention was to use the young people's own photographs as prompts but, upon reflection, it was decided that it would be more plausible for the initial questions to be rooted in personal experience (or could be understood as such), rather than the abstraction of photographs. For example, I first asked:

> 'Why are you glad you were born a girl/boy?'

I had originally thought about directly asking 'How are boys and girls different?' but decided against such a leading question which could have directed them to see boys and girls as fundamentally different, instead of asking them a question that was positively worded. I then went on to enquire:

> 'Would your life be different if you had been born a boy/girl?'

This was asked so their two responses could be aligned. The first question yielded positive answers for the first question and many young people also positioned themselves in relation to what they were not. This second question sought to encourage the young people to discuss the positive and/or negative effects of them changing sex and therefore how this now informed their construction of gender. This had the effect of engaging a more critical discussion of gender because they positioned themselves within the question and engaged with an analysis of how others' reaction to them contributed to gendered identity.

One of the main themes arising from the exploratory questionnaires was the gendered expectations and stereotypes that young people attributed to emotional and physical violence. Many of their answers perpetuated myths and stereotypes that are representative of patriarchal culture, such as that if a woman had done something wrong (such as have an affair) then it was acceptable to reprehend her with violence. Rather than accept these answers without recourse, the discussion groups provided a space in which opinions and ideas could be explored. Phrases were picked that demonstrated the young people both condemning and condoning violence, and were listed under the following headings:

> It is okay for a boy to hit another boy because...
> It is not okay for a boy to hit another boy because...
> It is okay for a boy to hit a girl because...
> It is not okay for a boy to hit a girl because...
> It is okay for a girl to hit a boy because...
> It is not okay for a girl to hit a boy because...

It is okay for a girl to hit another girl because…
It is not okay for a girl to hit another girl because…

Each heading, and its preceding quotes, was on a separate sheet which I laminated and used as a prompt. I randomly read a quote out and ask the young people whether they agreed or disagreed with it and why.

Vignettes

Three vignettes were employed during the discussion group session. Finch (1987: 105) describes vignettes as, 'short stories about hypothetical characters in specified circumstances, to whose situation the interviewee is invited to respond'. The vignettes were a means of generalising about situations rather than relating them to their own specific personal examples (see Stanley and Wise 1993). By using vignettes, young people had the space to analyse, define, explore and explain how they interpreted the situation using the discourses that they had available to them. Talking about situations from the vignettes also gave young people the opportunity to overcome preconceived assumptions about their age, knowledge or capabilities.[11] In a vignette there is no right or wrong answer – the whole process is made less school-like, which in turn empowers the participants (Hood et al. 1996; Morrow 2001). Young people, should they choose to, can talk through the characters. Barter and Renold (1999: 1) maintain that vignettes are helpful in research, 'to allow actions in context to be explored; to clarify people's judgements; and to provide a less personal and therefore less threatening way of exploring sensitive topics'.

There is a need to be wary of the methodological challenges of vignettes, particularly in concluding, 'that responses to vignettes will reflect how individuals actually respond in reality' (Barter and Renold 1999: 3). Even though asking what a third person would do is not the same as asking the participants directly (see Finch 1987), the young people related the situations to themselves, talking about what they would do and were therefore less likely to replicate public accounts of what they thought I wanted to hear. The vignettes were only one methodological tool of this research project, used as a stimulus to further discussion and to frame specific examples of abusive behaviour. Whilst there

11 Originally, when devising the discussion group topics from the exploratory questionnaire, I thought about using role-play in place of the vignettes. I decided against this for the following reasons: the groups would be too small; time constraints; didn't want them going off on a tangent; role-plays are more about play acting – it would be too hard to differentiate their opinions from their dramatic interpretations. It was important to find out what their opinions are rather than over emphasising attributes in their characters that make for good entertainment.

are power implications in the fact that I constructed the vignettes myself – albeit using ideas from the young people – they were used to generate examples of violent incidents, which the young people then discussed in more detail.

The vignettes were devised in response to two factors: Firstly by broadening the discussion topics to include actual instances of violence against women, discussion among the participants would be encouraged, and secondly by uncovering and exploring some of the stereotypes and myths demonstrated by the young people in the previous session, by using concrete examples (Hazel 1995a). Within the discussion groups, vignettes were used both to structure the sessions and also to bring together some of the young people's ideas and configure them for discussion. When devising the vignettes, care was taken not to structure them too tightly so as to allow for interpretation. It was important to include examples of both emotional and physical abuse.

The first vignette was a situation that related specifically to young people at a stage in their lives that they could recognise, incorporating a form of behaviour that was not physical violence. Their age was deliberately not specified but the term 'going out' was used so the young people could relate to the relationship. This vignette developed themes of possession and control using the premise of clothing.

> Claire and Lee have been seeing each other for four months. Claire's favourite outfit is her jeans and vest top. Lee has asked Claire not to wear the vest top because he says other boys look at her and he doesn't like it.

The second vignette was derived from the answers that related to the social practice of housework: whether boys and girls should be expected to do the same chores at home and the gendered assumptions that arose from this. When writing this it was envisaged that Lizzy was doing something independently for herself such as clothes shopping, juxtaposing this independent move with being 'punished' for failing to attend to Dave's needs. It was not expected that the young people would interpret shopping to mean supermarket shopping in anticipation of fulfilling Dave's 'needs'!

> Lizzy and Dave live in Glasgow. One day Lizzy goes out to the shops and when she comes back Dave asks her why dinner isn't ready. Lizzy says she has been busy and hasn't had chance to make anything. Dave slaps Lizzy across the face and tells her that she shouldn't go to the shops without asking him first.

The third vignette described a situation where a woman admitted to having an affair and her boyfriend punched her. The vignette focused upon the affair because this was the situation, if any, where young people were most likely to think that it was okay for a man to hit a woman. It was also important for Jamie to verbalise why he had hit Jenny, so the young people could discuss the word 'deserve'.

> Jamie and Jenny have been together a year. Jamie has just found out that Jenny has been seeing someone else. When he asks her, Jenny denies it at first and then admits she is in love with Roddy. Jamie punches Jenny and gives her a black eye saying that she deserved it.

The vignettes enabled the young people to explore what someone else should do, using their own beliefs and understanding about that particular situation, as well as provoking discussion of the issues raised and justifying their own reasons. For example, if I had said to a group of girls, 'would you do what a boy told you to?' most would probably have said no. However, in the context of a relationship where Claire is wearing a top Lee does not like/approve of, a significant number said Claire should either no longer wear the top, or she should put a cardigan over it – thereby doing what Lee had asked.

The discussion groups were rounded off by me giving the young people laminated cards with the terms: *Domestic Violence* and *Domestic Abuse* on them. Both terms were deliberately used to see if any distinctions were made, or if the young people were only aware of one phrase and not the other. The young people were asked if they had ever heard of either term and then asked if they knew what they meant. It was purposefully not done first so the young people wouldn't contextualise the vignettes using these terms – if they were not aware of them previously. This activity provided a means of 'rounding up' the examples discussed and presented a context for the vignettes. The discussions also highlighted the relevance of the terms to the young people: as a specific form of violence, as the only form of violence against women, as a lesser form of violence. The discussion groups lasted between 30 and 50 minutes and ended with me giving out the information sheet of websites and contact numbers and thanking the young people for their participation. All of the young people generally expressed an interest in what was to happen to the data.

The Pilot Study

The choice of school to use for the pilot resulted from circumstance. There were two schools within close proximity and the one that could begin the sessions earliest became the pilot. In qualitative research, particularly, there are so many factors involved, that unless each school and all the participants in the research are exact replicas, you can never anticipate all of the problems or hitches in your research design. However, the aim of the pilot was to directly ask the participants what they did and did not understand, and observe how they handled each of the sessions; also to flag up any issues concerning the methods and the young people's involvement. It was also an opportunity for me to think critically about how I presented myself to the teachers and young people, as well as working out the logistics and timing of the sessions. The following section describes the piloting of the separate parts of the study.

The Pilot Study: The Exploratory Questionnaire

The exploratory questionnaire was devised and piloted first. There was only one small change in wording from 'who are your friends' to 'name three of your friends'; as the original responses elicited the names of almost half the class. Revisions were made and then the final questionnaire was used with the four participating schools. One of the changes made as a result of this preliminary session was to give the questionnaire to the teacher at the same time as the rest of the class and not beforehand. This was because the teacher had requested to see the questionnaire when I originally visited. Following the pilot session, I secured the impression that several of the questions had been worked through with the young people, with the teacher believing she was helping me by 'preparing' the class. After a preliminary reading and analysis of all of the questionnaires in all of the schools (i.e. not just the pilot questionnaire), topics were identified and devised for the discussion group sessions.

The Pilot Study: Discussion Group Sessions

The discussion group topics were piloted with four groups (18 children) from the initial (pilot) school. Five changes came out of this:

- The first change involved the initial discussions around gender. I began by writing their responses down but this took too long and focused too much upon the act of writing rather than on the wider discussions. This technique was changed because the pilot highlighted it to be unnecessary, distracting and time consuming.
- The second involved the laminated sheets detailing perspectives on gendered violence. During the pilot sessions, the sheet was given to the young people to look through and comment upon. This tended to mean that they focussed upon those they disagreed with, or simply pointed to each statement flatly saying 'agree' or 'disagree'. The task also took far too long, which resulted in a loss of interest and boredom among the participants. In light of these failings, the session was adapted to include a randomly read out selection and the young people being to discuss them, resulting in much a more responsive and animated debate.

- The third change involved the vignettes. In the pilot sessions, the vignettes were alternated, choosing two out of the three each time. However, it was later decided to use all three, as a discussion of each situation was important as well as observing how the young people contextualised them in relation either to the one that preceded it or the one that followed that. It was deemed important to order the vignettes in terms of what could be termed 'gravitas' of the abuse, otherwise the young people may have their ability to contextualise the scene obscured by what had preceded it. However, if the emotionally abusive situation was discussed first, the comments tended to originate solely from that situation and not from its context within what they judged to be abusive situations.
- The fourth amendment was to focus the final discussion of violence upon the cards: Domestic Violence and Domestic Abuse, rather than using the young people's own drawings (which they had consented to be used) as a stimulus for discussion, as there tended to be more debate about their quality than the actual content.
- The final change that was made was the decision to have a set running order rather than randomly selecting the topics. This gave the sessions coherence in that I knew what we had covered and what we still had left to do. It also made the analysis easier in that the sections were more clearly defined and comparisons between the transcripts were less problematic.

Following the pilot, and the changes, the discussion group sessions were then undertaken with the remaining schools. The tape-recorded sessions were then transcribed verbatim.

Making Sense of the Data

The 'official' process of analysis began after the exploratory questionnaires and continued until the final drafts of the analysis chapters were completed and from the outset I kept a fieldwork diary detailing observations, ideas and meetings. In keeping with the similarities between feminist methodologies and children's participation theories, the suggestions for empowering the analysis process are again remarkably comparable (Stanley and Wise 1993; Oakley 1994; Thomas and O'Kane 1998). There are, however, very few guidelines on how best to conduct analysis, in part because of the magnitude of the task and diversity of subjects. Coffey and Atkinson (1996: 158) assert:

> Our task as qualitative researchers is to use ideas in order to develop interpretations that go beyond the limits of our own data and that go beyond the limits how previous scholars have used those ideas. It is in that synthesis that new interpretations and new ideas emerge.

There continue to be calls for participant involvement in the analysis process (Morrow and Richards 1996; Oakley 1994; Thomas and O'Kane 1998; Ward 1997). The time constraints of the fieldwork meant that was not possible on a large scale; however the young people did have the opportunity to (re)evaluate and interpret the comments they and others had made in relation to the discussions on violence, providing an element of 'respondent validation' (Guba and Lincoln 1994) as well as the means to demonstrate their own interpretations and meanings, 'researchers [...] are still assuming that a shared meaning attaches to words: that the question asked will be the one that is understood' (Hollway and Jefferson 2000: 11).

To re-familiarise myself with the participants in each group and remind myself of anything worthy of note – body language, arguments, unrecorded discussions – the transcripts were read and re-read alongside the fieldwork notes. This helped to further contextualise the transcripts. The process of transcribing was particularly tedious and longwinded. Even though the group sizes were comparably small, the mixture of competing and quiet voices meant that several parts of the tapes remained inaudible requiring constant listening and re-listening. During the transcriptions, I had made preliminary notes, which were then transposed onto the transcripts with additional highlighting and comments. Although the transcription process was a long and laborious one, it was useful in reinforcing familiarity with the data. Key themes began to emerge and these were grouped together. My analysis followed a similar route to that identified by Mauthner and Doucet (1998: 126–32) in their description of their voice-centred relational method:

- Reading for the plot – main events and sub plots, recurrent images, contradictions and metaphors in the narrative
- Reading for the voice of 'I' – the way the participants experience, talk and feel about themselves
- Reading for relationships with partners, relatives, children and social networks
- Placing participants within cultural contexts and social structures.

In following these themes I was able to distinguish the ways and words young people used to speak about violence, tracing the different and competing constructions. This method was also used to highlight how and when young people talked of violence, the contexts, the examples and the justifications used. It was important not to remove the quotes entirely from the context, for fear of changing the meaning or losing the young person's train of thought. It was also relevant to illuminate how the words spoken by the young person may have resulted from the response of somebody else. Again it was critical not to lose this sense of perspective within the analysis.

By reading and re-reading the data, other themes began to emerge that at first seemed isolated, but began to reappear in other transcripts when I looked for them. Very often some of the themes that were not immediately obvious came to light when I was totally immersed in the data. I kept a note of these themes, developing links between them, which in turn unearthed further examples. I could begin to identify emerging concepts piecing together what Mason identifies as the *intellectual puzzle* (2004: 159), all the while keeping in mind, that it was critical not to assume a relationship between things (Hollway and Jefferson 2000) or to take meanings for granted.

Part of this 'puzzle' involved returning to the theoretical literature in order to contextualise what the young people were saying. I also drew upon my own understandings, existing theoretical knowledge and the young people's contribution to generate and substantiate the conceptual frameworks that were emerging. Primarily the answers and explanations the young people gave were highlighted to see how they linked to existing theories. For example, their explanations of violence were initially positioned in relation to gender. Themes were then identified that remained outside of these frameworks such as age and time; space and location; distance and proximity. These themes kept reoccurring and conceptual links began to be formulated that were further endorsed by repetition in the transcripts. Bryman (2008: 391–2) maintains that the findings of research are to be used, 'to generalise to theory rather than to populations'. I understand this to mean that the strength of my data lies in its application to, and reciprocity of my generated concepts, rather than its repetition through numbers. Silverman (2000: 362) qualifies this with his advice, 'don't be satisfied until your generalisation is able to apply to every single gobbet of relevant data you have collected'.

In analysing the data, I was aware that my own interpretive account would be privileged, as it is here that I frame the young people's understandings within a conceptual feminist framework alongside my own experiential knowledge and beliefs. Throughout the fieldwork and the analysis process I felt the conflict between researcher and interpretive privilege. Opie (1992) warns of the limitations of feminist interpretations which I was aware of in structuring my analysis. Whilst I wanted to enable previously unknown or hidden knowledge to be liberated, I also was aware of the dangers of restricting the data to fit my feminist framework (ibid. 1992: 52). To illustrate this conflict, it is necessary to acknowledge the tensions between 'producing an analysis which goes beyond the experience of the researched whilst still granting them full subjectivity' (Acker et al. 1983: 129) whilst also recognising that, 'individuals do not necessarily possess sufficient knowledge to explain everything about their lives' (Maynard and Purvis 1994: 6). It is also significant to note that they may not have the interest or the energy to do so either! As such, this research and the subsequent analysis are my own interpretation of the data. I make no claims to objectivity, as I do not support the view that there is an objective truth to produce, but I do claim to have developed through my analysis, strong conceptual frameworks that aid in understanding what young people think about men's violence against women.

Validity and Reliability

Bryman (2008) maintains that the criteria of reliability and validity used for assessing much social science research are not always applicable to qualitative research (although this view is disputed; see Le Compte and Goetz 1982; Kirk and Miller 1986; Mason 2004). The same terms, when applied to young people and research, have been detrimental and used as a means to corroborate evidence of their unreliability and less than valid opinions. Bryman (2008) suggests appropriating Guba and Lincoln's (1994) critique of realism to develop alternative criteria by which to evaluate qualitative data and analysis. Guba and Lincoln's criteria focused upon the themes of 'trustworthiness' and 'authenticity'. The methods of analysis undertaken in my research are aligned with their criteria to highlight the ethicacy, the good practice and the detailed transparency of the findings and subsequent development of conceptual themes. The examples are not always specific as they permeate the whole research process, from the conception of the argument, through the fieldwork and onwards to the dissemination of the findings. Guba and Lincoln's (1994) criteria are listed below with some examples (in italics) of how my research adhered to their principles:

Trustworthiness

- Credibility: Good practice and respondent validation (*feedback from the young people during the discussion groups based upon their answers to the exploratory questionnaires*).
- Transferability: Make the process clear and provide rich accounts of the details of the culture (*detailed examples of this in this chapter and the following chapters*).
- Dependability: Auditing and keeping records (*detailed fieldwork diary; transcripts and additional notes; commitment to dissemination*).
- Confirmability: Letting the data speak for itself (*using large chunks of transcription to convey meaning*).

Authenticity

- Fairness: Does the research fairly represent different viewpoints among members of the social setting? (*Including all of the young people's voices and detailing sections where differing views are expressed*).
- Ontological authenticity: Does the research help members to arrive at a better understanding of their social milieu? (*The final section of the discussion group session enabled debate around differing terms and provided an opportunity for the young people to*

ask questions).

- Educative authenticity: Does the research help members to appreciate better the perspectives of other members of their social setting? (*The discussion sessions enabled other viewpoints, from other schools to be presented and debated. Also, there is the opportunity for differing views to be presented during the dissemination process*).
- Catalytic authenticity: Has the research acted as an impetus to members to engage in action to change their circumstances? (*The research has raised awareness of the issues among participants and encouraged debate and discussion. Dissemination of findings to encourage such impetus among young people, schools and education departments*). (Adapted from Bryman 2008: 376–80; incorporating Lincoln and Guba 1985, 1994)

This list is not exhaustive and has been modified further by social scientists. An addition relevant to this research is that of 'impact and importance'; of having significance in terms of theory development, the wider community and for practitioners (Yardley 2000). It is also critical to engage with the power 'in' the data. For example, the points at which some of the participants dominated the sessions and also the prominence given to certain people's words, over and above others. I was aware of my power to 'choose' and thus privilege one person's knowledge over and above another. A conscious effort was made to include quotes from all of the sessions and not just those that were 'eminently quotable' (Brown 2007).

Reflections on the Research Process

The main advice I would give to researchers embarking upon a similar task is to let the young people speak. That is, provide a space and ample opportunities for them to be heard and let this continuously inform the research process. This can prove difficult in an environment where both time and space are limited. Yet make the best of the time available by ensuring that young people are constantly involved, both within the research and outwith (to question the methods and reasons for the research). This is critical especially if there is not the time available for the young people to actively design the research themselves (as was the case here).

The main success of this research was the value of the vignettes. These short stories were used to contextualise specific situations of men's violence against women and to provide a starting point for discussions. The young people engaged with this method and were eager to debate their own opinions. However, when using vignettes, there is also the need for abstract discussion too, which is generally averted in much research with children and young people (Finch 1987; Hazel 1995a, 1995b, 1999; Hood et al. 1996; Morrow 2001). This is necessary, not only to explore how the young people may react 'in reality'

(Barter and Renold 1999), but also, in the case of this research, to explore the juxtaposition of the 'abstract' and the 'real life' examples. Here, a disjuncture was revealed between how young people constructed and understood men's violence against women, with the 'abstract' examples being 'real' and the situations in the vignettes more likely to be *naturalised*, *normalised* and in particular *justified*. The relationships created for the vignettes created a context in which young people justified the violent actions of the perpetrator and the apparent complicity of the woman.

Kelly (1988, 1994) maintains feminist research needs to reflexively include the researchers' problems and experiences too. There is a genuine need as a researcher to flag up your learning and highlight any weaknesses or flaws during your fieldwork, so you and others may benefit. I have chosen to highlight four areas which all relate to the issue of power. To conclude this section, I reflect upon the positive aspects of the research, as this is an oft neglected element of reflexive, qualitative research.

Space, Power and Privacy

The subject of space relates very specifically to the concept of power and a young person's right to privacy. The young people did not possess a space that they could call their own without being subject to adult scrutiny.[12] There were several times during the course of the fieldwork that I had to reassert their right to privacy. During the questionnaire sessions some teachers looked over the shoulders of the young people, read what they were writing or asked me who had written what. As the discussion groups were in separate rooms, I anticipated that any further invasions of privacy would be prevented. However, during one meeting with a teacher, prior to the discussion groups, I was asked to wait in the library where I would be carrying out the sessions. In the 10 minutes I waited there, as many people walked in. It was then I resolved to make notices: 'Please do not disturb, recorded interviews in progress'. Confidently believing this would solve the problem, I gave it little thought during the actual discussion groups, until the interruptions began. I was so surprised by the number of teachers who had very little respect for their pupil's privacy. Teachers walked in without knocking and remained undeterred when I explained we were in the middle of an interview, with some telling us to just carry on. Each time I made a point of stopping the tape so I could talk to the participants about why their privacy was important. Whilst I am aware of the need for access and the limited resources faced by many schools, there were teachers (and other pupils) who did

12 In comparison to the teachers who had the social space of the staff room as well as possessing the authority to create their own privacy in the classroom by shutting the door to keep pupils out.

not respect the privacy of young people. Indeed, Alderson (2000) goes so far as to assert that some teachers in her research believed they had an entitlement to be included in the details disclosed by their students.

Power: Gender Dynamics

When devising the groups from the friendship lists given to me by the young people, I noted that the majority of them were single-sex. Initially, and somewhat naively, I anticipated that this meant that many of the gendered dynamics would be tempered by the same-sex groupings. However, gendered power struggles did occur between boys and girls in the groups where there were both sexes and girls in these groups were silenced more than in other groups. Some examples in the following chapters illustrate the power dynamics around the competing masculinities present in all male groups, and how the hegemonic form (displayed using aggression and acceptance of violence) overrules the others. So the gender dynamics in the groups were not just created around masculinities and femininities, but different and competing forms of masculinities.

Power: The Researcher

There were very specific times during the fieldwork when I was aware that I, as the researcher, was in a position of power. An example of this was my realisation that I am an adult woman, with the means and verbal resources with which to defend myself and my gender. Towards the end of the fieldwork, I had one group remaining at Mary Magdalene Primary. It was originally meant to include three boys and two girls but one of the girls was ill, so there were only four in the group. We were discussing the second vignette (Lizzy and Dave) and an argument began between the three boys and the girl over who should cook the dinner in a relationship. I probed some of their opinions with phrases such as 'Can you tell me what you mean by that?' and 'Can you explain that for me'. Although I did not agree with what the boys were saying, I remained impartial. However, there came a point where, in retrospect, two things happened. I began to identify with the 11-year-old girl who was trying so desperately to argue that men and women should have equal roles within a household, and secondly, I began to feel the boys were bullying and laughing at her. So I intervened. I didn't want to say that she was right and they were wrong, but I wanted to enable the girl to get her point across in a powerful way. One of the boys had just said that men go out to work and women stay at home because if they both went out to work they would not have any dinner until later (and that was why women should make the dinner). I asked:

> Nancy: So is that not what happens in real life? Men and women go out to work?
> Craig: No, women mainly stay in the house.
> (Mary Magdalene School, Group 5)

I then asked for a show of hands, to indicate whose dad went out to work (all) and whose mum went out to work (all). I then let the discussion continue. I have wrangled over this interference again and again and have come to the conclusion that I was standing up for my 10-year-old self. Whether this is ethically sound is debatable, but I felt that the need to help the lone girl (and stop the sexist bullying) outweighed researcher neutrality. This illuminates the disjuncture between realities and their 'talk' among their peers. It also highlights the need to be aware of possible power dynamics within the groupings, as with hindsight I should not have let this particular discussion group go ahead.

Power: The Teachers

It is important to remember that power differentials in the research relationship are not only evident between the researcher and the participants; there are also power imbalances integral to the research process and there were those that had power over me. I found myself continually having to negotiate and will illustrate this point with two examples from the fieldwork. The first example was the power that teachers had when introducing me to their class and how this simple process could be so different. In one school, the head teacher (the symbol of authority in most schools) insisted on taking me to the classroom. She introduced me as 'Miss Lombard' and she explained the research. She presented me as being at university and thus very clever and then said 'some of you, not all, but some of you one day could be like her'. In another school, a teacher who had forgotten I was even coming, said 'hey come on in, this is Nancy everyone'. I explained the research very informally, stressing the importance of their own consent, their choices and involvement and they asked questions throughout. I had to work harder in the first school for them not to see me as an instrument of the school and for them not to feel bound by the roles dictated to them by the school environment; they put their hands up to talk to me even in the discussion groups and every time they referred to me it was as 'Miss'.

Another example of power negotiations was when one day I turned up at one school, having organised the friendship groups to begin the discussion sessions that day. Upon encountering the teacher, she presented me with a list of the groupings *she* had drawn up, excluding three, what she called, 'troublemakers'. Upon questioning her about it she said that two girls and a boy had been found with a pornographic magazine and she said she didn't want them to take part. I asked if they had parental consent and she said yes and I said that I thought they should still take part. She conceded, but said I shouldn't let them talk about anything sexual and if they did, for me to return them to the classroom. At the end of the discussion group, I asked if there were any questions. One of the girls in question said 'I think it's really good that you want to come here and actually listen to what we say'. The attitude of the teacher, coupled with what this girl said, really inspired me and assured me of the importance of my own and other research being carried out with young people.

Positive Reflections

It is all too easy to bemoan what went wrong and how you should have done things differently. Re-reading the comment above reminded me of many positive aspects of the research process. The enthusiasm of the young people was a constant theme throughout the fieldwork and can be attributed to much more than getting out of lessons. Many of the young people commented on how they appreciated having time out of the classroom to talk with their friends, take part in the research and having me listen to them. This zeal permeated all of the sessions and resulted in very few 'awkward' moments of 'shoe-gazing'. Indeed, one of the main difficulties during the discussion sessions was facilitating individual turns. For me this was proof that the methods chosen were appropriate because the young people were animated in their engagement of them. In hindsight, I can see that one of the most creative decisions I made, was to reflect the answers of the young people back upon themselves (during the discussion group sessions). This not only demonstrated their active involvement in the design of the discussion group topics, but also enabled them to critically challenge or agree with the statements of their peers. As a researcher, this provided me with a form of continuous analysis, whereby the young people were engaging with the meanings and interpretations of certain data and also contributing to the respondent validation. It also highlighted the danger of taking their opinions at face value, without providing opportunities for their own accompanying explanations and justifications which is a key feature in the methodology developed here.

Dissemination

A major part of the research process is the dissemination strategy. This was not 'tagged on' as an afterthought or something that came about because my findings were particularly spectacular; rather it was planned from the outset. It was vital to engage with those who had been involved in the research (either as participants or gatekeepers) and those who could use the research findings to further inform their practice, or to support bids for funding that identified need. The strategy therefore differed depending upon the audience, resulting in dissemination to the young people, who were sent a short report with the key findings and an explanation of what these meant; Glasgow City Council and all of the primary schools in Glasgow at a dissemination conference, opened by Johann Lamont MSP, where I presented the key findings from the research to 70 educational practitioners, followed by a workshop session organised in conjunction with Scottish Women's Aid (SWA) and Youth Lesbian, Gay, Bisexual and Transgender Scotland (YLGBTS); for practitioners at workshops, conferences and training events, including the development of training materials for Youth workers; the general public, through newspapers, radio, internet (blogs) and television; government – at debates at the Scottish Parliament and Welsh Assembly and talks at the United Nations and UNESCO; as well as ongoing engagement with the academic community through publications, blogs and invited conference presentations. The exploratory questionnaire has since been used in further research (see Raab 2007). After successfully obtaining a Beltane Honorary Fellowship, I developed a gender awareness training programme for primary school practitioners that will also be embedded within the Sexual Health and Relationships Education component of the Curriculum for Excellence.

Summary

To confront and challenge men's violence and its everyday occurrence and acceptability (Stanko 1985), we need to encourage the exploration and discussion of these issues, rather than hiding behind the veneers of incompetence and innocence which some adults appropriate in order to prevent young people's participation. Recognising and challenging these discursive restrictions was a critical part of the research. This chapter has explored the philosophical underpinnings to this research study bringing together key elements that are fundamental to feminist research. It is argued that feminist research and the sociology of childhood share key philosophies in terms of empowering participants and dealing reflexively with issues of power. It is these similarities that have influenced the research process and went on to inform the generation of the participatory methods used.

In providing an overview of the research and fieldwork processes, I have aimed to make the decisions, and the reasons behind them, understandable and transparent – and to recognise the subjectivity inherent in this research project. It is impossible to fully convey the dynamism of the methods and young people's enthusiasm to participate. It is generally easier to describe the shortcomings and the changes I would make with hindsight. Each method is not without its disadvantages, and although some problems could be anticipated, and to some extent dissipated (such as ensuring all participants were given the opportunity to contribute), others could only be grappled with at the time. Yet this is all part of the evolving research process, with honest reflection and reflexivity critical parts of this. The subjectivity involved in the interpretation and analysis of the data were made clear, with attempts being made to counter the powerful position of me as the researcher through the empowerment of the participants in the participatory methods and dissemination of the findings. The methods described here were a means of enabling the young people to engage with the research.

Chapter 4
Gender Constructions

Introduction

This chapter explores the competing means by which young people construct their own and others' gender identities. It is through constructing gender that young people understand power. This is the initial step in the process of analysing the pivotal relationship between young people, gender and violence. By looking at young people's perceptions of gendered behaviour their constructed understandings of male dominance and male power became explicit.

Young people construct gender discursively through their language and performances and institutionally through their positioning of their own identities in relations to social and cultural structures. It is not the intention of this chapter to focus upon other intersectional identities of self, such as class, ethnicity or ability, but where they are introduced as relevant either by the young people themselves or present as pertinent themes, they are discussed. The construction and negotiation of the young people's gender identities are presented here in relation to three prominent discursive themes:

- the embodiment of gender
- the performance of gender
- institutional regimes of gender.

It is necessary to note that these themes were not disparate, or progressive: the young people did not access or detail them linearly. Indeed, the themes were contradictory and interwoven, subscribed to and disregarded as the young people explored their own and others' constructions of gender. Ironically what these themes had in common were the contradictions. Yet what unified the themes were young people's constant construction of age (through the dichotomy of young and old) and space (through the binary of proximity and distance; lived experience and abstraction). The young people's own lived experience (as the basis of their knowledge) and the anticipation of their future lives offers a unique insight into their conceptualisations of gender.

The Embodiment of Gender

Discourses of Biology and the Physicality of Gender

The body was used as a starting point for gender difference, with the majority of young people accessing discourses of biology and physicality, positioning *all* boys and *all* girls as the same (but as different from the other). The young people readily accessed formal terminology to describe (male) hormones and the functions of the body revealing a sound knowledge of biological differences. However they were much less self-assured when it came to talking about male and female genitals as the extract below demonstrates:

John: You'd look different, you know...
Nancy: Different?
John: You know.
[Laughter]
Tommy: He means downstairs.
[Laughter]
John: He told me to say it.
Nancy: Okay so you'd be different 'downstairs'. Would that matter?
All: Yeah [forcefully and incredulously]
Nancy: Okay, why would that matter?
Tommy: 'Cause it's better having, you know, being a boy.
Simon: It's what makes you a boy.
Tommy: It's what means you're not a girl.

(Mary Magdalene School, Group 3)

Whether they had other words to choose instead of the vague 'downstairs', 'down there' and 'you know' was not clear but their inability and reluctance to share was obvious. This research was before the roll out of Sexual Health and Relationship Education (SHRE) in Glasgow for P1 to S6 and I was inhibited by introducing such words within a school-based context without prior approval. However, this problem of lack of words is well documented and not just in the academic literature (Moran 2011).

The differences for the young people were pertinent, but they rarely accessed a language with which to describe them, thereby ascribing almost a mythical status to their own indicators of difference. Participants were worried that even by talking about genitals they would get into trouble. It is significant to note that the young people had access to very few words to describe their own or other people's bodies and when they tried to, they were uncomfortable, demonstrated bravado or thought that I would chastise them for being 'dirty'. For many, these parts of their bodies were associated with urinary functions and sexual activities both of which had the connotations of being 'rude' or 'dirty'. The boys in the group above had actively tried to make me feel awkward, whispering, laughing and goaded by their friends to try and embarrass me because of the association of describing these parts of their bodies with being rude. These discussions highlighted the restrictions young people felt when talking about their own and others' bodies and their need for access to an acceptable language with which to do so. This confirms the endurance of the contested terrain that is 'sex education' and its dichotomy of whether it is to 'constrain' or 'empower' (Thorogood 2000; see also Moore 2012).

Although boys have more words with which to describe their bodies, they can be placed upon a (subjective) binary of childlike and inoffensive and adult and derogatory with only the term penis proving 'acceptable'. The same scale could be adapted for girls and with vagina being marginally acceptable but not wholly descriptive of what is there. The difference between these subjective binaries is the absence of any words for females that are used in a powerfully 'complimentary' or 'flattering' way to describe their genitals. These exist for men thus inscribing both the male genitals and the words with symbolic power.

Having a penis was identified as an important facet in the life of a boy and not one that the boys wanted to lose. The word penis was not used directly, only alluded to – often in a way that personified its presence. A penis was described as 'better', signalling a perceived advantage; its presence is what makes you a boy and not a girl. Girls were signified by their *absence* of a penis and not by the presence of something else (Braun and Kitzinger 2001; Cornog 1986). Interestingly, but unsurprisingly, there was no mention of the clitoris, the site of sexual pleasure for girls and women, nor was it alluded to (see also Allen 2004, 2005). Thus the hidden and private nature of women's bodies is a symbol of double jeopardy. The 'privacy' of their 'private' parts meant that not only were they hidden from view but they also had access to few words with which to describe them. Although identified as a symbol of 'difference', the lack of importance given to girls' genitalia instead creates it as an oppositional symbol, constructing girls as 'other' and deemed as absent or lacking. Having a penis was viewed as a symbol of freedom in terms of having the ability to pee where you wanted 'in bushes', 'in the park' and whilst 'standing up', none of which were freedoms afforded to the girls. The symbolic nature of the freedom provided by the phallus was viewed as further limiting to girls who could not exercise this same independence of, or within, their female bodies. For example, the expectation that their bodies should be hidden from the public sphere (discussed in Chapter 7) is in contrast to male appropriation of female bodies for public display (for example, mainstream media and pornography).

Girls' bodies were generally ignored with the gender difference invested in the adult bodies of women, which were then aligned with their reproductive capacity or biological functions, in particular periods, pregnancy and childbirth (by girls and boys). The role of motherhood was embraced by many of the girls (and highlighted by them as a positive reason for being a girl) with fatherhood rarely given the same credence and was never highlighted by boys as a reason they were pleased to be boys, suggesting that motherhood is strongly aligned with being a woman whereas the role of 'father' was not naturalised in the same way. When young people talked of their parents or parenting they did so in reference to 'mum', paralleling a woman's biological ability with her capacity to care.

While the joys (as described, and anticipated, solely by girls) of being 'a mum' were significant, the focus upon women's bodies was relayed in terms of physical pain and hardship:

Adam:	You have to go through *more pain* [if you are a girl].
Nancy:	Okay, more pain, what do you mean by that?
Adam:	Like if someone gets pregnant, then they are pregnant and then *giving birth*. You usually go through *pain* with that.

(Mountview School, Group 3, emphasis added)

Nancy:	Is there anything that you can do because you are a girl that you wouldn't be able to do if you were a boy?
Ruth:	Have babies. It's *unfair* because women have to go through *more pain* than boys do. Boys have to support them but women *have got to have the baby* and *go through* the pregnancy.

(Clifton School, Group 4, emphasis added)

In the second example, the role of the male in childbirth is introduced in terms of the expectation of his support (whether this is in a caring or financial capacity is not made apparent), but a heterosexual model of the family is clearly subscribed to, and expected. The term 'fair' is explored in relation to advantage and disadvantage and the inequity women experience in terms of the physical burdens of carrying and bearing children. That this burden carries on beyond the birth was exposed as an obvious dichotomy in the questionnaire responses when it came to expectations around childcare (see *Institutional Regimes of Gender*).

The expectation of women as carers was created and sustained because of the physical role they had already performed a status reaffirmed through much of the literature as a 'labour of love' (Graham 1983; McKie et al. 2002). Thus the inescapability of having to bear children was challenged as unfair, and an inequity of being female, but the 'naturalised' expectation of caring for the children was less so. It is significant to note the differing temporal labels (women alongside boys) implicating the ageless dividend of patriarchal power (Connell 1997).

The physical pain endured by (adult) women was listed as a reason why boys were pleased they were not girls and why girls wished they weren't girls either. All of the young people discussed (female) pain in one form or another (periods, pregnancy, childbirth) yet then proceeded to juxtapose this with the assertion that a gender difference between men and women was that men and boys were stronger, tougher and can endure more pain. Young people use the dualism, and the stereotypes invested in them, as evidence of gender difference. The young people interpret the physical pain some women may experience as a heavily gendered form of pain, which they naturalise and accept as women's 'lot'. The physical demands upon a woman's body were ascribed as 'natural' and a contributory factor to their inherent weakness. In contrast men's strength (embodied by the boys) was asserted as choice, a sense of power that they were entitled to because they were not limited by the 'naturalised' constraints of their masculinised bodies:

David: We are bigger.
Michael: We are stronger.
Iain: We get to be tough.

(Mary Magdalene School, Group 4)

They would then, however, contradict such assumptions, sometimes unknowingly and other times consciously, with their own experience and knowledge, utilising these to provide evidence to the contrary:

Tommy: You say all girls are weak but Stacey'd do you!
[Laughter]

(Mary Magdalene School, Group 3)

In the example above, the boys are talking about a specific girl in their class who does not conform to the attributes of 'femininity', and therefore they can use this embodied example of Stacey to contradict the stereotype. When constructions of gender, and power, were destabilised by their own experiential knowledge it became easier for them to do so. The implications of this for teaching practice are unambiguous.

Other physical variations discussed were outwardly expressive and culturally divergent but some of the young people talked about them as though they were fixed and stable indicators of what it meant to be a boy or a girl. This was because they were indicators that some of the young people embodied themselves; therefore they were talking about their own lived experiences of gender (for example, hair length, earrings, makeup, jewellery) many of which were also expressions of their movement into 'tween' age cultures (Russell and Tyler 2005). Others talked of dualisms that were either not clearly represented through their own physical appearances (muscles, hairiness or breasts) or were overtly challenged by group members. Young people propagated the alignment of the gendered self with physical appearance with the implication was that if your gender changed so would your appearance. In doing so, their discussions and understandings began to destabilise 'fixed' categories of physicality and gender difference:

Tommy: If you were a girl you'd have to have a shower when you get up and wash your hair.
John: And comb it.
Chris: And getting a haircut, that takes a long time.

(Mary Magdalene School, Group 3)

Nancy: Would your life be different if you were a girl?
Craig: You'd have long hair.

(Mary Magdalene School, Group 5)

Nancy: Would your life be different if you were a boy?
Farah: You'd have short hair.

(Baxter Road School, Group 2)

Lucy: [If you were a boy] you'd be colder 'cause your hair isn't long enough.

(Mary Magdalene School, Group 1)

Whilst it can be argued that this notion of hair length simply perpetuates stereotyped images of gender conformity, the operation of gender is revealed as a fragile construction that can be inverted through deviating slightly from the 'norm'. More than half of the young people equated being a boy with having short hair and being a girl with having long hair. The young people themselves did not equally represent this, and so challenged the conception, yet they still deemed it an accepted gender attribute. The boys in the following quote challenged this conception through revelations about their own hair length, conspicuous under their turbans.

Nancy: So why are you glad that you are boys?
Vikram: We can do more sports.
Adam: We don't have to have long hair.
Vikram: We have long hair but.
Adam: Do you?
Vikram: Aye, it's down to here [points to shoulders].
Sandeep: Mine is down to here [points to lower back].

Adam: Wow I never knew that did you?
Andrew: No.

(Mountview School, Group 3)

The surprise of the other boys in the group was equalled by their fascination and the two Sikh boys boasted their hair length to jostle for this unexpected hegemonic crown. Here, the cultural differences inverted gender expectation with the correlation of hair length alongside masculinity and power whilst also highlighting a level of cultural ignorance, as these boys had been peers, and friends, for more than five years.

Embodied Gender

In focusing upon the gendered body there is a need to make the necessary demarcation between the body as *determining* gender and the embodiment of gender as *socially constructing* of gender. This is to:

> challenge … the assumption that the biological make-up of our bodies is the 'basis', 'foundation', 'framework', or 'mould' of the social relations of gender. (Connell 1987: 67)

Hughes and Witz (1997) describe embodiment as a means of experiencing and understanding gender identity, as a *lived matter of gender*. McNay goes further to describe the intersections of embodiment:

> At the point of overlap between the physical, the symbolic and the sociological, the body is a dynamic, mutable frontier. The body is the threshold through which the subject's lived experience of the world is incorporated and realized and as such, is neither pure object nor pure subject. (McNay 1999: 98)

Young people constructed and experienced gender through embodiment. This binary is further compounded by the restriction of definition and language with which to theorise gender (Paechter 2006). Indeed our understanding of gender and gender identity is hindered and:

> exacerbated by our inability to define either masculinity or femininity except in relation to each other and to men and women … This is because masculinity and femininity are not just constructed in relation to each other their relation is dualistic. A dualistic relation is one in which the subordinate term is negated, rather than the two sides being in equal balance. (2006: 254–6)

As such it is difficult to construct gender as anything but dualistic and in relation to the 'other' (generally masculine) identity and as situated within a heterosexual framework.

Recently theoretical focus has returned to the body in terms of deconstructing essentialist arguments of the fixed body but also conceptualising the body as located in space (Young 1990; Valentine 1996; Rose 1997). Analysis of the body is critical in understanding young people's gender constructions in terms of space and time. For example, violence is a means of disrupting space and of damaging bodies, and changing bodies represent the physical passage of time. The body is a part of space in terms of being a localised entity but it is also a temporal concept in that it changes and develops. It performs and it can be institutionalised. It is critical to further examine the concept of embodiment using the lens of temporality in terms of understanding the body as transitional, for example becoming 'more gendered' over time.

Grown-Up (Gendered) Bodies

The fragility of construction was again exposed when gender was linked with the physicality of the body because none of the (grown-up) examples described by the young people were representative of who they were. They traded upon stereotyped notions of grown-up bodies and dichotomous views of what it means for men and women to have perfect bodies. This was a tactic used by many of the young people; they looked to the future to access physical differences between men and women, or as a means to consolidate the differences they perceived already existed. Such differences were representative of what they were to 'become' highlighting their own dichotomies of young and old with becoming more gendered. Renold (2005) also noted the:

> illusion of size and strength [as] … a constant battle and the tension between the 'ideal' and 'lived experience' of doing 'manly' masculinity confronted boys daily, both in their failure to meet 'hegemonic' standards of 'older' masculinities and in their inability to convincingly demonstrate their difference from weak and passive femininities. (2005: 81)

The manhood many of the boys described was unachievable in their present state of an 11-year-old body and but the gender differences were ever present. This proposition of 'creation' has been replicated in studies looking at boys and young men yet failing to examine whether such expressions are the authentic voices of the boys interviewed, or an investment in public discourses of esteemed (adult) masculinity. O'Donnell and Sharpe (2000) argue that boys have not yet solidified their masculine identity, but by suggesting this, they are defining masculine identity as a fixed and stable concept *at some point.*

It is important therefore, to recognise that the development and application of masculinity for both boys and men, is an active and ongoing construction in relation to their embodied selves (young and old), the social definition of their environment (school, work, home) and the shifting social, cultural and historical contexts (Connell 2002, 2005) and that women and girls should experience the continued construction of their own gender identities in this same way, rather than always in relation to 'the other' (Holland et al. 2004; Renold 2005; Sharpe 1994). At present little is made of the power held by younger men (boys) and the control they may perpetrate over their (female) peers. This is because the concept of hegemonic masculinity tends to locate the concept of hegemony within a static temporal framework of adulthood (examining time in reference to epochs but not within, for example, the temporality of the life course). This begs the question of whether there is the possibility of constructing a 'younger' hegemonic masculinity, or whether this, like theoretical notions of hegemonic femininities is inherently contradictory.

It can therefore be argued that masculinity is often constructed as a masculine 'adult' identity, with physicality being 'fully' achieved through the embodiment of adulthood. These constructions of masculinity, although conceived around performances, can also be essentialised as biologically determined. It is interesting to note whether there is a difference between how boys see themselves now and in the future, judging forms of masculinity to be more achievable through adulthood. For example, work looking specifically at the relationships between normative gender identity and violence, has succeeded in generating assumptions of masculinity as an 'adult' identity to be achieved with prestige but also age (O'Donnell and Sharpe 2000; Swain 2003). For example, McMahon (1993: 691) argues that many definitions of masculinity are in reality 'descriptions of popular ideologies about the actual or ideal characteristics of *men*' (my emphasis).

Although Connell asserts that masculinity is a 'life project' (1995), many forms of masculinity are still constructed as adult endeavours and this was how many of the young boys in particular constructed it – as something that was achievable only by grown-ups[1] with 'natural' masculinity fixed by adulthood. In this way, masculinities are judged as being biological endeavours fully achieved by the embodiment of adult men's bodies and adult men's prowess. Thus much work, by focusing upon young people's own constructions of their masculine identities (Kehily et al. 1997; Mac an Ghaill and Heywood 2007; Nayak et al. 1996) and indeed femininities, has overlooked how the gender identities of childhood and adulthood merge or intersect and the implication this has for the continuation of (men's) violence.

---

1 Girls incidentally saw both men and boys embracing forms of masculine identities.

The physicality of men was discussed in terms of muscles, visiting the gym and being fit. Women were positioned in opposition to this in terms of super diets and striving to be 'skinny'. Several of the boys talked of the correlation between women striving to be skinny and the recent deaths of models from anorexia.

Therefore in a similar way that men, defined in relation to hegemonic masculinity are keen to disassociate themselves from all things feminine (Connell 2001), there are implications here that women choose to be smaller, skinnier and thus less like a man. These differences of physicality also alluded to differences in power. When fitness was discussed in terms of women's health, it was suggested they visited the gym to 'burn off calories', thus to make them thinner (and weaker) rather than fitter and stronger. But in the examples used, the people were actively constructing their own bodies and choosing to physically change their appearance. In doing so, they are destabilising gender by demonstrating its creative fluidity, whether this is to conform or deviate from the gendered norm:

> Nicole: I suppose it depends on the person, not the gender. It's people that are different.
>
> (Mountview School, Group 1)

Here, Nicole, whilst deconstructing gender as an absolute attribute, recognises that people themselves are not constitutive of gender stereotypes and so this in itself cannot be seen as a basis for difference and opposition. She encapsulates the attitudes of many of the young people in that their developing sense of self or selves were fluid, but were increasingly finding that they were limited in having to navigate their notions of self through narrowly defined channels of fixed gender identity. For many this culminated in constructing their own gender identities in opposition to what they will become – as (gendered) adults. Thus they were eager and able to destabilise gender categories through their own life experience examples but often relied upon stable and rigid categories to understand and construct explanations for others. Young people found it hard to move past the physicality of the (adult) body. This was less so with regard to muscles and hair, which could be changed. However genitalia and biology were understood as fixed and stable indicators of difference, linking gender immutably with sex and the role of women to have and care for children. Young people found themselves much more able to (re)produce gender as a socially constructed product of choice and constraint when explored through the discursive frame of performativity.

The Performance of Gender

Gendered Clothing

Young people constructed gender through a performative framework of fashion and clothing examining the role of gender expectation in conformity and choice:

Nancy:	Is there anything that you can do because you are a girl that you wouldn't be able to do if you were a boy?
Yolande:	Clothes.
Nancy:	What do you mean?
Yolande:	Like most boys don't wear skirts.
Siobhan:	But see girls can wear trousers.
Chrissie:	The only time a boy can wear a skirt if he wants to be a boy is a kilt or unless it's a joke.
Lindsay:	And we've got more options.
Siobhan:	Yeah we can wear boys' clothes, shorts, trousers, anything.
Lindsay:	'Cause it used to be women would only wear skirts and dresses.

(Clifton School, Group 4)

A salient point from the quote above is the awareness of the construction of gender through clothing. What a boy wears *makes him* a boy. Thus if a boy wore a skirt he would be 'a girl' yet the sentiment that wearing a kilt is 'the only time a boy can wear a skirt if *he wants to be a boy*' shows an active choice in gender creation. All of the groups denied that boys 'could' wear skirts except to make people laugh or 'be a girl' unless it was a kilt.[2]

Stacey:	Boys can't wear skirts.
Emma:	They can. Kilts.
Stacey:	A kilt's a kilt. It's not supposed to be a fashion item.
Nancy:	How is a kilt different from a skirt then?
Emma:	Because it's bigger.
Cheryl:	Kilts are traditional.
Nancy:	So boys are okay to wear kilts but not skirts?
Cheryl:	Uh huh. 'Cause if a boy wore a skirt, they're gonna think some awful things about him.

[Laughter]

(Mary Magdalene School, Group 1)

2 All of the groups made the association between the kilt and a skirt but its recognition as a symbol of national dress, and therefore tradition and history, located it firmly within a masculine identity.

The 'freedom' and wide range of clothing options afforded to girls was juxtaposed with the regulations enforced upon boys who were limited to what they could wear and restricted from items identified as 'feminine'. In the questionnaire, the young people all thought that it was okay for a girl to wear a blue t-shirt but most disagreed that it was okay for a boy to wear a pink t-shirt.[3]What is female is labelled as such, whereas everything else is assumed to be neutral, that is, male. The reasoning here suggests that it is okay for girls' to 'go against' expectations and transcend stereotypes but that a boy has to regulate his masculinity by avoiding all things feminine. Wearing clothes or colours that were meant for girls was labelled as 'gay', 'not right', 'a joke' and 'wrong' by boys and girls alike.

One boy, Jack, perceptively described the reasons in terms of conformity and the transience of gender performativity and creation;

> Jack: But if everyone else was doing it, then it would be alright. Yeah. And if like everything had changed and there was nobody saying that you couldn't then ... boys would probably wear skirts, if you know what I mean ... and they wouldn't see anything wrong with it.
>
> (Clifton School, Group 3)

When questioned who made the rules, the young people aligned their construction with 'higher forces', 'the big cheeses' and 'playground politics'. Thus their association with a fixed gender order limited the possibility for change in the minds of the young people and they conformed because they didn't question this, 'that's how it is'. This is hopeful for the challenge of the gender order by 'authority' as a means to overcome stereotypes but it does rely upon consistency. Yet their belief that a boy wearing a skirt destabilises the gender order by resisting the innate and embracing the construction transcends gender as a 'natural' concept, suggesting there is nothing inherent to the body that dictates gender, rather that gender is constructed through ideology and discourse.

But this 'equality' of opportunity (in relation to girls and clothing) proved hollow, as when asked if this freedom translated into other areas of life, the answer was a resounding no. The wider structures of choice relating to clothes for girls were not as broad when framed by moral gender codes.

---

3 The colour blue is less aligned with masculinity as pink is with femininity. Blue, as a colour can stand alone, pink however is always positioned on a binary with blue, even if blue is absent. Pink as a colour is also sexualised in terms of its alignment with homosexuality (and thus femininity) and the 'pink pound'.

Empowering Girls through Masculinity?

A useful label accessed by some of the young people to describe girls who performed masculinity was that of 'tomboy'. This phrase was appropriated in two ways: firstly, to describe girls who deviated from normative definitions of femininity, and in doing so, label their actions as exceptional, and secondly, to highlight the distinction of acceptability between *girls acting like boys*, and *boys acting like girls*.

Shona:	Boys aren't scared to do things. Like they'll jump into hedges and that. Girls wouldn't do that.
Alice:	I jump into hedges.
Shona:	Yeah, but you're a tomboy.

(Mary Magdalene School, Group 2)

In the above quote, Alice is demonstrating that not only boys do these things, that girls do them too, thus the example does not coincide with her own lived reality. However Shona's retort is that Alice is an exception to other girls, she is a tomboy, a girl with proclivities for masculine attributes. By doing this, Shona regulates Alice by defining her as different, rather than viewing her behaviour as a means to consolidate her own version of femininity. A further illustration of this behaviour is girls who openly thrived on being 'boy-like'. For the girls who embraced this label, or that of 'tomboy', it was a deviation from constricted femininities where they could be physically able, strong and good at sports. But by aligning these attributes with traditionally masculine behaviour, these girls could not be viewed as girl-like. Therefore such girls were forced to 'choose' whether they wanted to continue with their performances of strong, assertive and independent identities or subsume them in pretending they were unable or unwilling to do these things to conform to a suitable feminine gender identity. Ringrose and Renold (2012) have taken this discussion further, questioning why when girls challenge gender normatives they have to do so within the confines of masculinist constructs. Their thesis is that girls need more ways to be subversive and there needs to be more gender categories than the existing binaries where girls either have to be one thing or nothing.

In the example below Stewart questions the dichotomies of gender, asking why girls can act like boys, with little consequence, but boys can't act like girls without being emasculated:

Stewart:	You get tomgirls, I mean girls who are tomboys, which is a girl with like all the rough and tough and stuff. But say if you had a

tomgirl, a boy who liked doing girl stuff, people would just call him gay, and then he'd get bullied.

(Clifton School, Group 5)

Thus, Stewart acknowledges the performative elements of gender but also recognises that such performances are strictly regulated. Young people were more able to discuss their own gendered diversity but relied upon stereotypes when discussing 'others'. Their juxtaposition of abstract and experiential knowledge is explored further using the example of emotion.

Emotion

The expression of certain emotions was initially constructed as a key difference between boys and girls. Emotions were placed, directly and indirectly on a binary scale of positive and negative, strength and weakness, anger and crying, talking and not talking with girls described as more emotional and facing fewer societal restrictions in being so. Within the confines of acceptable masculine emotions, the young people placed 'anger'. Unlike other (feminised) or 'soft' emotions, anger was judged a safe emotion to express as it is aligned with masculinity, masculine display and was not classed as 'weak'. This ability to openly show (soft) emotion was viewed by both boys and girls as a positive attribute of being a girl. Yet boys also identified girls' tendency to do so as a weakness:

Jason: Yeah 'cause like then they'll start to cry, like babies and then people know they are after attention sometimes.

(Mary Magdalene School, Group 3)

Not showing emotion was not viewed as an inherent feature of being a boy, rather a performance prescribed by societal restrictions and the confines of others' expectations of masculinity:

Shazia: Like boys, they don't, they don't express their feelings because if they do that to another boy, they'll think that they are not tough. I think that's what boys like to do. They try to act tough. But girls, they can just express things if they are sad.

(Baxter Road School, Group 2)

Melanie: … boys don't really cry much. Or if they do you don't see it.

Aimee: They don't show their emotions as much.

Melanie: Yeah, like girls are more open about their thoughts and stuff whereas boys seem to keep it to themselves. I mean, I don't know, but it seems like that.

Karina:	Uh huh. And also it seems like, I don't know, like by not showing it they'll impress other boys and if they do their friends will think they're stupid.
Melanie:	Yeah the boys in our class are like that.

(Clifton School, Group 2)

Yet they also revealed instances of their own (and others') emotions that resisted these limiting binaries. Thus they would challenge their friends' prescribed and limiting notions of gender using their own lived experiences but were more reluctant to do this if they did not have access to alternative (experiential) scripts with which to resist gendered stereotypes. In one all-male group, the boys talked about how crying was a positive way to release your emotions challenging its construction as 'unmasculine':

Ewan:	It's always better to cry because, erm … it's like you have it all in your mind if you don't cry 'cause you are always thinking about it. If you cry, it could sort of … the feeling just sort of goes away and it's a lot easier than bottling it all up.

(Clifton School, Group 3)

The same boys also saw crying as a means to manipulate others, to get attention and to make others feel sorry for you; attributes more traditionally associated with femininity. There was also recognition, by this group and others, that crying was a degendered activity (or should be):

Joe:	Some girls try and hide it. Some girls don't. Some boys do and some boys don't. It depends on what type of person you are.

(Clifton School, Group 3)

It is significant that Joe, above, and other groups talked in terms of young people crying. They did not therefore discuss the possibility (or indeed acceptability) of a particular age group (grown-up) or gender (men) demonstrating emotion in this way and whether this would be viewed as weakness or not. The majority of young people expressed an understanding of emotions as a performative element of gender. Their understanding was that there were performances that had to be adhered to in order to portray an 'acceptable' gender identity. Yet through the labelling of boys who did express 'negative' emotion as 'wimps' or 'sensitive boys', there was a conformity to an ideal of masculin*ity*, that was to be either aspired to or held in esteem. This was an ideal that constituted both physical and performative elements of what it is to be a 'man'. It was this acceptance of, and aspiration to, this one form of masculinity that highlighted power relations between boys and girls but also between and among boys. Although all of the boys accessed and displayed a plurality of masculine identities it was this limited and singular form that many attained to. One of the ways young people relayed this masculine performative trait was in terms of 'showing off'.

Forms of Expression: 'Showing Off'

Sport (and in particular football) as show*man*ship enables boys to show off their skills, demonstrate prowess and potency as well as dominating the school playground area, allowing for clear demonstrations of masculine identity:

> Vikram: When we do sport, people get to know about you more. If you are a girl, you don't show what you can do … like in football.
>
> (Mountview School, Group 3)

Boys exude more confidence because they believe that the area and the game is theirs, regarding girls as inferior because of this. For girls, boys showing off performed two purposes: to show the girls they were better than them and to demonstrate their superiority to other boys, a perfect example of Connell's (2005) hegemonic masculinity:

> Katie: Boys like to show you that they can do it. They show off and tell you that you can't do it and that they are better than everyone else.
>
> (Hardcastle School, Group 1)

Girls also expressed how they found the changes in boys' behaviour and performances of machismo particularly frustrating. Many of the girls talked of a different presentation of self by the boys when they were in a one on one situation with them:

> Cheryl: When a boy's with his pals if a girl talks to him he'll say, 'shut up you nutter'. Like John Travolta in Grease, you know, where he acts all proud in front of his pals? But when it's just a boy and a girl, it's totally different. It's like they talk and everything.
>
> (Mary Magdalene School, Group 1)

There is a contradiction between a boy's own presentation of self and his public persona, which appears to be evolved of many more identities particularly if there is an audience to perform to. Whether these are normative constraints of a masculine identity or a desire to be judged differently, or both, this was a gendered aspect picked up on by girls, about boys. 'Showing off' can be viewed initially as a means to exude confidence and demonstrate ability but both boys and girls acknowledged that boys were also constrained by it in terms of only being able to perform a certain sort of behaviour; a very limited masculin*ity*. The disdain of girls at the boys' displays of masculinity through the medium of showing off can also be viewed as their challenge to this gendered ritual through a resistance of such performances.

Institutional Regimes of Gender

During the discussions there was a general awareness of men taking advantage of women through both their expectations and positions and that boys, because of these structures, had greater power (Daniel: 'People accept boys better'. Mary Magdalene School, Group 5). There was also an awareness of the inequities of the system and that it was girls who were penalised (Shazia: 'Girls have hard lives'. Baxter Road School, Group 2) by male power. Several of the boys maintained that if they were girls they would 'fight for equality', demonstrating awareness that there is a fight to be fought yet that it is a struggle for women alone. Such statements imply that the disadvantages women experience are for them to rectify themselves rather than changing the power imbalance with men per se whilst also labelling men and women as monolithic groups. The wider structures of power explored are now analysed in terms of the interlocked regimes of gender: school, friendships, work, home, family and relationships.

School and Peer Friendships

The school as a public site is influential in the lives of young people. It is a place where young people spend much of their time, where they learn alongside their peers (and adults) whilst creating and maintaining friendships. One of the main themes that weaved between all of the groups was the separation and division of space. This extended to the use of toilets, 'boys' and 'girls' and the playground. A large part of the playground was defined and dominated by the boys. The space, the boys and the football were concurrent. The area was so clearly demarcated for this purpose that it was not questioned or mentioned by any of the boys who were involved in it and who took it for granted. This finding replicates much other research that has looked at boys and girls use of playground space (Karsten 2003, Swain 2000, Thorne 1992). Not only did the majority of boys dominate this space but they also actively excluded the girls:

Shona: Sometimes when boys are playing football and you ask to join in, they say no 'cause you're a girl.

Nancy: And what do you think of that?

Shona: Well I don't think it's really fair 'cause we let them join in with our games, so why shouldn't they let us join in?

(Mary Magdalene School, Group 2)

By this girl (and others) having to request permission to join in the football, the boys are actively in a powerful position where their authority of 'the pitch' is not questioned, and their power has prevalence in their reluctance to 'allow' girls to take part. This girl, and others, did attempt to challenge the powerful gendered dynamics of the pitch, yet it was difficult to do so in an area that was so heavily gendered and normalised as not 'their space to play'.

This is an area that has much research devoted to it but it is relevant here for three salient reasons. Firstly, it was one of the most prevalent issues raised in all schools and the fact that it still is means that little has changed. Secondly, this was an issue raised wholly by girls who see it as unfair, yet the democracy of the playground is not even thought about by boys who view it in terms of their entitlement. The need to make the many voices of girls heard here is imperative. Girls' views are clearly being silenced at worst, or ignored at best. Thirdly, there is the assumption that the space and the games of football played there both belong to the boys.

Football was not only gendered institutionally, as demonstrated above, but was also regulated ideologically (see also Swain 2003). This was done both by those with the power (the boys who played football) and those without (the girls who wanted to play football). This exclusion of girls is directly related to the gendered limits imposed between boys and girls by boys. Playing football and other athletic sports were anticipated as activities girls could not compete in because they were (assumed to be) lacking in competence, a daily revival of Young's well known work (1990):

Grace: Like some sports … you can't do because you are a girl.
Samia: Aye.
Kirsten: Like in the playground and stuff like that. Boys say you can't do it, because you are a girl.
Samia: Aye, it's not fair.
Nancy: So it's not fair? Is it true that you can't do those things?
Grace: Yeah … no, well it's true they don't let you.
Samia: I mean you feel a bit uncomfortable with the boys around 'cause if it's just us girls, you just do it, but if the boys are there, they start laughing.
Grace: They say you are doing it wrong, that you can't do it. You feel ashamed to do it. They just start laughing so you feel uncomfortable to do PE or sports activities and stuff.

(Baxter Road School, Group 4)

The boys described here are actively ridiculing the girls and attempting to control their behaviour with disparaging remarks. This example, and others that reflected the sentiments expressed here, highlight that it is the boys who are restricting the girls' behaviour and not necessarily girls' lack of belief in their own abilities, although this obviously has some relevance. Freedom of space and movement is available here for certain boys to define their own masculine identities, which they then, in turn, actively restrict girls from doing the same. This regulation through the boys' sense of entitlement is all too recognisable for the girls. It is through the boys' regulation of the girls' behaviour, that the girls are beginning to internalise conflicting messages about their own interests and abilities. Girls are relegated from joining in or prevented from doing so as they are identified as not being good at sport by boys (Stewart: 'The boys would maybe tease you if you tried to join in'. Clifton School, Group 5) and through internalising a lack of belief in their own ability (Cheryl: 'Boys aren't scared to do more things ... they can fly over walls with one hand, I can't do that'. Mary Magdalene School, Group 1). This goes a long way to construct negative gender attributes and further consolidate an already rigid gendered hierarchy.

As well as being regulated by boys, girls also regulated themselves. When asked what they liked during the exploratory questionnaire sessions, the favourite sport of boys was football. The favourite sport of girls was also football but this is not represented by the number of girls enabled to play the sport within schools, either during games or break times. What is of interest here is that the number of girls who said that they liked football during their individual questionnaires did not proffer this same opinion during the discussion group sessions among their peers (with two exceptions). A reason for this may be linked to the close association of football with a masculine identity and thus an unacceptable form of femininity.

Thus it was frequently intimated by girls that they do not have the opportunity or are excluded from sporting activities both within the school playground (Meera: 'They won't let us play'. Baxter Road School, Group 2) although a number of girls had found clubs that welcomed their membership:

> Chrissie: It's quite nice when they are mixed because you have more control, you can learn more. And you can show that you can do the same things that boys can and they can see that.
>
> (Clifton School, Group 4)

In extolling the benefits of mixed membership, girls feel that they have more control in terms of being involved without boys informally limiting that. It is significant that it is not only being able to do the same things as boys that is important, but crucial that boys are aware of it too, thus overcoming their preconceived notions of girls' capabilities using lived examples as proof of their knowledge.

There were boys who resisted the stereotype that girls could not play football or other sports, challenging the myth with evidence of their reality to the contrary, as well as recognising the obstacles girls faced:

Louis: Girls play sports as well.
Cameron: I suppose, eh, football's a lot sexist, eh, to get into football teams.
Louis: There's like no girls in the football team.

(Clifton School, Group 1)

Paul: Boys play sport and that makes them fitter.
Iain: So do girls.

(Mary Magdalene School, Group 5)

Several boys acknowledged that they needed to be better than girls in 'masculine' fields such as football else risk being feminised. There were also those boys who recognised this competition but did not feel the pressure to conform:

Cameron: The guys called us sissies … but actually they [the girls] were actually [*sic*] the better players.

(Clifton School, Group 1)

The boy above is arguing that gender here was irrelevant; recognising that just because he is a boy doesn't mean that he should necessarily be better than the girls taking part, that ability transcends gender.

The division and symbolism afforded of gender was firmly entrenched within young people's friendship groups. All of the young people viewed their friends as integral to who they were and saw friendships as transcending the boundaries of school, community and home. One of the first things identified by the participants when asked if their lives would change if they woke up as the opposite sex, was that they would have different (same-sex) friends thus creating a constriction of gendered friendships.

This gendered nature of friendships was linked to the need for commonality between friends, for example, that only girls liked sleepovers and shopping and only boys liked football. But when this issue was explored further many of the young people's interests crossed gender boundaries and were not always shared by their friends:

Karen: I mean me and my friends, we don't really like the same things but it doesn't really matter.

(Mountview School, Group 2)

Therefore this gendered division of friendship groups was less about polemic gender interests and more about gender expectations and maintaining gender boundaries; boys are friends with boys, girls are friends with girls. Thus because the young people viewed themselves as oppositional, they already anticipated that they would not get on. At the age of 11 and 12, same-sex friendships were most common with only a handful of young people identifying close mixed-sex friendships (The lists of friends on the exploratory questionnaires confirmed these separate friendship spheres). In her work with primary school children, Renold (2005) found that alongside friendships being gendered they were also sexualised (the dominance of the heterosexual framework in the lives of primary school children is discussed further in Chapter 7). Where it did not already exist there was a belief that friendships 'became' single sex ventures as the young people grew older, demonstrating the temporal expectations of adult relationship:

> Siobhan: Like when you are younger, you are friends with everyone, you know girls and boys. But when you are older you can't. I mean all my friends are girls now.
>
> (Clifton School, Group 4)

Here Siobhan expresses a clear division between getting older and the expectations of single sex friendships, a view that was shared by others in the fieldwork. Within these separate spheres, myths were perpetrated about the nature of friendships and particularly relating to their break-up. Both boys and girls labelled girls as the most 'manipulative' and 'emotional' in terms of holding grudges and refusing to make-up. This was reflective of anticipated roles in heterosexual relationships where girls were viewed as nagging and more capable of emotional abuse (see Chapter 6). Boys, in opposition, were labelled unemotional and 'not bothered' about falling out with friends. Yet the lived examples saw little evidence of this, instead highlighting alternative 'stories' with boys telling of upset and heartache over their fallings out with friends:

> Sonny: I hold grudges very strong … I wouldn't make up and then after a while I might tell them why I was lonely.
>
> (Clifton School, Group 3)

Girls, rather than embodying the fickleness they were labelled with, would talk about the importance of friendship maintenance in their lives:

> Lindsay: If me and my friends ever argue over the same boy, we made up this wee stupid rule, 'friends are forever, boys are for whenever'. And that's true. It's better to have your friends than a boyfriend'.
>
> (Clifton School, Group 4)

In the same way that friendships were heavily gendered spheres, by implication mixed-sex friendships were defined by heterosexuality, in terms of role and expectation. That is, friendships between boys and girls were constrained by anticipated gender roles that the young people were bound by to act. Fancying boys was deemed 'natural' for girls whereas boys were ridiculed for expressing desire for relationships. This can be interpreted as boys being reluctant to align themselves with girls (the 'feminine') over boys (the 'masculine'). Yet there was also a difficulty, for boys, in overcoming this disjuncture between the separate spheres of male and female, spending so long distancing themselves from girls and then wanting to 'fancy' them.

During discussions of personal relationships all of the single sex girl groups broached the subject of boyfriends eagerly and without prompting. It was this confidence that was recognised by boys and girls alike. They talked of the politics of 'going out' with boys and were nonchalant about approaching boys or asking them out. They were not embarrassed to say who they fancied or who they were currently going out with. Cultural norms still often position men as being the initiators in relationships with women in the passive role, waiting to respond. Here, girls, in relation to the boys, took the initiative and were in control of creating, sustaining and ending the relationships. Further to this, cultural investment in the relationship talk provided a stalwart for friendship sustenance, one that boys were reluctant or unable to engage in with their friends. This could be seen as one of the commonalities of girls' friendships with other girls:

Elizabeth: Girls will talk to their friends but boys don't tell their friends anything 'cause it's embarrassing.

(Mary Magdalene School, Group 2)

Dougie: Say like erm someone fancies someone, right. Like a girl. If a girl said to her friends she fancied someone they'd all be like, oh cool, but if a boy said that, they'd tease him.

(Clifton School, Group 5)

The depth of girls' friendships and the trust they shared can be directly linked to the previous discussion of emotions. Girls did not identify boys as sharing the same emotional intensity with their male friends as they did with theirs, particularly in respect to the support and advice given regarding personal relations. Girls indicated this was a reason they valued their friends and pitied boys for not experiencing the same levels of intimacy. In their constructions of gender identity, the young people have tended to align girls with privacy, in relation to their bodies and the expectation of their role within the private sphere. Yet here it is boys who are associated with privacy in terms of their emotional intimacy. Again this is an idealised and restricted construction of masculinity, reinforced by young people's expectation and anticipation of it with limited options for alternative or more attainable masculine identities.

Girls have not been encouraged to keep these spheres of boys and girls separate to the same extent and that is one of the reasons why, for this briefest of times, they have the control. Therefore it is construed 'normal' for them to want a boyfriend and to define themselves in relation to this. Girls are thought of as lesser, or lacking, because they were not made whole by a relationship – in the same way that children have been viewed as 'incomplete' adults. Thus this is why girls are not ridiculed in the same way that boys are because they 'need' the relationship to complete themselves. This also has serious implications for girls feeling pressured to make relationships work at any cost and not 'giving up' on it. Even though girls were initially viewed as being in control there was a duality between their actions and their perceived motives. Girls were viewed as confident and strong in pursuing active relationships but their reasons for doing so were based upon feminine weakness and a need to be loved:

> Stacey: … a boy'll say to a girl, I love you but he doesn't mean it. He just says it to make her feel better.
>
> (Mary Magdalene School, Group 1)

This need to be loved, but not to be sexualised (by others) encapsulates the double standard of girls and their reputations which is discussed later. It is in this entwining of reputation, entitlement and heterosexuality that parents' played an important role. Parents were salient models for the constructions of heterosexual identities, both as a mould to replicate and as a creator of rules. For boys, advice or instruction from parents was given little heed; girls however repeated much of the advice imparted, particularly from their mothers:

> Alice: My mum, she told me if someone ever said I love you before you are ever married, she said just never listen 'cause all they want to do is kiss you or have you.
>
> (Mary Magdalene School, Group 2)

Although the girl is advised to 'resist' the role of the man is still positioned in terms of entitlement – wanting what is 'rightfully' his. As the above quote illustrates much of the advice expiated the predatory role of the male, viewing men with suspicion and advocating repression (or total absence) of their own sexual desires. Girls were thus positioned upon a binary scale between models of childhood innocence and in possession of insatiable sexuality that was in need of constraint, and that it was their responsibility to manage this.

The Home and Familial Relationships

Gender demarcated the home environment, through the division of labour to parental expectations. Age also intersected with gender creating a disjuncture between the idealism of their future gendered expectations and their own experiential and realised realities. In terms of their everyday lives, the young people discussed parental expectations maintaining that girls in the family were treated more leniently in terms of discipline:

> Dougie: Everyone expects boys to be the worst.
>
> Stewart: My dad always thinks that because I'm the boy, I must have done it.
>
> (Clifton School, Group 5)

However underlying this 'leniency' is an expectation that it is the girls' role to behave better than her male siblings and that boys will be unruly and misbehave more. The gender order was most closely replicated in intimate domestic structures and through parental expectation of these roles. Several of the boys commented that they had household duties to perform and girls rejected the notion that housework was solely 'women's work'. The vast majority of the young people agreed that boys and girls should help out at home and do the same household jobs. However, this gender ideal was not replicated in the reality gleaned from the responses in the questionnaire. Much of the work in the home was divided along gender lines, with women (or female cleaners) doing the bulk of the chores. There was a slight incline in the amount of housework parents expected from their daughters than their sons (although age could have also been a factor here) yet on the whole the share of duties remained constant.

There was a marked division between the groups in terms of those who acknowledged the inequality of role expectation and allocation and those for whom these roles were normalised. In such cases the roles were unfair but remained unchallenged because they were 'naturalised'. The young people quoted below debated women's greater 'independence' as a result of not being restricted by the expectation of being the breadwinner:

> Shilpa: [As a woman] you don't have to work all that hard. You cook and clean and you can have a job as well but you don't have to. But you look after the baby.
>
> (Baxter Road, Group 2)

> Shaheeda: We do the housework and boys do the hard work. They go out to work and we only have to do the housework.
>
> (Baxter Road, Group 1)

This inverted equality argument puts forward the view that women have more freedom because they are not rigidly defined by prescriptive (paid) working roles. However, the lack of opportunity faced by women and the inevitability of a woman's dependence upon a male breadwinner failed to be challenged in this assumption of 'freedom'.

In the quote below, the gendered inequality is recognised through the preposition that when men are in relationships there is an expectation that women will fulfil this role, that it is her role to do these things. When men are alone and not positioned in relation to women, they can take on this role but it is the stereotyped and unified concepts of masculinity and femininity, as constituting the heterosexual matrix that creates and sustains this gendered expectation:

Meera: When men or boys have a girlfriend, they expect them to do everything, to clean, go to work, look after the children. Then you would get home and have to have everything ready, have food ready. Boys can do that stuff too, they just can't be bothered.

(Baxter Road School, Group 2)

Rachel: That's what I don't see. Every time there's a couple it is always the woman who needs to make the dinner. And wash and cleaning

Craig: Most of the time 'cause the man is stronger and the man can do more work.

(Mary Magdalene School, Group 5)

At this point in their lives (the present) the young people were most likely to view their gendered identities as constantly evolving and more fluid, with a range of identities available to them rather than being constrained by a singular identity. Yet these identities became more rigid and less plural when framed by age, relationships and familial responsibilities. The heterosexual partnership and the gender roles within become more structured, fixed and rigid and acceptable for the young people (male and female) when aligned with marriage, the private sphere of the home and children.

This dichotomy of expectation between the present and the future, young and old and individual and relationship also contributed, in part, to girls' early recognition of systematic gender inequalities. They saw themselves as more equal now than in the future. Age intersected their constructions of gender in that the more adult the woman – the more fixed and restrictive her gendered identity became. This understanding of the female role also demonstrates the duality between 'them' and 'us', the girls want to be equal but they do not always see other girls as being so. For boys, hegemonic masculinity was mobilised around traits that they identified as being encapsulated by grown-up men; marriage, home and children rather than themselves as 11- and 12-year-old boys. Rather than seeing it as an aspiration, they were more likely to view this 'ideal' masculin*ity* as static, fixed and to some extent inevitable as it was bound up in their futures as men.

Even when framed by rigidity and inevitability marriage was still seen as the culmination of the heterosexual ideal. Marriage was a significant milestone in a person's life and one which the majority of young people anticipated for themselves. For many there was an understanding that marriage was sacrosanct over and above other forms of relationships. This became obvious when young people relied upon the status of a relationship to determine a woman's actions as the example below illustrates:

> Siobhan: [Following the third vignette] I mean if they had been married or whatever then she should have tried harder, to be with her husband.
>
> (Clifton School, Group 4)

In this quote, not only does Siobhan reinforce the importance of marriage and in making a relationship work, she also implicates the woman (in this case Jenny) as being responsible for her own victimisation. Whilst this view of marriage was most widely shared in the Catholic school, many of the young people in the non-denomination schools also held marriage in the greatest esteem, but in doing so, limited the actions and the choices available to the women in such relationships. There were few alternatives to the institutionalisation offered, with one boy discussing the concept of monogamy as a choice rather than a fixed notion:

> Sonny: If I had a boyfriend and we said we could see other people and we did then that would be okay. But if I had a boyfriend and we said let's just see each other and then I ran off with somebody else, then that wouldn't be fair.
>
> (Clifton School, Group 3)

In this extract, Sonny presents a progressive view of a relationship based upon mutual responsibility and compromise rather than overarching monogamy. What is also of interest here is Sonny's positioning in terms of a role where he had a boyfriend, thus further deviating from a monogamous heterosexual institution.

Work

There were several of the girls' aspiration choices that overlapped with their male peers: scientist, musician, doctor, police officer, teacher. These generic professions have gone some way to sustaining gendered career paths and are no longer seen as the domain of one sex over the other.

Yet, while all of young people agreed that girls can be doctors, the majority disagreed that it was okay for boys to be nurses, a traditionally female profession. Here, this is again reflective of aligning boys with femininity and the young people's reluctance to do this. This was again demonstrated when young people were questioned if it was okay for a man or a woman to give up work to look after the children. Many agreed that both 'parents' could or just the woman. However, none of the young people agreed that just the man could give up his job to look after the children. To agree with this statement would be to dislodge the breadwinning status of men and to align him with a traditionally feminine childcare role. Within this discourse is the supposition that men have choices in terms of their employment roles, but that this does not extend to choosing not to work. The roles of employment and sexuality are bound together in the portrayal of acceptable male identities. This was also significant in how young people distanced their own present beliefs with the reality of their future representation of their gendered lives. It is also interesting to note that many of these young people are the embodiment of the inequalities that their own mothers face. This was the one area of the research where the class divisions between the schools were most apparent, and for that reason needs to be highlighted here. Whereas the differences between the career choices of boys in all the areas was negligible, the contrast between the girls was stark, with the girls from the more deprived areas being much more likely to opt for traditional (part time) jobs offering lower pay and fewer prospects. Both the boys and girls living in the more deprived areas of Glasgow were more likely to ascribe to the traditional male breadwinner model with the female in a dependent care giving role.

Women's inequality was clearly represented in young people's understanding and constructions of gender through the public sphere of work.[4] This was generally because they were aware of unfairness in terms of wages or position and it could clearly divided in right and wrong along gender lines:

Jason: Men earn more money.

(Mary Magdalene School, Group 3)

Ruth: If there is two different jobs, like a factory job I think they [men and women] should get paid the same for doing the same

4 Although these answers could be interpreted as reflecting reality and an acknowledgement that men do earn more money than women those who are reluctant to challenge this status quo are enabling women's subordination to continue through their acceptance of the normality and the gendered status quo.

job, but they're not. ... There are things men can do that women can't because of privileges that men get.

(Clifton School, Group 4)

Joe:	Most bosses are men now like ... and so if somebody was going to get a promotion, they might put a man up instead of a girl. Then the man gets it and men have more power.
Ewan:	It's awfully weird because there's slightly more females than males.
Joe:	But men still have the advantages.
Nancy:	So does that mean you are pleased to be a boy?
Joe:	No.
Ewan:	No because it's unfair.

(Clifton School, Group 3)

The final example above clearly illuminates that the boys are aware that it is their access to and retaining of power that positions men in more privileged positions. Whereas some viewed this as unfair, other boys did not question this entitlement.

What the discussions of work and equality brought to the fore was the disjuncture between what young people believed (the idealism of equality) and their lived real choices (part time poorly paid work). On the whole, jobs chosen by boys generally required university education (lecturer, architect, designer) and/or intensive training or apprenticeships (plumber, mechanic) or great sporting talent (professional football player, rugby player). What was most noticeable was that while girls did choose some, if fewer, jobs requiring similar training and skills, their choices were much less ambitious. The majority of their aspirations were traditionally feminised jobs with lower skills and pay (nursery nurse, nurse, shop keeper, housewife). Others didn't even specify a particular occupation, simply writing 'part time work'. Not one of these options was listed by any of the boys. What this demonstrates is that a significant number of girls were already aiming much lower in their aspirations and expectations than their male counterparts, anticipating less pay and part time work they can combine with other traditional caring roles required of them, implicating themselves with the systematic inequalities of paid and unpaid labour. They saw inequalities as existing simply between high wages and privilege and did not question the realities that contributed to this inequity such as opportunities, childcare, qualifications and access. Such inequities were normalised into the reality of life and then replicated by the young people through their own anticipated job choices.

Summary

This chapter has highlighted different sites of gender construction demonstrating how gender is constantly negotiated and shifting in young people's identities and definitions. It has identified how gender is constructed by the young people in different ways, through physical embodiment, performance and institutionally and how it can at times be obscured by other, more prevalent identities, such as class.

Oppositional and differential discourses provide an easily accessible and coherent framework for young people to construct their own and others' gender identities. These frameworks rely on common sense assumptions and the perpetration of myths that normalise dualisms. This duality generates dynamics of power though the positioning of gender attributes upon a binary. In this research the young people used the body as a starting point for their investment in a 'difference' discourse. The language they used to represent their own and others' bodies provided a means to maintain such dichotomies and generate oppositional concepts. Young people were most likely to espouse notions of distinction upon (sexualised) adult bodies that were different to their own. This then created a binary of young and old through their alignment of boys with girls. So although a category of distinction was still employed, it was one in which their own (young) gender identities were constructed as transient and in opposition to the 'other' (adult) fixed gender categories.

Young people were keen to explore performative elements of gender such as appearance, actions and interests embedding their constructions within their own lived reality enabling them to destabilise fixed notions of gender. By viewing gender as a socially produced category they could explore ways in which their actions and performances contributed to the differences they originally identified as inherent.

They viewed the external gender role of 'other' be that of boys, girls, grown-ups or future roles as much more limiting, stable and singular. What became clear through the analysis is that all of the young people accessed a discourse of dualistic gender; that is gender as operating within two levels, whether this be reality and image, young and old, present and future, now and becoming, radical and conservative. The young people, at times, described very radical, progressive and feminist understandings of gender in both its construction and performance. Yet, while their own experience and knowledge was at times quite radical, and their own identities were more fluid and open to negotiation, their adult trajectories promoted much more conservative stereotypes. For example, they were much more limiting, rigid and quick to regulate the actions and constructions of others if they did not meet with their own common sense notions and expectations of the gendered world. Therefore, institutional gender regimes (of which the adult world was key) were where the limits of gender construction were upheld through adherence to authority, perpetuation of myths, possession of power and normative constraints.

Chapter 5
'Real' Violence by 'Real' Men: Naturalising Masculinity

Alice: Violence is where two men are hitting and the polis come and put them in the jail.

Mary Magdalene School, Group 2

Introduction

This chapter explores the ways in which young people construct and understand violence and how they appropriate 'official' definitions to explain what they term 'real' violence. It is maintained that the young people were most likely to label actions from which they were physically and emotionally distant, as 'real' violence.

This chapter begins with an overview of the ways in which the young people defined and understood violence and violent actions. The next chapter looks more specifically at their own 'naming' of personal examples. To 'define' is to give a definition of, or determine the nature of, whereas to 'name' is to *personally* identify the characteristics of something. Whilst the power to define violence is often a function of privilege and authority there is no single, universally acceptable definition of violence (de Vylder 2004: 65). As such, definitions and meanings of violence are dependent upon the individual's position or standpoint; violated, violator, witness (see Burman et al. 2003; Hearn 1998) and also the present context in which it occurs, as well as the cultural context (tradition, belief, violation of rights). Young people are rarely located in these positions of power; as such they can be readily influenced but not necessarily determined by them. The young people were able to 'define' violence when they witnessed it either in an abstract or physical form but were more reluctant to define it as violence when they had any involvement. This was particularly the case with the boys.

Lived Examples versus Abstract Reasoning

The term 'lived experience' is not necessarily describing experiences of violence but is a pragmatic description, which takes the view that the young people's own lived experiences and knowledge are critical in informing their own views. The term also encapsulates the transitory framework set out at the start of the book where young people draw upon their past experience and present knowledge alongside the anticipations of their futures to understand violence and more specifically men's violence against women.

Trying to Find the 'Correct' Answer

An eagerness to find an *objective* way to describe violence was demonstrated by the majority of the young people, highlighting their need for a 'right' answer or what Michell (1999) calls their 'well-rehearsed public knowledge'. This also illustrates the preferential position of accepted definitions of violence, as opposed to violence as named by the young people themselves:

> Michael: Is violence a rule because if it is you are not meant to break a rule?
>
> Nancy: You tell me? Is violence a rule?
>
> Michael: Yeah. If you smashed a window, you'd get a fine. So if it's against the rules no one should use violence.
>
> Nancy: What happened if you smashed a window to rescue somebody?
>
> Michael: Then you'd no get a fine. So I suppose it depends on why.
>
> (Mary Magdalene School, Group 4)

Michael also appealed to me, as an adult and symbolic teacher, to provide him with the 'right' answer. Of course, as was demonstrated throughout, definitions of violence are subjective and the naming of actions as violent, is dependent upon a range of factors including context, intention and motive (Stanko 2003). Inherent within this is the acknowledgement of young people's lack of power in defining violence for themselves.

Once the young people recognised that I didn't have a right answer in mind the concept of one objective definition of violence began to be problematised by them leading to more nuanced debates, but there was still an over-reliance upon official definitions to confirm what they thought:

> Katie: It depends on the reason you are doing it. Like if you mean it or not.
>
> (Hardcastle School, Group 1)

> Elliott: Someone might think it's violent and someone else might not.
>
> (Hardcastle School, Group 2)

Hearn (1998: 16) produced a typology of criteria that had to be met for something to be defined as violent and this criteria changed; culturally, politically, legally and historically, including the recognition by a third person that the 'acts, activities or events [are] violent'. Yet the intention is not always clear, in that many actions attributed with violence are not recognised as such and the power of naming also needs to be accorded with the definition. For the young people, because of their status as children, they are not accorded the power to define; rather they (as in other areas of their lives) are superseded by generational power. This has further implications for how they understand actions that conform to 'real' actions and, crucially, those which do not. This meant that young people defined acts as violence which had already been labelled as such by others. For example acts that had received media coverage or involved actions that incorporated recognised indicators of violent behaviour. These recognised indicators began to form a pattern, or what I came to term a *constellation of factors*.

A Constellation of Violence

When talking of violence, young people were not always comfortable with their own knowledge, or doubted their authority to 'name' for themselves. Instead, they held rigid definitions of violence where certain criteria had to be met before actions could be validated as such. In this way young people defined violence as a prescribed framework of factors that fitted into existing common sense notions. A *constellation of factors* was generated, which had to be in place for the young people to 'define' an act as 'real' violence: gender (men); age (adults); physical actions; spaces (outside) and consequence (chastisement, physical injury, intervention by authority). In other words, for an act to be counted as 'violent' it typically had to fulfil certain criteria (which can also be identified as those acts most likely to be represented in crime statistics and in the media). It had to be performed by adult men in an outside space, involving physical actions resulting in visible injury, ending with police intervention and consequence such as an arrest.

When this model was deviated from, for example with girls as the actors, or where intervention did not follow, the young people were less likely to label these incidents as 'real' violence. Also incidents that were experienced by the young people themselves ('named') were less likely to be labelled as violence, particularly if they involved girls as 'victims' (of male peers' actions) and where there was no official consequence (such as the intervention of a teacher). They also accessed this restrictive model of violence, to understand domestic abuse and to frame women's use of violence as indicative of their quest for gender equality. I assert that such a model further impacts upon the minimisation of women's experiences when the violence does not fit within the framework of what is 'real' (see Krahe and Temkin 2009; Radford and Stanko 1996; Russell 1990).

These examples were juxtaposed alongside their own narratives of *lived experience* where violent actions were proximate to their own lives. These instances were most likely to be labelled as 'unreal' violence. The violences that are described in the next chapter are 'named' violences; that is those examples that were outside of this framework but still existed (and were experienced) within their everyday lives.

Defining 'Real' Violence

Adult Men

This next section looks at 'real' violence in terms of how it fits into young people's constellation of violence. Gender was prolific in their discussions of both young and older men engaging in 'real' violence, endorsing an anticipated and acceptable form of masculinity, to the extent that such behaviour was naturalised. Bowker (1998) argues that the link between masculinity and violence is strong, presenting a more deterministic argument that draws heavily upon biology. In his book he asserts that when a man's sense of manliness is perceived to be challenged, some men react with what Bowker calls, 'hyper-masculine behaviour', emphasising those aspects of masculinity which for them encompasses a real man, such as violence. For the most part, young people's definitions of 'real violence' centred upon adult men and their adult male strength:

> Monica: Violence is like men, hitting and kicking.
>
> (Clifton School, Group 2)

> Elizabeth: Men start the violence 'cause they are bigger and stronger.
>
> (Mary Magdalene School, Group 5)

Violence is judged to be a conduit through which men can display certain forms of masculinity. In this way, violence is privileged as a demonstration of physical strength, prowess and power and centred around being an adult man. Yet it is important to note that violence perpetrated by men was naturalised by the expectations of their fixed masculine role:

> Shilpa: Men punch, but men can take it.
>
> (Baxter Road School, Group 2)

> Eloise: It's men that do the violence.
>
> (Hardcastle School, Group 1)

This alignment of violence with positive implications of power, is positioned alongside the implicit assumption that men are never 'victims' of violence as to be so would demonstrate weakness. So in this sense, men are the hegemonic actors in violent situations; they are violent but they are 'meant' to be therefore there are no victims.

Violence was conceptualised as a means by which to indicate gender difference through the physical embodiment of (male) power. This was a power afforded to adult men by both boys and girls and to boys by girls. For many of the young people, there was a 'natural' linear progression from boys growing up into men and becoming (potentially) violent. As such, violence was naturalised through the appropriation of particular identities: gender and age. It was also naturalised by its link to adult male bodies that were deemed naturally stronger and therefore more able to 'give' and 'take' violence. In her work, Chung (2005) identified that essentialist ideas about gender were dominant in young people's understandings of men's use of violence. In this study violence was naturalised by age, whereby the young people aligned adulthood with the potential for violence. In short, the age (adult) and gender (male) of a person were prerequisites to violent behaviour being naturalised and judged as being 'real'.

Boys and girls both understood adult men's violence as a natural occurrence whereas boys judged their own (and other boys') violence to be a performance through which to illustrate and validate power. Many of the boys saw masculinity as a singular and fixed identity, achievable only by adult men, whilst the girls judged masculinity as an identity encompassed by adult men *and* boys, demonstrated through physical, violent actions. Girls also experienced this form of masculinity in their present lives and anticipated it in the future. Whilst boys aspired to it (or believed they should) in their present lives, they determined that it was only achievable by adult men.

Boys and Violence

This naturalisation of gender endorsed the view that men and boys were more violent and that (for girls) being a boy was synonymous with this kind of behaviour. It also further validated the model of 'real' violence adhered to by the young people:

Meera: If you were a boy, you'd be going around hitting and punching each other

(Baxter Road School, Group 2)

Grace: It's not *natural* for girls to hit each other but … it's *natural* for boys to hit each other 'cause they are always fighting…

Kirsten: I haven't seen one girl who has actually physically fought with another girl.

(Baxter Road School, Group 4)

Grace mentions the notion of 'naturalness' and aligns violence with the essence of what it is to be a boy. By making this link with such action being 'natural', it is deemed irrevocable. In this sense, the perpetration of violence is not questioned rather its presence in the construction of masculinities is validated. Again all of the young people with very few exceptions saw violence as being natural for men. The girls were also likely to label boys as being violent whereas boys were more questioning of this – seeing violence as a learned behaviour.

Violent Masculinity: Natural for Men, Practiced by Boys

Young people sought to naturalise violence as a prerequisite of masculine identity, reinforcing 'naturalised' gender differences to do so; using the notion of being 'a man' to explain predispositions to violence. In all cases, an understanding of violence was sought outside of the individuals' own sphere of knowledge, focusing upon, and illustrated with, *abstract* examples of violence and violent behaviour. These intrinsic attributes of *masculinity* were also drawn upon to explain girls' violence (as unnatural or 'non' violence) because of their lack of masculinity. It was also evident in their 'naturalised' endorsements of gendered hierarchies of violence and the codes that had to be adhered to. The term 'masculinity' as opposed to socially constructed *masculinities* is used here (see, for example, Connell 2005). It was through the discursive framework of social constructionism that the concept and position of 'men' and 'masculinity' began to be questioned and challenged, in the same way that feminists and childhood theorists had sought to deconstruct the categories of 'woman' and 'child'. Prior to this men had been accepted as gender-neutral subjects; the bench mark on which all 'others' were measured. Deconstructing 'men' and 'masculinity/ies' has been an important step forward in the theorisation of violence (Segal 1997; Hearn 1998, 2001; Connell 1993, 2000).

Yet these 'naturalised' examples of violence jarred with discussions of their own lives and experiential knowledge. For example, when the young people talked about boys they knew (or their own experience of being boys themselves), then the discussions of 'naturalised' violence transformed into socially constructed and performative attributes of what it was to be a man – attributes that were considered both desirable and unobtainable constructions, for example, boys who struggled with the expectation that they should perpetrate or experience violence because of expectations around their gender.

Masculinity was a trait associated with adult 'men' and it was anticipated that boys needed to 'perform', 'pretend' and 'practise' being men, acknowledging a disabling and unobtainable hegemonic 'ideal'. For Connell:

> 'Masculinity', to the extent that the term can be briefly identified at all, is simultaneously a place in gender relations, the practices through which men and women engage that place in gender, and the effects of these practices in bodily experience, personality and culture. (Connell 2005: 71)

Kimmel argues that masculinity is defined by what it is not, rather than what it is: 'being a man means not being like a woman' (Kimmel 1994: 126), with Morgan (1992) asserting that masculinity is something men 'do' rather than what they 'are'. In this sense, much of what men 'do' can be defined as violence (see Hearn 1998). Connell asserts that power is the defining feature of hegemonic masculinity with this power symbolised through enactments of violence. For Kaufman:

> The equation of masculinity with power is one that developed over centuries. It conformed to, and in turn justified, the real-life domination of men over women and the valuation of males over females. (Kaufman 1999: 62– 3)

Connell's (1995, 2005) theorisation of hegemonic masculinity as 'the cultural dynamic by which a group claims and sustains a leading position in social life' (Connell 2005: 77), has proved of critical importance as a way of understanding the construction of gender identity and the valorisation of violence. Connell's term refers to the most dominant (and dominating) form of masculinity, which structures power relations among and between other masculinities and femininities, and legitimates the use of power and control (see also Kimmel, 1987). Indeed it guarantees (or is taken to guarantee) the dominant position of men and the subordination of women (Connell 1995: 77). Masculinity theorists have identified heterosexuality as being a fundamental component of hegemonic masculinity (Connell 2005, 2000; Epstein 1997; Flood 1997, 2009a, 2009b; Mac an Ghaill 1994; Stoudt 2006) constructed in opposition to all things 'gay' or 'girl like'. According to Messerschmidt:

> [o]ne of the ways then, to validate masculinity at school is to express and define yourself as heterosexual both by degrading homosexuality and by exaggerating heterosexual practices … the cool guys are not only tall, strong and athletic but are actively and publicly involved in heterosexuality. (2000: 300–301)

Much was made of the connection between being a boy and being 'tough', a description that alluded to physical strength and a willingness to fight. Although the generic label of 'tough' was associated with boys, not one individual boy within any of the groups was labelled in this way during the sessions. Therefore, the label represented a construct rather than a lived description of one's actions. Yet the generated abstract identity was a powerful aspiration and an attempt to achieve it was necessary:

Tommy:	If you are a boy *you get to be tough* and if you are a girl you sit like this but you are gay if you do it.
Jason:	Yeah, if you have your hands clasped and your legs crossed you are gay
Tommy:	'Cause that's what girls do.

(Mary Magdalene School, Group 3)

For the group above, toughness was an undisputed prerequisite of being male. Being unable to demonstrate this construction of masculinity, aligned you with the feminine and more significantly with 'being gay', the antipathy of all things boy-like. The construction of a masculine identity operates here simultaneously on two levels, defining what you are in terms of what you are not (a girl or gay), and the disjuncture between the constructed reality (toughness) and the lived experience of being a boy.

Therefore, in constructing or aspiring to this normative gender role boys and men are encouraged to denounce all things not endorsed by this rigid heteronormativity (Warner 1991). Warner (1991) coined the phrase 'hetero-normativity' to illustrate the gender norms, practices and institutions that privileged heterosexuality. Engaging with the ideas informing heteronormativity is relevant here to illustrate young people's interactions with gendered norms and practices and how these locate them within certain (heterosexual) sexual spheres. Heteronormativity, whilst describing the power of heterosexual normativity as a discursive concept, implies that all things are fixed within that framework of understanding and that heterosexuality is a stable construct.

Swain (2003: 302) identifies the demonstration of physicality among boys: strength, speed and the ability to fight, as being a key signifier in 'successful masculinity' used to construct hierarchies of hegemonic and subordinate masculinities and one of the means to demonstrate this is through the 'showing off' of such attributes. Swain found that in his study of primary school boys:

> There were some boys who deliberately cultivated aggressive 'macho' forms of behaviour, which they saw as a way of establishing their masculine authority. Toughness seems to characterise much of their attitude and relations to other boys, though this was scarcely ever directed at girls. (Swain 2004: 175)

Frosh et al. (2002) identified 'being hard' as a key aspect of 'popular masculinity' that served to regulate boys' behaviour. McCarry (2003: 223) also concluded that the young people in her study, accepted male violence as part of male identity. Indeed they 'conceptualised power and superior status as intrinsic to masculinity'. Most boys in all these studies admitted to not possessing the necessary attributes to achieve this status. It is significant however, that whilst all men benefit from what Connell (2001: 40) terms, 'the patriarchal dividend'; the advantage men in general gain from the overall subordination of women, not all men are equally privileged within or by patriarchal relations.

Several of the girls saw this propensity for being able to commit violence in a positive light, and talked in terms of wanting to be a boy so they could be physically stronger and more able to defend themselves. For boys this association with strength and toughness was identified as potentially disabling. They recoiled from the assumption that because you were a boy you had to be violent. This uneasiness could explain why boys 'put off' this expectation until adulthood:

> Paul: One of the things I don't like about being a boy is like well men they get a reputation from a few people and you don't hear of many women doing it but you hear of a lot of men … after that, like people think that almost every single boy could be like that so that's how they get their name for it.
>
> (Mary Magdalene School, Group 4)

The expectation to be violent was associated with not being weak. One boy describes how his dad expects him to be able to put up with physical violence from his sister, explicitly because she is smaller, a year younger, and importantly because she is a girl:

> Stewart: Me and my sister fight sometimes, right erm and because I'm bigger, she, like my dad expects me to be able to kinda take it and he says like, you're bigger, you should, it shouldn't affect you.
>
> (Clifton School, Group 5)

Many of the boys involved in this research were grappling with both the implications and realities of hegemonic masculinity identities. When girls talked of violence they talked of 'boys' as well as 'men'. Boys were much more likely to only refer to 'men', deliberately redefining the boundaries of violence to intimate 'the other' and to exclude themselves from it:

> Dougie: Like it's the same between a man and a woman and a bigger boy and a littler boy. Everyone would blame the bigger boy.

Nancy:	So you think that people always assume that it's the man?
Dougie:	They do, like the bigger person.
Stewart:	It's normally 'cause the men who are causing the violence are bigger and stronger.

(Clifton School, Group 5)

Although in the example above the boys talk about the gendered nature of the expectation of violence, what they actually refer to is the size of the individual as being indicative of their propensity to commit violent acts. So, although individually they challenged stereotypes (in not wanting to be associated with an expectation to be violent), they were still aligning violence with size and physical strength, and thus hegemonic masculinity.

As highlighted in Chapter 4 there were several contradictions in what the young people said. Many were eager to equate men as naturally violent. Young people's models of 'real' violence were only able to explain men's use of violence as a natural phenomenon rooted in their physical prowess and power – men use violence because it is innate in their biology. Young people used the dualisms, and the stereotypes invested in them, as evidence of gender difference:

Sam:	Girls being weaker than boys. Is that not a bit of a myth?
Nancy:	What do you mean?
Sam:	Like it's a bit of an idea that someone made up?
Nancy:	What do you think?
Sam:	You can both be equally as strong, sometimes girls and women can be stronger.

(Mountview School, Group 2)

These quotes illustrate a disjuncture between their abstract reasoning – that 'real' violence involves men, who are naturally stronger and more powerful – and their lived reality – that the girls and (boys) they know do not all fit this description. In the second example, the boy questions the myth of 'weakness' but seeks my reassurance when doing so, as it is an attribute so deeply embedded within acceptable femininity, that to argue against it appears perplexing, even though his own knowledge supports his belief. This demonstrates the strength of the role of authority in challenging both gender norms and stereotypes (the symbolism of gendered power was engrained and therefore much more difficult for the young people to challenge directly and sometimes even to recognise (see also Spencer et al. 2003).

Young people found it hard to move past the physicality of the (adult) body. This was less so with regard to muscles and hair, which could be changed. However, genitalia and biology were understood as fixed and stable indicators of difference, linking gender immutably with sex and the role of women to have and care for children. The symbolism of gendered power was engrained and therefore much more difficult for the young people to challenge directly. Yet it became easier for them to do so when constructions of gender and power were destabilised by their own experiential knowledge. This illustrates the disjuncture between 'real' and 'unreal' and 'common sense' and 'experiential'.

Their own position within childhood presents an uneasy dichotomy between the proximity of what they know and experience, and the distance of abstract examples that are culturally endorsed and reinforced. What they experienced as gendered young people, was for them not representative of what they were to become. The fluidity of their own gendered experiences jarred with the rigid frameworks of adult gender roles. For example, the young people traded upon stereotyped notions of grown-up bodies; they looked to the future to subscribe to physical differences between men and women, or as a means to consolidate the differences they perceived already existed. Such differences were representative of what they were to 'become'.

'Outside' Spaces

The age of people also determined the spaces they occupied, which in turn impacted upon the spaces which the young people identified with violence:

Nancy: And where does most of this violence takes place?
Shona: Anywhere. On the street, in the park.
Alice: In the pub, when they are drunk.

(Mary Magdalene School, Group 3)

Alice mentions alcohol as a factor in violent behaviour, but it is contextualised as being within a pub (and therefore in an adult environment). Adulthood is also supposed through her use of 'they', thereby associating alcohol with 'other'. What is interesting is that although young people did make links between alcohol and violence nobody used it as an explanation for violence or to justify violent behaviour. When alcohol was mentioned or people referred to as being drunk it was as an addition to the violence that was already occurring. Drinking too much alcohol was viewed negatively and the combination of violence and alcohol even more so. None of the young people spoke about drinking alcohol themselves.

The association of outside space with violence was a prominent theme in their discussions. Young people spoke of violence happening 'anywhere' but then limited it to places where it was seen and witnessed. Therefore, for them violence predominated public spaces because that is where it was most visible.

Much of the violence participants had personally witnessed involved teenagers and young adults (boys and men older than the young people themselves). The acts were committed in public places, where young people hung around together in the evenings and at night, such as school playgrounds and parks. Although the spaces are open to the public, at night these are places generally closed off and only frequented by young people and teenagers. Thus these spaces can be said to constitute private areas for the young people during these times. This theme can be seen to introduce the idea of private behaviours in public places thus transcending spatial dualisms.

Here it can be argued that there is an inversion of public and private spaces with displays of private behaviour in public places; for example teenagers in parks, drinking, sitting around, sexualised behaviour, arguments and physical violence:

> Dougie: You see it [violence] outside and you see it in the park. Neds fighting. You see it on the street.
>
> Stewart: And at school. They get on the roof and throw slates at cars … and they just don't seem to care at all 'cause the janny [janitor] comes out and the police come but they just do it again.
>
> (Clifton School, Group 5)

It is important at this point to note that many of the young people interwove the term 'violence' with 'fighting'. That is, when asked about violence they replied substituting the word violence with fighting. At first I thought that this endorsed it as a physical activity but then realised, and was convinced by the young people's discussions, that fighting can be verbal and emotionally based too. Whilst not encompassing as many acts or behaviours as the term 'violence'; 'fighting' was a word that the young people felt more comfortable in using and accessed it to name certain behaviours and actions that they viewed as 'violent' as well as explicitly using it to describe actions by young people.

Young people also described school as a place where they witnessed violent behaviour and the main actors in these situations were boys. The majority of descriptions of violence at school followed a prescribed model and can also be framed by the constellation of violence model used by the young people. The only difference is that the main actors are not adult men but boys. The framework of violence described by young people involved two or more boys, fighting physically in the yard or in an area of the school that was not (or very rarely) the classroom. The same use of outside space where the actions were witnessed by others is important here. Teachers or dinner ladies were the figures of authority who first recognised the actions as violence and then went on to define them as such to both the children involved and onlookers. They then broke up the violence and the boys were chastised. This meant that there was a consequence and official sanction for their behaviour, again reaffirming for others that such actions are both violent and wrong:

Eloise: John and Harry were punching each other in the playground and lost golden time.

(Hardcastle School, Group 1)

Russell: Davie pinned that boy from P4 against the wall and the teacher made his mum come in.

(Hardcastle School, Group 2)

Debbie: After playtime [when there had been an incident involving two boys] the teacher talked to us all in class and told us we shouldn't do that.

(Mountview School, Group 4)

Without exception, this cycle of events was followed and replicated in all schools, when relaying tales of incidents involving boys. This constellation of factors, including the defining of the behaviour as wrong and subsequent consequences from a person in authority was critical in framing the issue for girls. Boys, however, were more likely to define chastisement or consequence as becoming 'more serious' with age.

Age as More Likely to Determine Consequence

The following quote highlights the young people's (boys') reticence to align their own behaviour within prominent cultural discourses when there was no official consequence defining it as violent or violence such as the police or the court system. For them authority and the invoking of a consequence framed an incident as violence. Such actions and spaces were more generally occupied by adults. Age, therefore, was a salient factor in young people's defining of violence:

Jack: Like me and my friend fight, but that's not violence. Violence is something bigger. Violence is where you end up in the jail.

(Clifton Group School, Group 3)

This reluctance to label their own behaviour as violent (especially when it involved the victimisation of their female peers), also illustrates the young people's casual normalisation of their actions, which is analysed in more detail in Chapter 6.

As has already been highlighted, age or adulthood and being a man were the prerequisites to actions being defined as violent. For example, the behaviour undertaken by the young people themselves and their peers was not in itself judged by them to be violent, because in their there was a lack of involvement from the authorities other than school.

Some of the consequences of violence were only seen to come into being with age, such as the legal system (being arrested or sent to prison). Therefore, the self same behaviour was 'allowed' if you were too young to face legal repercussions. For example, there were young people who, because of their age, did not think that the system of law applied to them, either as perpetrators or as victims:

Craig: If a boy hits a girl well that's it, but if a man hits the woman he can go to jail for it.

(Mary Magdalene School, Group 5)

Whilst this raises important questions about their own rights (and their lack of knowledge of such rights), it also creates and sustains a belief among young people that 'real' violence is rarely committed or experienced by them personally because the acts are not always witnessed, labelled or condemned by 'authority' (with the exception of school based violence for the boys). Young people here both anticipated and accepted the role of (adult) authority in defining 'real' violence for them.

The Authority of the Media in Defining 'Real' Violence

Young people's knowledge of violence was drawn from their everyday lives, some of which was informed from powerful media discourses (such as street crime, the use of weapons and 'stranger danger'). Their adherence to this limited model of 'real' violence, perpetuates the skewed perceptions of the perils of 'stranger danger' and the potential threat of public space, both of which are perpetuated in the media but rarely reflected in lived experience (Kitzinger 2002; Scott 2003; Stanko 1992).

Many of these representations of violence were negotiated through discussions with their peers, who were influential in the process of helping to define violent actions and behaviour. The media is judged as having a powerful ideological role in informing the young people's perceptions and understandings and this has been seized upon in prevention campaigns, although its success is debatable (see Gadd 2013). The media has also been blamed of creating and sustaining climates of 'acceptable' violence. The proliferation of social media use predates this research and much has been written since that contributes to the debate (De Block and Buckingham 2010). The role of personal media in creating normative and relational contexts for abuse is an emerging area of research, although for others, fears around its influence have been overstated (Livingstone 2002, 2008; Livingstone et al. 2010). The use and abuse of mobile media is not reflected upon here. That which does exist looks at it in terms of risk (Benotsch et al. 2012) and tends to focus upon teenagers (Lippman and Campbell 2014).

Media as Boundary of 'Real' and 'Unreal' Violence

For the young people their use of media related to TVs, computers, books and newspapers. They initiated discussions of the media and talked of events and examples they had seen. The young people also used the media to create boundaries of 'real' and 'unreal' violences that they are able to subscribe to and distance themselves from. For example, the media was viewed as a tool that disseminated 'real life' stories through represented realities (such as soap opera storylines) and the reality of life in a represented form (such as news stories). News stories and documentary programmes about real life violence were quoted as providing the young people with knowledge and understanding. They were also aware of issues such as domestic violence because of story lines in soaps that had tackled them, such as *Eastenders*, *Hollyoaks* and *Coronation Street.* Also, there were discussions of pop stars such as Rhianna and the abuse she experienced from Chris Brown. Less popular, but still a useful resource was printed media, with several of the girls talking about the books of Jacqueline Wilson.[1]

TV programmes were excellent vehicles for detailing patterns of abuse. The behaviours depicted occurred over a period of time – although it was often one particular incident that the young people would focus on (the 'worst' bit as they saw it). Those examples covered in the media (such as Rhianna's abusive relationship) had the propensity of making the violence seem like a 'one-off' event that had (often) involved the police rather than a pattern of 'less newsworthy' abusive 'coercively controlling' behaviours.

Yet at times, it was unclear to me (and them) where these discursive boundaries of the 'real' and 'unreal' were drawn. It also became necessary to question the legitimation young people sought from these discourses to justify their dismissal of the perpetrators' actions (see the *Eastenders* example below).

Young people however, are not merely objects of the media; they did not accept everything that was presented to them without challenging it. Instead, they actively negotiated with the media and the representations of violence they encountered. This agentic status is further demonstrated through their peer relationships with whom they engage when accessing the media representations. This was illustrated in their talk of characters in books and films, when discussing their competing abilities at playing video games and their engagement with soap story lines:

1 *Lola Rose* by Jacqueline Wilson tells the story of Jayni/Lola Rose who escapes from her abusive father, and, together with her mum and her brother, starts a new life.

Tommy: That's like in Eastenders, wee Mo.
[laughter]
Tommy: And Trevor beating her up.
Jason: She wasnae eating her dinner and he smashed her face into it [laughter].
Nancy: Why do you think he did that?
Jason: Because she didnae like it and it was all sticky and ewughh … it just looked disgusting and she didn't eat it and she said I won't eat it and he took a fluke [a fit of anger] and went mental. It was funny man!
[Laughter]
Nancy: Okay, so you are all laughing? You say it was funny? Why was that funny when Trevor did that to her?
Jason: 'Cause he shoved her head in her dinner.
Tommy: I mean you knew it was acting but if it was real, it wouldne be.
(Mary Magdalene School, Group 3)

The example above was one of many episodes over a period of months exploring the abusive relationship of Trevor and Little Mo and was shown at least four years prior to the research being undertaken. Even though the programme contextualised the abuse as continuing and cumulative, the young people still judged Trevor's behaviour as taking 'a fluke' (an immediate, uncontrollable rage). This suggests a sudden reaction from Trevor rather than sustained and systematic abuse. More worryingly however, and a recurrent theme among many of the boys' groups, is the labelling of his actions as 'funny'. The group justified this by labelling the whole scenario as 'not real' and therefore it was okay to find it funny.

The category of 'unreal' is a broad definition used by the young people to describe actions which are not real (for them) and therefore 'fictitious'. It is also a term used to describe those actions which others may 'name' as violence (for example girls naming actions perpetrated against them by boys) but are not 'defined' by others as such, because they do not fit in with the constellation of factors that constitute 'real' violence (see next chapter for further elaborations of this point). It is unclear whether the boys here labelled the actions of 'Trevor' as 'unreal' because it was a soap opera on television, or because it did not fit into the realms of what they considered 'real' violence (that is, separating their understandings of 'real' physical violence from that of pushing Mo's head into her dinner).

There were some young people who actively engaged in questioning and challenging the powerful discourses of the media and what they perceived as media bias; for example, the power of the media in defining what was violent. For example, several of the groups talked about the prevalence of stranger attacks (real violence) in the news as they appeared more 'newsworthy', as opposed to examples of intimates ('unreal'):

Sonny: Like if a stranger hurt you, like that one in the news, [name], she got stabbed in the neck. The reason it was on the news was because it was a stranger. If it was someone close to you it'd be out of anger usually.

Ewan: Yes those are the ones we hear about, when you don't know your attacker and it's not your fault.

(Clifton School, Group 3)

Here Sonny makes two very separate points. Firstly, he recognises the newsworthiness of a stranger attack as opposed to violence perpetrated by an intimate. By making this distinction, the media is categorising violence and thereby generating a tier of seriousness and blame. Secondly, Sonny contextualises intimate violence as occurring because of anger; that intimates provoke reactions and that this is a causal response. Therefore, by this reasoning, because strangers do not know each other personally, they cannot anger each other and so the explanation for the violence comes from elsewhere and this lack of explanation makes it more noteworthy.

The media perpetually bolsters the moral panics over violent video games and their impact upon children and young people (see Cohen (1972) for an overview of media amplification and Barker (2001) for a critique of Newson's report looking at the impact of violent films and games on children and young people). As is demonstrated below, young people viewed video games as offering 'unreal' depictions of violence, and one in which they were all too aware of the adult – imposed moral panic over their inability to distinguish between representation (unreal) and reality (real). Yet the young people believed it was the adults who failed to see the distinction between 'real' and 'unreal', not themselves:

Davie: Parents always worry and say you shouldn't play stuff like that with the shooting and all. Do they not know it's a game? It's not real?

(Baxter Road, Group 3)

Any talk of video games was generally initiated by me, but always assigned to the same category of 'unreality' by the young people. In general more boys than girls talked about playing such games and divorced them from the reality of 'real life' situations or examples of violence. Thus video games were not ascribed as sources of information of violence, rather accessible representations of violence that were fundamentally not real but 'games'. Therefore, although video games have been defined as 'violent' the young people did not name them as such. The young people, who spoke about them, also attributed any link between the two as being already exacerbated by a propensity to violence, rather than being a direct result of the video game. This demonstrated a realisation of, and attribution of their own agentic status rather than them simply being seen as objects of socialisation:

> Cameron: Like shooting games. They say that it makes you kill people and things like that but it doesn't.
> Nancy: Do you play games like that?
> Cameron: I've got one, yeah. It's just a game. It's not gonna make me go out and shoot someone.
> Louis: Yeah, only if you are crazy.
> Christopher: Yeah you have to have some sort of problem.
> Cameron: Like violence in them already.
>
> (Clifton School, Group 1)

However, Cameron's final comment attributes violence as a biological factor that is inherent, lying dormant until reacting to a trigger (a further example of a 'natural' male reaction). Conversely this example also epitomises the atypical perpetrator and is representative of arguments against the censorship of video games. Upon initial analysis, young people used the media to classify that which they understood as 'unreal' violence, illustrating their own ability to differentiate between 'reality' and 'representation'. It then, however, becomes more complex. 'Real' is that which is culturally endorsed and that which adheres to their constellation of factors; 'unreal' becomes the category used to name that which is not judged to be violent; that which falls outside of the 'official' definition.

Constructions of Gender as a Binary

In the following quotation, Kate locates her understanding of violence against women, within binary concepts of femininity and weakness.

> Kate: It's wrong for a boy to hit a girl because the girl might cry.
>
> (Baxter Road School, Group 5)

Alongside the implicit acceptance of normative masculinity and the alignment of this construction with power, is the perception that men's violence against women is wrong *because* of the perceived weakness of females. Therefore, women are complicit in their own victimisation, because they are not strong enough to counter it. Although Kate and others challenged the perpetration of physical violence, the gendered practices which contributed to it were rarely resisted. Kate was not alone in this conceptualisation of violence against women. Many of the participants concurred that girls (as opposed to boys) would be more likely to be hurt during physical violence, that females were physically weaker and that male violence against women was mismatched and unfair. Here, Shona locates her understanding of men's violence against women within binary concepts of femininity and weakness. This was a view shared by the majority of participants, who concurred that girls (as opposed to boys) would be more likely to be hurt during physical violence, that females were weaker and that men's violence against women was mismatched and unfair, as boys (men) are bigger and stronger than girls (women). So although the young people were most likely to challenge physical (as opposed to emotional) violence, they were less likely to overtly resist the gendered practices which contributed to it.

The construction of violent behaviour was also a means of endorsing gendered performances of violence along the binary lines of physical and emotional. There was a perpetual assumption that boys and girls express violent behaviour in different ways, and that these ways directly correlated with their gender:

Daisy: I think girls show it in a different way.
Nicole: Yeah they do.
Daisy: I think boys are more physical and girls are more verbal, yeah.
(Mountview School, Group 1)

Shazia: Girls just shout at each other, they don't fight.
(Baxter Road School, Group 1)

Ruth: Boys get into a lot more fist fights. With girls it's more sort of, erm, verbal arguments than physical.
(Clifton School, Group 4)

Alice: Girls use talking not violence.
(Mary Magdalene School, Group 2)

The assumption that boys are more physically violent and girls express violence verbally feeds straight into the gendered dichotomy, and positions girls and boys yet again as oppositional. It also incorporates much of the embodied gender stereotypes of boys and girls being different in terms of strength and physicality, and therefore having little option but to maximise their gendered attributes, boys through physical (powerful) means and girls through (softer) more emotional dialogue. Whilst it is important to recognise the different spheres of abuse, in terms of physical and emotional, positioning them upon a binary simply further divides them, as separate, and tiered, violences.

In the extract below, the group explored the tensions between constructed images of gender and reality:

Sonny:	Not all boys are stronger than girls, it depends who it is. Some girls are very strong … it's just most men don't want to be shown up.
Joe:	Yeah they don't want the girl to beat them 'cause it's wrong.
[Laughter]	
Sonny:	Well it's not wrong but the men think it's wrong.
Joe:	It's totally humiliating for them.
Ewan:	To be beaten by a girl. You'd get teased and stuff if you got beaten by a girl.

(Clifton School, Group 3)

Here Sonny rejects the notion that all men are stronger than all women, insisting instead that this is an image that some men portray, and it is important for them to continue in their representation of this image, otherwise their masculinity may be questioned. The other boys do not engage with Sonny's slightly more sophisticated argument maintaining instead that men would be humiliated should a woman 'beat' a man, whereas Sonny understands that it is the representation of gender, and the expectation this entails that results in this apparent 'humiliation'. For him, this humiliation results from boys not being able to exert their power over girls, and from girls being viewed as more powerful, thereby positioning boys in opposition to them and as weaker. Weakness then is judged as even greater as boys start off from a much more powerful position and their descent from there, serves to highlight the fragility of their masculine identity.

Young people found themselves much more able to (re)produce gender as a socially constructed product of choice and constraint when explored through the discursive frame of performativity, and when it was aligned directly with their own experiences. This was the framework they used to explain the use of violence to 'show off'. Several of the girls picked up on the performative elements of masculinity, intimating that boys frequently showed off in all areas of their lives, often in attempts to 'prove' their superiority:

Aimee:	If you were a boy, you'd be showing off. To prove that you're better than girls.

(Clifton School, Group 2)

Julia:	Boys always just want to show that they are the best.

(Hardcastle School, Group 1)

This consolidates the earlier points in Chapter 4 made about boys' presentation of self through the performative strategies of 'showing off' in terms of only being able to perform a certain sort of behaviour; a very limited masculin*ity*.

'Equalising' Violence

Women and girls rarely featured in young people's examples of what constituted 'real' violence. Violence used *by* women was difficult for the young people to conceive of, as it did not conform to their own linear model of 'real' violence (i.e. involving men) and was not necessarily something they always had knowledge or experience of. Instead, it was constructed alongside what they did know – that men are 'naturally' violent. Such an assumption automatically positioned women and girls as going against both nature and 'acceptable' forms of femininity. Therefore, when violence was linked to girls, it was seen as wrong and deemed unnatural, because of its 'inherent' constitution as an indicator of masculinity, and its confirmation of the existence of dichotomous and fixed gender identity.

On the few occasions where girls were described as being physically violent, the terminology used was very different, as the example below highlights:

Fatima:	If it's between girls and they are *actually fighting physically* then it's *actually intense* but if it's boys fighting it's *just* a fist fight and things like that.
Nicole:	Because when I was going home the other day, by the junction, there was a girl having a *cat* fight with another girl and it just got out of hand.
Fatima:	Girls from that school have got quite a bad reputation, *going down the street* and *swearing* and *making a noise*, *giving grief* and *breaching the peace*.
Nancy:	Can I just pick up on something, why do you call girls fighting a cat fight?
Fatima:	I don't know that's just what they are called.
Nicole:	I think it's off the television, like in the movies they call them cat fights and I suppose they think it's cool.
Nancy:	Okay. Would you ever call two boys fighting a cat fight?
All:	No.

(Mountview School, Group 1, my emphasis)

Although the group talk here about girls fighting there is very little mention of their actual actions. What they do mention, as a means to explain the bad reputation these girls have (swearing, breaching the peace, making noise), does not correlate with the negative labels they then accord them. Yet it is the deviation away from an acceptable form of femininity that warrants such condemnation. The girls in question were in an outside space (the street) *and* making noise thus drawing attention to them being in a public space. During the session, by questioning their use of the label 'cat fight', I was attempting to get the girls to deconstruct their gendered use of the term and the implications of labelling girls as 'cats'. The use of the term echoes the previous discussion where types of violent actions used are dependent upon gender. Thus cat fighting implies scratching, biting, spitting and caterwauling. This again divides boys' and girls' behaviour. Boys are viewed as using more 'heavy' types of violence such as kicking, punching and hitting, but which is not given an animalistic comparison – it is viewed as a more 'naturalistic' behaviour and thus not in need of a comparison to give it meaning.

The 'deviant' behaviour of girls fighting is framed by the expectations of acceptable femininity. During the exploratory questionnaire, violence between girls was deemed 'not right' and 'wrong' with justifications such as 'girls are supposed to be polite' and 'girls shouldn't behave like that'. Yet when the young people were confronted with these justifications during the discussion group sessions, they were more likely to challenge these limited constructions of femininity, thus opposing abstract notions of girls, by grounding their knowledge within their own lived experiences of knowing or being a girl:

Samia: Girls don't have to be polite, saying that's just sexist.

(Baxter Road School, Group 4)

Shona: Not all girls are polite, just like not all boys aren't.

(Mary Magdalene School, Group 2)

This illustrates the discrepancy between girls' own proximity to their lived experience of being a girl and the distant abstract examples used to perpetuate stereotypes. As such, the social sanctioning of gendered violence is constructed along the lines of gender equality in terms of only being able to be violent to other people within your gender groups (again this relates back to the 'naturalisation' of gender). As long as an equality code is adhered to and men are only violent with other men and women are only violent to other women, and these boundaries are not transgressed, then violence, to some of the young people, is acceptable:

Michael: If it's a boy against a girl, he should go and get his sister or something.

Nancy: Why?

Michael: 'Cause it's a girl.

Nancy: So is it okay for a girl to hit another girl?

All: Yeah.

(Mary Magdalene School, Group 4)

In this example there is an acceptance (and expectation) that family members (although often victims or perpetrators in sibling violence) will support you at any cost in your quest to equally match gendered fights. Many of the young people agreed with such sentiments and espoused a discourse of gender 'equality' in violence. This violence was generally more acceptable when it involved people who were equivalents, not only physically but also along gender lines:

Sandeep: It's usually girls that hit girls and boys that hit boys.

(Mountview School, Group 3)

Some groups reiterated the alignment of 'equality' in violence during the discussion of the third vignette, believing that the violence used by Jamie against Jenny should have been instead used against Roddy, as they were more evenly matched, as men. Implicit in the theme of equality through violence is the image of men fighting over women.[2]

Summary

In this chapter, the relevance of young people's constructions and understandings of violence is identified, alongside the significance of the processes involved in 'defining' violence. Data illuminates and demonstrates how the young people judge violence through an adherence to a constellation of factors. These need to be in place for them to 'define' actions as violence: two or more (adult) men, physically fighting, in a public space, with injury and/or official consequence.

It is asserted that young people are more able to define violence that has happened to 'others'. This incorporates 'other' people, 'other' outside spaces; 'other' people's homes and 'other people's' violence. This 'otherness' also relates to adults in terms of the young people giving more validation to the actions and experiences of adults than their own. The closer the young people were to the individuals and situations they identified (in terms of age, gender, knowledge of) the less likely they were to identify actions and behaviour as violent and in doing so 'naturalise' what they term 'real' violence making it less likely to be challenged. The next chapter highlights such a position results in young people's failure to recognise their own experiential knowledge (achieved in the process

2 Although this may engender 'romanticised' notions of duels and knights in armour, the patriarchal reality is that the woman is constructed as a possession to be won.

of 'naming' violence) or leads them to conclude that their own experience is defined as less significant.

Young people draw upon gender, age and space to understand men's violence against women; their constructions of it are dependent upon highly gendered codes, age (in terms of their envisaged fracture between childhood and adulthood) and space (which they construct using distance and proximity). Their constructions are interweaved, with their understandings of gender cognisant with the temporality of the life course (young and old) which also impacts upon their understanding of space (near and far) which destabilises traditional notions of public and private spaces.

The next chapter looks at how young people are more likely to normalise their own experiences of 'violence'. In doing this, young people begin to legitimate those types of violence that do not fit into their constellation framework. Age and gender are part of the defining of what is violence, but as the following chapters reveal it also illustrates that they can be used as part of the justifications of, and for violence.

Chapter 6
Processes of Normalisation: Distancing 'Unreal' and 'Proximate' Violence

Domestic abuse is associated with broader gender inequality and should be understood in its historical context, whereby societies have given greater status, wealth, influence, control and power to men. It is part of a range of behaviours constituting male abuse of power, and is linked to other forms of men's violence (Scottish Executive 2000: 5).

> I define coercive control as a strategic course of self-interested behaviour designed to secure and expand gender-based privilege by establishing a regime of domination in personal life. This definition incorporates three facets of women's experience that are obscured by the violence model: that the oppression involved is 'ongoing' rather than episodic (a 'course of conduct') and resulting harms cumulative, that it is multi-faceted, and that it involves rational, instrumental behaviour. (Stark 2013: 21)

Violence and Abuse

A decision was made early in the research to ask young people directly what they understood by the term '*domestic abuse*'. As illustrated in the previous sections, many of the young people correlated violence with physical acts. Both words (violence and abuse) were originally introduced because of the Scottish government's focus upon domestic abuse and it was significant to note how the young people negotiated both terms. Whilst their understanding of each was multiple and varied, the common denominator between their suggestions came from the clear demarcation of the terms 'violence' and 'abuse' and whether they saw any difference between them. Violence was described as '*actual violence*' and linked with physicality in terms of hitting, punching, kicking and injury. Abuse was aligned to emotionality and verbal arguments as well as physical violence:

Alice: Violence is hitting and abuse is annoying someone, harassing them and then ending up hitting them.

(Mary Magdalene School, Group 2)

John: Domestic abuse is where you get hit all the time just for stupid things.

Simon: No abuse is where they insult you and violence is when you get hit.

(Mary Magdalene School, Group 3)

Differences between violence and abuse were identified in terms of the intensity and prolonged nature of the actions. Violence, in general, was described as a one-off isolated (physical) action such as the (apparent) isolated incident they heard about in each of the vignettes:

Jack: I think the vignettes were talking about violence, but not abuse, they weren't abusive 'cause *abuse is further than that.* Like more, it's more of I don't like you smack, punch, push down the stairs and then they might break their back and they are paralysed.

(Clifton School, Group 3, my emphasis)

Abuse was seen as a series of prolonged and cumulative actions that began with words but could progress into sustained acts of physical attacks:

Shazia: Because if someone uses physical abuse once, then they're obviously going to do it again.

(Baxter Road School, Group 2)

Daisy: *Abuse is a more general term than violence.* Like it covers if I was her husband [points to friend] and I was saying horrible things to her and she would start to believe it, so *abuse covers that and the violence as well.*

(Mountview School, Group 1, my emphasis)

Will: And *abuse is like swearing at them all the time, making them do stuff, calling them names.*

(Baxter Road School, Group 5, my emphasis)

In the extracts above, an awareness is demonstrated that the violence perpetrated by men and experienced by women is part of an abusive cycle, that increases in severity and frequency over time.

Yet how the young people conceptualised 'violence' and 'abuse' changed again when they were aligned directly with the term '*domestic*' (in keeping with the Scottish government's strategy). All groups linked 'domestic' with the site of the home, either through their knowledge of the word or the association of it with other words, for example, *domestic* pets. This can be related back to the earlier discussion of violence and 'space', where young people rarely acknowledged the home as being a site for 'violence' unless it was prefixed with the word 'domestic'.

When asked about the terms *domestic violence* and *domestic abuse* at the end of the session, half of the groups had not heard of either phrase. Of the nine groups that were aware of the terms, three groups said they didn't know what they meant. The remaining groups suggested an array of definitions ranging from child abuse, emotional and physical violence and violence within the family. The link between domestic abuse and child abuse has been highlighted before and flags up early feminist concerns with the infantilisation of the term.

For most of the young people, the description 'domestic' primarily alluded to the sphere of the home and the family within it, rather than intimating the nature of the relationship between victim and perpetrator. Therefore the young people's initial focus was upon the space in which the violence and abuse occurred, over and above the nature and relationship of the participants.

In doing this, their conceptualisation of such behaviours was limited by the physical space in which it occurred. Through the notion of 'distance', it was easier for the young people to accept actions as violent when they took place away from them, e.g. in outside public spaces. They struggled slightly with the conceptualisation of violence within the sphere of the home, as this was a place that they were proximate to (and for many was an apparent place of safety)– so they linked it to 'other' people's families or used justifications (see Chapter 7) to explain it.

The private space of the home was constructed as a degendered space, where the young people's main differential of power was structured by chronological age. They were most likely to venture that violence in the home occurs between parent and child or was equally divided between spouses. Thus, their understanding of the power differentials arises from their own readily visual and experiential contrasts of physical size, emotional power and authority. This then fed into their biological constructions of men as strong and powerful and therefore the most likely to be violent:

Nancy: And who does this kind of violence?
Tommy: The men.
Chris: Not always, it could be a stressed out mother.
Simon: Aye, hitting her boy.

Chris: The man could hit the woman, then the woman is taking it out on the children.

(Mary Magdalene School, Group 3)

Monica: An adult hitting another adult.
Aimee: No it's an adult hitting a child.

(Clifton School, Group 2)

When young people discussed examples of domestic abuse (involving women as victims), they assumed that the similar model of consequence would be followed – indeed this was a marker whereby they judged the validity of the scenario and they were less likely to justify the violent actions if the police were involved (official consequence). As such, the intervention by the woman to stop the violence, or the police to intervene, substantiated the notion that the violence was 'real'. Several groups of girls were eager to explain how they would readily leave a partner if he became violent. Their anticipations of what they would do if they experienced violence, followed a clearly designated model of options, including telling somebody, calling the police and leaving the abusive partner:

Shona: Well if he [Dave] won't apologise, I think she should leave him and tell someone about it.
Nancy: Who should she tell?
Shona: Her ma, or if it's a really bad hit, the police.

(Mary Magdalene School, Group 2)

Meera: I would go to the police.
Farah: Actually, when people are in that situation, they might be too scared to go to the police.
Meera: I'd ring the police and leave. That's what I would do anyway, other people might not. I can't say for sure that's what I would do, as that's in the future, when I'm older. But right now I would say that I would.

(Baxter Road School, Group 2)

Young people proffered the options as if they were very clear cut. However, Farah in the example above recognises the level of fear the woman may be experiencing and the determination it would take for her to go to the police. Meera, upon contemplating this, accepted that how she would react might change when she was older, when confronted with the reality of an abusive relationship and the constraints that the reality would impose. This also illustrates the differences between how girls constructed their own present, gender identities as fluid now – but as fixed by heterosexual relationships when they become adults (see Chapter 4). This quote, as well as highlighting the distance of time (adulthood), also 'others' the violence because it is happening to 'other' people. It is not violence that is occurring in young people's own temporal or spatial spheres. In the quote, Meera is aware that this option was not always available for all women to take. However, her faith (and that of others) in the criminal justice system does not waver. In the quote below, Meera believes that if Lizzy tells the police she is fearful, the police will automatically deal with Dave and rectify the situation. There is a clear demarcation between right and wrong, a belief that the police will act and that the perpetrator will be taken away.

There is also an element raised here about women and their choice to stay with violent partners, situating the perspective within a violence-prone discourse. Even when this did happen, the prefix of 'domestic' and their association of it with the home minimised the violence for some of the young people:

Cameron: Domestic violence isn't like just doing each other in, it's just *attempting* to.

(Clifton School, Group 1, my emphasis)

Stewart: [talking about a TV programme] it was on about domestic violence *but there was a lot more serious things than that. That was one of the minor things.*
Nancy: What was one of the minor things?
Stewart: Like stamping on her head.
Dougie: Yeah like the other stuff was *more serious*, like stabbings.

(Clifton School, Group 5, my emphasis)

Both examples of violence in the second extract sound 'serious' and it can only be surmised whether Stewart labelled them as less so because of the link between the violence being categorised as *domestic* or because of the gender makeup of the couple. It is also interesting that his example of the more serious violence involved a weapon. The immediate consequences of violence, such as the injuries that were inflicted by physical violence formed part of the constellation of violence adhered to by the young people. For many of the participants, injury was the factor by which to judge how serious the violence was:

Sarah: You never know, 'cause some boys. I mean it might be a knife, it might be a gun or anything. You never know and if one of them pulls out a knife and stabs them *then that's just taking it too far* and you hear about boys murdering other boys …

(Mary Magdalene School, Group 1, my emphasis)

Sarah places degrees of violence and injury upon a graduating scale, with murder being the ultimate consequence. She also genders the violence by contextualising her example with male actors. In this sense, Sarah labels violence as being more common and most serious when boys are involved. It is also important to note that her example is placed within a media discourse of 'you hear' where she is not relating what she knows but what she has been told to fear.

Descriptions and depictions of injury in the young people's pictures and stories were commonly used to tell the story, but also as an indication of the level of violence. Because of the nature of their drawing, much of the violence was depicted in a 'cartoon' style, with very graphic depictions of injuries, such as beheadings, loss of limbs and lots of blood. Such pictures were indicative of the sensationalism in newspaper stories. Often the pictures were taken to a neat and logical conclusion of 'happy ever after', with the victim going to hospital to get better and the perpetrator apprehended by the police. To an extent, this could be seen to demonstrate that whilst the consequences of violent behaviour are understood they are not always wholly comprehended:[1]

> Meera: See if she [Claire] says I don't want to be with you 'cause you are telling me what to do, he could make something up and say he is going to kill her or batter her in and if that happens she could tell the police and they can sort it out.
>
> Shazia: And they can just get his mum and dad up there to sort it out.
>
> (Baxter Road School, Group 2)

This belief in authority is also reflected by Shazia, who thinks that Lee's parents, once they are made aware of any wrong – doing, will chastise Lee and make sure it doesn't happen again. This comment is reflective of the young people's position in society, where parents are the primary figures of authority and where their children are still ultimately their responsibility. This discourse of being in charge and being able to enforce their authority is paralleled with the relationship between Lee and Claire and the 'power' he has, or tries to have over her. This is again reflected in some of the young people's understandings of child and parent relationships, where there is less a relationship of equality and rather one of authority:

> Lindsay: It's basically a man hitting a woman or a woman hitting a man or hitting the children in the house. But it's not going on in public so say someone came out with a black eye, if someone asks what

1 I would also contend that drawing a gory picture was perhaps easier and more fun than relaying a verbal argument. Also see Chapter 3 for discussion and reflections on the methods.

happened, the woman automatically makes up a story that something happened to them.

Ruth: People who take their anger out on people that haven't done anything and the woman might cover it up saying she fell.

(Clifton School, Group 4)

Interestingly, when discussing cases in the abstract young people were more likely to suggest a woman being abused should contact the police. Ruth's description above is also important in highlighting her belief that the woman will have done nothing to exacerbate the actions of the abuser. Both of these reactions were supported by others, but not reiterated in the examples discussed in the vignettes. For instance, in the vignettes where various examples of women's experiences of abuse were discussed, the strength of the conviction to contact the police was not reiterated. This highlights the importance of the context of the vignettes as opposed to discussing the examples within a vacuum. They set up a relationship in which the violence occurred to provide a context; but many of the young people saw this as providing a background which they then used to generate excuses and justifications on which they could base the man's violent 'reaction'. (See Chapter 7 for further discussion).

Approximately half of the young people described domestic violence and abuse as gendered. Those who did not were more likely to describe men and women using gendered tactics; men being physically violent because of their strength and women being emotionally abusive because of their lack of strength and/or power.

In many of the cases where young people sought to degender violence they instead succeeded in further engendering it through the perpetration of stereotypes. When young people did locate violence within a gendered framework, they often positioned women as powerless, rather than focusing upon the man's use of power:

Craig: Abuse is when you've got a wife and you are a man and you keep on hitting her and that. And if you keep on pushing her, then she doesn't say anything and he just keeps on doing it until she gets sick of it. Then she can't take it anymore and so she'll do something to herself.

Nancy: Like what?

Daniel: It happens to some children, if they get bullied so much they might commit suicide 'cause they are so mad.

(Mary Magdalene School, Group 5)

It is interesting here that Craig begins his discussion in the first person and goes on to describe the violence that he in the first person would perpetrate. He then changes to the third person as the violence escalates. In this way, Craig is implicating himself in the action of being 'a man', but using the third person (the 'other') to distance himself when the violence becomes too 'real'.

Domestic abuse was situated within the young people's constellation of violence when it conformed to the specific framework. That is when the violence involved adults, when it was in a space away from them (outside from them) with physical evidence (injury) confirmed by authority (the police) and official consequences (arrest and prison). Such a model only enabled domestic abuse to be judged as a specific incident rather than a pattern of behaviours and also relied upon the successful intervention of authority. So therefore when it did not conform to this framework (as domestic abuse generally does not) the young people were less likely to label it as 'real'. This lack of recognition (of behaviours outside of this constellation) meant that they often lacked an official structure with which to name their own experiences.

You Can't Hit a Woman: Gendered Moral Codes

Yet the display of such behaviour was subject to strict gendered codes and rules. Within these boundaries, only certain performances would be judged positively, whilst others could serve to stigmatise the man as weak. Young people maintained that labels such as *girl beater* and *lassie basher* were used to shame boys who are violent towards girls:

> Jake: If you hit a girl then everyone will start calling you a lassie basher.
> Nancy: Right, and is that the only reason you wouldn't do it? Because of the names?
> Jake: No. It's because if you hit them, then they'll go and tell on you and then you'll get into trouble.
>
> (Baxter Road School, Group 3)

Here, the power of labelling is significant, but not as much a deterrent as Jake's own preservation of self through not wanting to get into trouble. He positions himself higher than girls in that respect. His reason for not being violent is not a moral one, rather he does not want to get into trouble. Also, if he does not get into trouble – and is therefore not chastised – the violence remains 'unreal'.

It became clear that the labels were a means by which to question their masculine identities and it is here, not in their actions of being abusive to girls, that the label becomes derogatory. Only men who are not 'man' enough to hit other men are violent towards women. It is not the violence against women that is condemned, but their inability to be 'naturally' masculine and thus compete with an 'equal'. Girls are described as 'weaker' than boys and by implication, are placed on a binary scale where boys are judged as 'stronger' and ultimately seen as 'superior'. Thus if the violence deviated from prescribed models of definitive masculinity (for example the involvement of a woman as the victim of violence), the violent behaviour was no longer a means by which to demonstrate masculinity; rather it became an affirmation of weakness and therefore aligned with femininity:

Chris:	If a girl hits a boy it's probably because he has done something, and you can't really hit her back 'cause she's a girl.
Nancy:	Why can't you hit a girl?
Chris:	Because everybody, because everybody in your school will start calling you a girl beater.
Nancy:	So if people didn't say that, if they didn't call you that name would it be alright to hit her?
Chris:	No, it doesn't make much difference. It doesn't make you feel stronger hitting a girl, it makes you feel lousy.
Jason:	You can't beat a boy so you have to beat a girl.
John:	'Cause they're weaker.
Nancy:	Sorry you just said it's 'cause they are weaker?
Jason:	They are!
Nancy:	Why are they weaker?
Jason:	They are.

(Mary Magdalene School, Group 3)

The unacceptability of men's violence against women is expressed here in terms of any boy who hit a girl would experience a reverberation of violence against himself as he has gone against a code that condemns men hitting women. Boys can't hit girls because other men who are defending their own, and others' masculinity, will attack them. Thus, and it is this 'moral' opposition that should prevent men from being violent towards women. In our society the dominant social construction of masculinity rewards aggression (Connell 1987, 2005; Brownmiller 1975) and femininity is often constructed as passive, fearful and dependent (Connell 2005).

So there is conflict between those boys who think hitting girls goes against a moral code and simply highlights weakness, and others who think that being violent towards girls is justified because it is a means by which to construct their identity. There was very little discussion of an alternative conceptualisation of masculinity, where the use of violence was always judged as wrong regardless of gender or the perceived positions of power. Thus, there is a disjuncture between the two registers of male violence and female weakness and whether they can be combined to promote a positive male identity.

Whilst their rhetoric says one thing, the everyday discussions of their violence against girls in the playground, is judged by the boys as an acceptable form of behaviour. This is because the boys judge themselves to be more limited in their conduits of identity, whereby they must construct it in the few ways available to them including demonstrating their potential power over those nearest to them, and those perceived as the weakest (and therefore the least potential threat). An alternative masculinity presents itself as a means for them to react to men's violence against women and 'protect' the vulnerable.

Iain: See a boy can hit a girl but he'd normally get leathered.

(Mary Magdalene School, Group 4)

Yet even though this stigma of boys hitting girls was perpetuated, boys also had the power to normalise the violence, as and when it suited them to do so. Therefore, the power to label, but also the power to define that label was theirs.

Discussion of gendered moral codes around violence focused upon imagined examples as detailed earlier or deviated no further than a complicit first person 'I' before the narrative hurriedly returned to the safety of abstraction. However, the contradictory norms and rules that operate around violence became more personalised when several groups of boys talked about violence they had perpetrated.

John: Like girls won't talk to you for ages, just 'cause you've given them a bruise on their arm …
Tommy: Yeah and like … are you recording this bit.
Nancy: I'm recording it all.
Tommy: Like when [whispers name] threw that bottle at her and she wouldn't talk to him for over a week.
John: Yeah.

(Mary Magdalene School, Group 3)

Here the boys are discussing girls' reactions to their actions against them. There is a reluctance to use the word 'violence' here, as it is not a term mentioned by the boys themselves, but they clearly describe violent behaviour that has inflicted injury or has been aggressive in some way. What is significant is the blame the boys attribute to the girls because of their reactions. They normalise their own behaviour but describe the reactions of the girls as 'over reactions' to what they see as everyday interactions between boys and girls. Thus because it is the girls' responsibility, the fragility of their own masculinity (demonstrated in this display of power and violence) is still intact. Yet there is a certain amount of acknowledgement that the behaviour is wrong, because they do not want to incriminate one of the boys involved and so they whisper his name. Again, the fragility of masculinity is highlighted through the subtle susceptibility of violence as both a badge of honour, or as a means of highlighting weakness.

> [men's violence against women] is something that normal, ordinary men do routinely on a very substantial scale because they want to, because they think they have a right to and because nothing effective is done to stop them. (Itzin 2000: 378)

Naming 'Unreal' Violence

The concepts of time, space and gender illustrated in the previous chapter can also be drawn from young people's accounts to explain 'unreal' violence. This was behaviour that did not fit into their linear model of violence in terms of the actors, spaces and intervention. 'Unreal' violence signifies the proximity of the young people to the violence. That is, behaviour that was close to them in terms of temporality (it happened among young people, peers and siblings), spatially (in locations close to them) and both between and among the same gender. The proximity of the young people to violence directly impacted upon their naming of it. That is, the nearer they were, the more likely they were to minimise or normalise the violence. The theme of distance applies both literally, in terms of closeness and theoretically, in terms of recognition of self in factors precluding to violence (such as age or certain masculinities). The role of those in authority was also relevant in this framing of violence, with their 'official' recognition of it providing credence to the naming of it – or not.

Violence that was labelled 'unreal' represented the actions that the young people were most likely to normalise. They called this 'dummy fighting', 'pretend' and 'unreal'. All of these actions took place among their peers and siblings in their own spaces; playgrounds, homes and community streets. Crucially, these actions were not labelled or condemned by adults or those in authority as 'violence'. This lack of validation resulted in young people accepting and minimising their own roles of perpetration and victimisation.

There was a disparity between how the boys and girls defined and named violence. Initially both boys and girls located violence using age and gender – men's involvement defined an action as violent. All of the discussions identified violence (in its perpetration and victimisation) as being an activity defined by the participation of adult men. In this way, violence is located as being in the 'future', temporally distant from their own lives as young people. However, for girls, violence and violent identities had more to do with gender than age. They described violence as being perpetrated by both men and boys. Boys excluded themselves from this model, because they assured those in authority that their violence was not 'real' thereby distancing their actions from condemnation by authority.

Much of young people's lack of power is discussed in detail in the methodological literature, but is often ignored theoretically. What is of interest here, is how young people replicate existing models of adult power in their own definitions of violence but were able, through the friendship based discussion groups, to explore their own understandings and 'name' violence for themselves, in much the same way that feminism sought to accord women with this power (Dobash and Dobash 1992; Kelly 1988).

Girls' Experiences and the Power of 'Naming'

For girls, their understanding of violence was located within their past and present experiential understanding, which also served to inform their anticipations of the future. Childhood theorists have long argued that young people use their experiential knowledge to make sense of their lives (Adam 2002; Brannen 2005) and in this way, models of temporality are also pertinent in understanding how girls make sense of violence. That is their own past and present experiences of how boys act towards them, and the discursive reasoning they apply, work together to enable them to make sense of this 'unreal' violence, replicating Kelly's work (1988: 23) on women's recognition of abuse 'at the time or later'.

Yet the girls often found that their own experiences of violent (male) peers, was invalidated by the lack of adult recognition (and definition) of the actions. So because of this, girls were likely to also define 'real' violence as distant from them, in terms of the temporal and spatial phenomenon of adulthood, whilst finding their own 'named' experiences as ignored and minimised (Kelly 1988; Radford et al. 1996a) by those with the authority to do so.

It is significant that the model of 'real' violence that both boys and girls adhere to does not always reflect their own lived experiences. That is not to say that the young people themselves do not see or experience violent acts for themselves; rather it emphasises the discursive power of the adult world in firstly defining the violence, through for example disproportionate media reporting, and secondly the role of adults in validating certain actions as violence, and others as not, through their authoritative intervention.

Existing studies (Burman et al. 2006; Burton et al. 1998; Dublin Women's Aid 1999; Kelly et al. 1991; McCarry 2003) that have focused upon young people have tended to ask closed questions about experiences of violence or have anticipated their 'future' reactions. It is pertinent that young people's present experiences, and their own and others' invalidation of these, are fully brought to light here.

Normalising Violence

The second half of this chapter looks at how young people normalised certain forms of 'violence'. Here the processes of normalisation draw upon feminist theories and incorporate the means by which events, actions and behaviours are slotted into categories that are known, recognised and taken for granted, particularly in relation to expectations of gender. Within their own personal narratives, the young people revealed accounts of behaviour that could be construed (but not always named by them) as violence they had witnessed, experienced or perpetrated which was most likely to occur between themselves and their peers or siblings. It was these forms of behaviour that they tended to normalise because they did not fit into their linear models of 'real' violence (see previous chapter). The behaviour that was normalised was either happening among siblings (within the home), or among peers (with boys as perpetrators and girls as victims). This was in stark contrast to the same behaviour but that it crucially involved other people (distanced from themselves) and which was therefore defined as 'real'. In these situations the young people defined these forms of behaviour as violent or violence. The following chapter explores how young people used gender and age to justify the same (normalised) violent behaviour among adults, which in turn, endorses and stabilises men's power.

This section looks at examples of violent actions that were normalised by the young people. Although this is behaviour that I have identified as violence (not the young people), it is crucial to note that the self same behaviour, when occurring among different actors, in a different space was considered violent by the young people themselves. This process of normalising, illustrates how the spatial positioning of violence – in this case proximity – affects how the violence is named. Whether the actions are experienced differentially because of this, is highly contentious, as it could simply be argued that such actions were not validated by 'others' and therefore classed as 'unreal'. In this way, although the naming of the behaviour as wrong is critical, the spatial, temporal and relational aspects impact upon young people's means to do so. These actions were proximate to the young people and perpetrated by those known by them and close to them. They occurred in spaces that were relevant and normalised – homes, schools, playgrounds, involving those of a similar age, but not always the same gender. Because all these factors rendered the experience as common – it also colluded to construct the experience as invisible and therefore 'unreal'. Many of the young people were adverse to physical violence that resulted in pain or physical injury, and their discussions in the groups reflected this stance. However, time and time again, the same young people told of their violent interactions with their siblings. Such interactions were either regarded as acceptable forms of violent behaviour (dummy fighting), because it was confined to the sphere of sibling relationships, or it was not labelled as violent at all, amalgamated into normalised sibling behaviour. Although not overtly recognising this behaviour among themselves – the young people's descriptions of dummy fighting or pretend violence, often replicated many of the gendered dynamics that they go on to describe in adult gendered violence.

'Unreal' Violence between Peers

Several of the young people disclosed violence that they had used against their peers and that they felt justified in doing so:

Sandeep: You sometimes hit a girl if you get annoyed if they say something to you.
Nancy: So you hit a girl if they say something that annoys you?
Sandeep: Yeah.
Vikram: Sometimes you can hit hard and sometimes you can hit not very hard.
Nancy: Right okay, so you are saying it's okay to hit a girl if the girl …
Sandeep: No it's not okay to hit a girl, but it's okay if they annoy you.
Nancy: So if you have a reason.
Both: Yeah.

(Mountview School, Group 3)

In this example the boys have made a demarcation between their reasons for violence but do not seem to identify the contradictions in their understanding. They say it's wrong to hit a girl, but it's okay if she annoys you but they still insist on perpetuating the belief that hitting a girl is wrong. The fact that they put themselves at the centre of the decision making on defining whether the girl is in need of being hit, is a powerful position for them to be in, but also one which they believe is their entitlement. They also discuss different degrees of hitting; hard and not very hard, revealing behaviour and actions that they have put thought into and undertaken. By discussing and constructing this continuum of violence, they are placing themselves in control of decision-making. It is a controlled behaviour and not a reflexive reaction. The nonchalant way in which the boys discussed this and explained it, was disarming as most of the previous discussion had been condemning of violence. Here, girls were classed in the very way that makes them not part of the category that they were alluding to; second-class citizens. This is a very powerful position that is occupied by some of the boys here. That they do not question their position is indicative of their sense of entitlement:

Will: Boys aren't girl beaters unless you really want to hit one.

(Baxter Road School, Group 5)

Chris: I wouldn't hit a girl, but I would if she did something to me.
(Mary Magdalene School, Group 3)

The second quote from Chris highlights the difference between rhetoric and reality. He begins by saying what he thinks he should say and what is expected of him, but then deviates from this with his own belief that he would react with violence if a girl provoked him. Thus Chris portrays himself as very moral, (he would not hit a girl) framing his belief within the moral discourse of (honourable) men shouldn't hit (vulnerable) women. But this discourse reveals itself to be morally bankrupt, when Chris highlights he would have to go against this morality, if the girl *forced him* to hit her because of *her* actions. This is an example of the double jeopardy of womanhood; not only does the girl victimise *herself* through 'aggravating' Chris, but he retains his power because he has been forced to go against this unspoken rule to defend his masculinity, because of *her* behaviour.

As has already been highlighted through the discussions of violence, the media and computer games, young people are more than capable of separating what happens in a media form (such as the TV) with what happens in reality. They generated a division between the games they play and what they do in their real lives. They also perpetuated this divide in relation to real and pretend fighting, to describe the aggressive play (particularly boys) shared with their friends. Although not overtly recognising this behaviour among themselves, the young people's descriptions of 'dummy' fighting or pretend violence, often replicated many of the gendered dynamics and actions that they previously described:

Iain: Because boys always use carry on fighting and say I hit him it wouldn't really hurt him. Boys always carry on fight. If I go and hit a girl, they start crying and say that I am abusing her.
(Mary Magdalene School, Group 4)

There is an obvious disjuncture between what the boy labels as carry on fighting and what the girl(s) he hits feels. Iain labels 'carry on' fighting as an exclusively male activity and one in which girls do not belong, as expressed in their adverse reaction to his 'carry on'. Iain describes hitting girls in a very nonchalant way and is incredulous at their reaction with the fact that they cry, which for him, proves their weakness What is of note here is the appropriation of the term 'abuse', that the girls use to name his behaviour; a label which Iain does not recognise from his own behaviour and one that he does not agree with. Although he mentions his action (hitting) and their naming of this (abuse) within the same sentence, he denies the link between the two, thereby distancing himself from 'real' violent behaviour. Of significance here is who has the power to define? Whose definition is the more powerful and whose naming is heard and reacted upon? Through his denial of wrongdoing, or at least in denial of the labelling of his behaviour, Iain is blurring the boundaries between what constitutes violence and who has the power to name it as such:

Emma:	And the teacher says don't do fighting but they do it for real and just say its dummy fighting.
Cheryl:	If you've seen their faces it's really real.
Stacey:	If it's fun fighting that's okay, but if it's real it's not.
Nancy:	So if they are just pretending …
Emma:	Sometimes they do it with us like sometimes they come up and punch you [all talking at once].
Cheryl:	And I say just 'Go Away!' And he just ignores me and keeps on hitting me.
Nancy:	And is he doing that or is he pretending?
Cheryl:	He pretends that he is doing it but it is really sore.
Stacey:	You try and get them to stop but they keep doing it.
Lucy:	He wants to have fun with you, so he just goes up and does it.
Cheryl:	I was going to Sarah's house once and he kept threatening me and following me and I was like, no! Just go away!

(Mary Magdalene School, Group 1)

The above example gives three different constructions of violence that is named by teachers (authority), the boys (perpetrators and victims) and the girls (victims). Although the boys pretend the fighting is not real, there is a question whether this is so or if this is a tactic to placate the teachers. The girls experience the fighting as real and name it as such. They do not like it, are hurt by it and actively try to stop it, either individually or collectively. These violences are physical as well as threatening behaviours, including stalking. Here, as in much of the other discussions, the focus is on physical behaviours, with less emphasis (although present) on emotional abuses.[2] Yet although the girls name these actions as violence, it is portrayed as less serious or not violent at all, by boys and by some of the teachers. In this extract the voices of the girls are not heard, their naming of actions and their experiences of them appear not to carry the same weight as boys at their school, who are viewed as more likely to be involved in violent acts, but with other boys.

2 There was no mention during any of the sessions of economic abuse. The young people participating were all too young to have legal paid employment and all lived at home with parents or guardians. Discussions around the economic element of gender construction through paid work revealed the continued adherence to a gendered and class model, despite some changes in education and labour market activities by women.

Kelly used this focus upon the daily, the mundane and the normalised interactions between women and men to enable women to highlight and name their experiences. Her continuum was originally devised as a theoretical framework that succeeded in merging the gendered spheres by illuminating the notion that men's normative behaviour and women's oppression crossed these spherical boundaries. In doing so the continuum facilitated the labelling of apparently 'normal' behaviour as part of men's ability and choice to control, conceptualising commonalities experienced by many women and men in their day to day lives:

> Enab[ling] women to make sense of their own experiences by showing how 'typical' and 'abhorrant' male behaviour shade into one another. (Kelly 1988: 75)

In developing this framework, Kelly sought to highlight that these examples of male behaviour, however commonplace for men and women, were not normal and not acceptable and needed to be challenged and named as wrong.

Brothers and Sisters: 'It's Just What They Do'

In all of the young people's narratives they talked about violence that was 'not real', 'a kid on' or 'carry on' or 'dummy fighting'. They associated this form of 'violence' with their peers, other young people and particularly with their siblings:

> Raswana: If it's your brother, you just fight 'cause it's for a wee laugh, but you never actually fight properly like punch punch 'cause I could never hit him back like he hits me.
>
> (Baxter Road School, Group 4)

> Nancy: So are you saying, have you ever hit someone?
>
> Monica: Well no, not like that. I can't think of anyone. I mean there's my brother, but that's because he's my brother.
>
> (Clifton School, Group 2)

Here, and in countless other examples, the techniques of normalisation are employed to downplay the seriousness of the violence or the significance of the victims. This view was further endorsed by the actions and reactions of others, for example friends in the discussion groups. They were already aware of the examples that I was being told, and often joined in on the telling. The stories were sensationalised through descriptions of physical actions and injury, but their understanding of the 'sibling relationship' meant that notions of serious violence were downplayed:

Shona: I mean, I only fight with my sister, but that's because she is really annoying.
Stephanie: Her and her sisters nearly kill each other. I went to her house and they were literally punching each other.
Shona: I was. I was really angry.
Laura: And that other time. You got that black eye off your sister.
Shona: Aye, I did.

(Mary Magdalene School, Group 1)

Tommy: When me and my brother were fighting I split my knee.
Chris: My brother smashed my head off the table.
Jason: I pushed mine and he made my arm go black and blue. Then my mum came in and stopped us. She doesn't like us fighting.

(Mary Magdalene School, Group 3)

During this final discussion the crescendo in machismo was evident, with each boy trying to outdo the last with the extent of their fighting, and judging the levels of violence by how badly they were injured. What it highlights however, is the levels of violence that are occurring within homes between siblings, that they and their families often deemed normal, particularly between brothers. There were various informal gender rules among brothers and sisters (usually created and maintained by parents) based upon binary gender stereotypes of strength and weakness endorsed in the earlier examples and averting violence from within the family (e.g. you shouldn't hit your brother). The fact that Jason (above) says rather nonchalantly that his mum doesn't like fighting, puts her in an isolated position within a household that perhaps deems such activity as 'normal' and judges their mother to be oversensitive in her adverse reaction to it.[3]

Indeed it was mothers who were judged to be the person most likely to stop violence between siblings, or to prevent it from happening in the first place. Whilst mum could often be seen as a figure of authority to stop the violence from escalating, she was also positioned as a killjoy, thus reinforcing the 'unnatural' alignment of women and violence:

Nadia: When I hit my brother, he doesn't hit me back.
Nancy: Okay. And why do you think that is?
Nadia: 'Cause he knows that he is stronger than me and he knows I would tell my mum.

(Baxter Road School, Group 1)

3 She is deemed 'unnatural' in her reaction, but 'natural' in her caring role as a wife and mother.

What was particularly surprising was the extent of the violence between adults and their younger siblings. For example in the extract below, Cheryl talks about her brother with whom she has a 10-year age gap:

> Cheryl: I was fighting with my brother yesterday and my mum had to split us up, and she was like that, you're brother and sister and you should get on. But see if my brother was fighting with his pals, he's 21, he could get the jail.
>
> (Mary Magdalene School, Group 1)

Here, Cheryl relays how age can be a factor in different definitions of violence and how when you are older you are subject to legal sanctions. She is also aware of how the private act of fighting with her brother, to the extent that their mum has to intervene, is viewed differently to a public act of violence with his peers. Thus the interplay of age, gender and relationships affect how young people name violence.

The 'unreal' or dummy fighting at home between brothers and sisters was mentioned by all groups and always normalised as within the parameters of 'normal' sibling behaviour. This is an area that has received relatively little theoretical attention. Burman et al. (2003) mentioned that much of the violence girls experienced was from their peers and siblings, a finding that was affirmed by Batchelor (2007) in her thesis on girls and prison. In her book *Siblings: Sex and Violence* (2003), Mitchell examines the issue but very much from a psychoanalytical perspective detailing the latent violence within this form of family relationship.

The notion of distance can also help in understanding the young people's conceptualisation of temporality in terms of adulthood and adult relationships being 'far away' concepts. Girls used the distance of time in particular to help them to understand their own experiences of 'normalised' violence. Using the perspective of time, they were more able to comprehend what had happened to them.

'Proximity' and 'Unreal' Violences: Conceptualising Space

It is crucial to not only label specific behaviours of men as wrong, but also to make visible how such actions can be named, defined and understood, how they can be presumed to mean different things and take on different meanings, and being named in entirely different ways depending upon the spatial, temporal and relational category. For example, the 'same' behaviour that a man exhibits to an unknown woman in a street, can be categorised in a different way (by him, by her, by bystanders) from that behaviour exhibited by a teenage boy at a house party with a girl he knows (by him, by her, by bystanders). So even though Kelly would argue that it is the 'naming' by women that is critical, the spatial, temporal and relational aspects of the actions would impact upon her doing this, and so need therefore to be considered as part of her naming. Bowlby et al. (2010) examine spaces and places as shaped by processes operating inside and outside of its boundaries. These spaces and places are understood and experienced differently by different people and the same people at different times. This assertion illustrates how temporal, spatial and gendered understandings may be used to assess the validity and seriousness of the actions. As such, we need to be aware of how these different understandings could influence young people's own *naming or defining* of violence and how their own position in childhood may further impact upon this.

Valentine (2007) developed her theoretical position on intersectionality and identity through the significance of space in subject formation. The main theoretical relevance here is the construction of space and identity as being co-dependent, with location being constitutive of identity and not incidental to it. Whilst this can be seen to reinforce the binary spheres of public and private, it also illuminates their significance. For example, Valentine demonstrates the fluidity of spheres, in that they are defined by the social and spatial implications (for example childhood) and not through the embodied individuals within them. Valentine goes on to argue:

> The identity of particular spaces – the home, the school, the workplace ... are in turn produced and stabilised through the repetition of the intersectional identities of the dominant groups that occupy them such that particular groups claim the right to these spaces. When individual identities are 'done' differently in particular temporal moments they rub up against, and so expose, these dominant spatial orderings that define who is in place/out of place, who belongs and who does not. (Valentine 2007: 19)

Valentine helps to theorise how matter out of place (where something is uncommon) renders it visible within the spatial ordering in society. Thus, where violence is commonplace or thought to be so (outside and in public) it is spatially acceptable and recognised as common (which we can link back to Kelly's continuum's shortcomings), yet when violent behaviour is commonplace, but occurring within invisible spaces such as the home or within intimate, peer or sibling relationships, it is rendered invisible because it is normalised.

Space is used here to theorise both violence and childhood. It incorporates the notions of distancing (Young 1990) and proximity as well as physical locality, dimensions of the public/private as well as young people's own personal sense of proximity and distance. The concepts of distance and proximity are combined, to theorise young people's use of physical and abstract space and spatiality. For example, the notion of 'othering' is represented through *proximity* (me; near to me) and *distance* (them; away from me) to explain their *spatial* constructions of violence. 'Othering' is also accessed to conceptualise the *distance* and *proximity* of the *temporal* (young and old, present and future) as understood within the young people's own life course. As such, young people conceptualise violence in their own and others' lives, using space as a frame to understand violence, looking at where it happens, what that space represents, whether it constitutes violence or not (because of the connotations of that location), and their own relationship to it.

Ways of Talking, Ways of Laughing: Creating Proximity and Distance

There were many occasions when the young people used laughter or joking throughout the discussion groups. Some of the times I was included in their laughter, and other times they were laughing at remembered and retold stories from their friendships. Laughter was an integral part of the sessions and a means of enabling the young people to relax and distance the research from the classroom. It was also a critical aspect in how they talked about violence. However, there were a couple of occasions when laughter was used to exclude me as the researcher, and at times I felt, me as a woman. It was then that I felt uncomfortable, self-conscious and angry. I also felt that when this happened, the boys involved held the power, leaving me powerless. One such example is described below;

> [During the reading of the third vignette, the five boys all begin to laugh at the point where Jamie punches Jenny. The boy reading the example cannot finish reading it and I take the card from him and re-read the vignette, whilst all of the boys continue to laugh. I look and feel increasingly uncomfortable (but try not to show it)].
>
> Paul: I think in the last one [Dave and Lizzy vignette] he shouldn't have hit her, but in this one he should.
> Nancy: Can I just ask you why you were laughing at this one?
>
> [The group continue to laugh but try harder to hide it]
>
> Nancy: I'm not telling you off, I am just interested in why you are laughing.
> David: 'Cause it's funny.
> Nancy: Okay, and why is it funny?
> David: Dunno.
> Michael: I was just laughing 'cause he was laughing.
>
> (Mary Magdalene School, Group 4)

During this session I felt excluded and self-conscious; I noted that all the boys were united in their laughter. Yet listening to the session on the tape, I became more aware of the complexity of their interactions. While laughter was used to unite the boys, it was also used as a tool to distance them from the seriousness of the violence.

This was not the only example of laughter. There have been other extracts where the laughter of the young people has been conveyed within the context of their discussion. Groups of both boys and girls used laughter to laugh at their own jokes, at each other and examples of abusive behaviour. When laughter followed descriptions of abuse or comments about what should happen, I felt annoyed, uncomfortable and saddened. However, I only ever felt uncomfortable in the all-male groups. This was when I was most aware of my gender and their power within the group.

Other descriptions of violent behaviour framed by laughter served to negate the 'seriousness' of the actions. When Simon disclosed how his relationship with his best friend was based upon their shared violent behaviour, he ended by laughing,

> Simon: I always used to fight with my best friend [name]. We'd be fighting and swearing at each other but the next day, we'd be friends [laughs].
>
> (Mary Magdalene School, Group 3)

Whether Simon uses laughter to distance himself from the unacceptability of the aggression in the friendship (as he does with his use of the past tense), or in his awareness of the futility of his actions is not wholly clear, but his willingness to talk about it is apparent. This readiness and ability to talk (by Simon and others) served to counter the myths of 'innocence' and 'ignorance' as perpetuated by common sense discourses around children and violence.

This form of 'distancing' from the violence using laughter differs from the other techniques used by the young people. Those techniques use temporal, spatial or gendered distance to separate themselves from the violence. In this way laughter is used for several reasons, nervousness, bravado, camaraderie and to neutralise their own personal feelings within the narrative. Whilst such examples were infrequent, in contrast to their continued use of time, space and gender, they are still significant to illustrate some of the methods young people deployed to talk about violence, and in particular their own lived experiences of violence.

The young people disclosed many examples of violence that took place within their own homes. Often, this was done in relation to siblings, with the behaviour being neutralised as normalised sibling behaviour, as discussed above. In the same way that the methods used to relay this behaviour was done in a jokey, nonchalant manner, this tone was continued when young people attempted to disclose instances of abusive behaviour from their fathers to their mothers or their own parents' abusive behaviour towards them:

> Michael: My mam batters me but she calls it discipline. I call it child abuse or child assault. If I do something bad then she hits me (laughs).[4]
>
> [Rest of the group laugh]
>
> (Mary Magdalene School, Group 4)

In this example, Michael discloses the violence he experiences from his mum. He began very seriously, but then turned his disclosure into a 'joke', or something deserving of laughter. Both he and the group were beginning to feel uncomfortable and this feeling was dispersed through the laughter. However, others in the group recognised the seriousness of Michael's account in the group by nodding in agreement, before the cue to laugh was instigated. The means of using laughter as a tool for sharing and distancing oneself from the reality of violence was a means of normalising the actions for others. Although the violence they described was a 'normal' part of their life, they recognised that it was not normal in the lives of others, and as such felt the need not to draw attention to it. Thus by downplaying it or attempting to make a joke, they diffused the situation with laughter. However, the following examples highlight a different tone and serves to illustrate how young people's labelling of such actions differed. Here young people share tales of their friends:

> Adam: My brother's best friend has one of those things, what are they called [injunctions] because he gets beaten up by his dad.
>
> (Clifton School, Group 3)

> Ruth: Our friend said her dad was hitting her and I didn't know what to do. And then it stopped for ages and she didn't want to ring Childline 'cause she thought she might get taken away.
>
> (Mountview School, Group 4)

Although the tone is stark in comparison to Michael's disclosure, the theme of distance is still very apparent. The groups discussed sincerely and sombrely,

4 In this quote, Michael discloses abuse he is experiencing at home, even though he attempts to make light of this by introducing laughter. At the end of this discussion group, I asked Michael to remain behind on the pretence of helping me tidy up. I spoke to him about what he had said and asked if there was anything he would like to talk to me about. He said no. After this, I spoke to the head teacher about what Michael had disclosed and she assured me that the school were already aware of this issue.

aware of the gravitas of the situation faced by their friends. But because what was happening was happening elsewhere, to someone else, in someone else's home, the proximity of the violence was far away and therefore outside of their own spheres. This is not to say that the self same people discussing these situations were not experiencing them too, but the tales they chose to share highlighted the distance and the boundaries drawn by violence. The situations discussed were labelled as 'serious' and 'heavy', making the contrast between the discussions even more stark.

These quotes illustrate the departure from abstract cases into 'lived realities'. The examples above highlight the 'unreal' transcending into the 'real' and are underlined by young people's sense of bewilderment with how best to cope. This is all the more pertinent, especially because it does not 'fit' with common sense and culturally endorsed definitions of violence, that their linear model of violence helps them to understand. This shift to the personal cannot be normalised, naturalised or justified – the processes by which young people understand violence. As such, they are left with few means by which to make sense of it.

The manner in which many of the young people spoke about violence and violent behaviour was open and honest. Their willingness to divulge personal stories and experiences, as well as reflect upon and explore wider issues countered myths of their 'innocence' and 'ignorance'. Yet within their discussions of what they labelled as violence, the focus was not on themselves, and rarely the individuals concerned, but upon the space in which the acts occurred and the young people's proximity to it. The theme of distance and proximity was used as a measure by which violence could be labelled as such. Thus the greater the distance, the further away they were; outside spaces, other people's homes, violence as happening to others, the more likely the young people were to name the actions as violence. Very often their own experiences, particularly in relation to siblings, or girls' examples of boys' behaviour towards them, were defined as less significant by either themselves, other actors or both.

As in any research study, there are the voices of a minority that still need to be represented. In this study, the number of young people who could give clearly defined examples of domestic violence/abuse, relating it to the gendered dynamics of a relationship and the man's use of power and control is significant. The young people who labelled domestic violence in this way could relate it back to the examples within the vignettes; they focused upon the abuser and his abuse of power and would argue to exonerate the woman from blame. I would surmise that the young people who could name domestic violence most likely were near to it, in the respect that they had the experience of it happening in their families; to them and to their mums:

Christopher: Controlling a woman and hitting her and won't let her out and he makes her do stuff and sorta just abuses her.

[Clifton School, Group 1]

Gayle: I mean that's what men do to mums, I mean like women. Just like shouting and controlling what she does. It's not fair on them or the children.[5]

[Baxter Road School, Group 1]

This presumption is not indicative of the number of young people who were actually living in abusive households. Indeed it is argued that there were many more than the few who could name the violence as such.

Summary

This chapter provided an analysis of the differing forms of identities accessed and subscribed to by the young people, in their understanding and explanations of men's violence against women. As the previous chapter highlighted, the young people are able to define violence that is distant from them – spatially and in terms of temporal distance (e.g. among adults). Yet when the same actions occur within their own experiential spaces and among those close to them (such as peers and/or siblings), they are more likely to normalise them as 'unreal' and not violent. It is argued that these examples of normalised violence are such because they do not fit the standardised constellation structure of age (adult); gender (man); space (public); action (physical), and, crucially, are generally without official reaction or consequence. This not only results in girls in particular being unable to access a framework by which to make sense of their own experiences, but it also serves to invalidate and minimise many of the young people's own experiences of violence and violent behaviour.

5 Although Gayle did not directly disclose, her 'slip up' revealed that her mum and their family may have been experiencing domestic violence. As with Michael, I asked Gayle to help me tidy up and spoke to her. I also reiterated the advice and information on the sheet 'Who can I talk to?' I spoke to the head teacher who was again aware of Gayle's 'family problems'.

Chapter 7
Heterosexuality, Gender and Adulthood: Justifications of Violence

Introduction

This chapter draws, in the main, from analysis of the vignettes and as such the examples of domestic abuse. It is argued that heterosexuality is the main framework through which young people understand violence against women; that is they examine the motivations of the individual through the context of heterosexuality. Justification is a form of explanation that entails using and endorsing inequality to explain violence. Men are placed in a position of power and women in a subordinate role with violence used by men to consolidate their position. The concept of heterosexuality both naturalises and normalises these inequities, to the extent that for many of the young people the violence and abuse appears a valid action and reaction to the context.

The justifications they offer fit into the following discursive themes; male entitlement, obedience, regulation and control; ownership and possession and 'blaming' women directly for the violence. The chapter concludes with an analysis of the dissenting voices; those who did not think men's violence against women was ever justified and purported women's choices and autonomy as being all important.

To begin it is essential to analyse how young people understand and experience heterosexuality as this impacts upon how they generate their techniques of justification. The differences between their 'present' and 'future' identities (identified in Chapter 4) are pertinent. The significance of their temporal identities 'me now' and 'future me' highlights the need to theorise young people in terms of both their position in childhood and their anticipation of adulthood within the transitory framework introduced in Chapters 1 and 2 and further considered in Chapter 4.

Young People and Heterosexuality

Chapter 4 set out how young people construct their own and others' gender identities. The findings here consolidated much other research that demonstrates how young people use the framework of heterosexuality to contextualise their own gender roles (for example, Renold 2005). Binary positions (which are encapsulated by heterosexuality) are endorsed and naturalised to the extent that heterosexuality is not viewed as a position but as the normalised entity from which other forms of sexuality are deviations. The cultural dominance of heterosexuality is also legitimised through laws and legislation that prioritise marriage and nuclear family units. Heterosexuality is also replicated within a framework of stereotyped gender role acquisition that perpetuates the roles of male breadwinner and female care giver which in turn reinforce the public/private dichotomy.

It is imperative here to highlight the difference between researchers using heterosexuality to define the differences between young people and the young people defining themselves in relation to that. One of the main issues that is constantly reiterated is that some boys are judged as actively constructing their sexualities (however confined they are by the restraints of masculine identity) whereas girls are always judged as being constructed in relation to it. Holland et al. (2004) made reference to this incongruity faced by men resisting normative definitions of masculinity and heterosexuality:

> Men are then in contradictory situations in which they suffer from being socially pressured into a narrow and constraining conception of masculine sexuality, but they also benefit from social arrangements which systematically privilege the male over the female. (155)

By moving away from the restricted binary confines (as a means of description and definition) it is argued that young people also use a matrix of time and space to position themselves (not always in opposition to each other) but upon a complex interaction of spatial and temporal positions that can transcend binary dichotomies.

Although in much work exploring young people and gender, heterosexuality is the normative framework for young people to construct their own identities and performances, the temporality of the framework is often overlooked. That is, although there is an expectation that young people will position themselves within its regulated boundaries, the key is that it is done so age 'appropriately'.

The young people actively constructed and anticipated (hetero)sexualised relationships, informed and defined by a man and a woman. Heterosexuality was not considered an 'ideal', rather it was unquestioned as 'normal' and 'natural' (see Chapter 4 for the 'naturalising' of gender). Illustrated in the quotes below is the acceptance and perpetration of heterosexuality and its internalisation by society:

Cheryl: Boys like girls.
Lucy: And girls like boys.
Cheryl: And if you didn't, you'd be gay.
[All laugh]

(Mary Magdalene School, Group 1)

Tommy: I wouldnae bother being a lassie.
Jason: You'd have to have a boyfriend though.

(Mary Magdalene School, Group 2)

The normality afforded to heterosexuality is demonstrated within the second quote, where the implication is that if you did change sex, your partner preference undoubtedly would too; alongside the implication that to be a woman you would have to have a man to make you complete. The matter of fact mantra of the first quote, does not question this heteronormativity, rather the group laughs at the anticipation of any deviation from it.

When homosexuality or 'being gay' was mentioned in the discussion groups it was done so in ways that connoted derision or humour. On these few occasions that alternative lifestyles were mentioned, the young people appeared to have limited scripts or experiential knowledge to access. However, there was one group where alternative sexuality was mentioned and a positive discussion ensued:

Fiona: There's nothing wrong with being gay
Stewart: True, but a lot of people think that there is
Dougie: Yeah, a lot of people get teased
Stewart: There was that programme, *Playing it Straight*. It's on on a Friday night. If the gay guy got picked by the women then he'd get £100,000. If he was straight he'd have to split it fifty-fifty. But the gay guy won, she thought he was straight. But he gave her the money because he just came on the show to prove the point that gay men weren't sissies in everything as people expected them to be.
Dougie: And that's good, because a lot of people, I don't know why but they say that gay people are different from other people.
Stewart: And they say they can't help it but that's like racism, judging people because of that.

(Clifton School, Group 5)

This discussion was generated when talking about young people's own relationships with each other.[1] The young people reject the view that gay men are 'different' or lacking, by equating homophobia with racism. This succinct discussion about 'deviations' from the norm is incredibly articulate and thoughtful. Although one of the girls initiated the discussion, it was the two boys who agreed and went on to articulate their reasons why. That one of the boys, Stewart, was popular and a hegemonic male is of course relevant, for his ability to take such a stance, yet be wholly distanced from it. However, the other boy, Dougie, did not fit this mould and argued as strongly and as confidently as his friend.

Present and Future Identities

With very few notable exceptions, heterosexual frameworks defined almost all of the young people's expectations of relationships, both in the present and in the future (see Chapter 4). Hatcher (1995: 187) views 'romantic' relationships as a 'crucial context for the formation of gender identities' and the means by which adult ideologies, the media and youth culture permeate into the cultures of children (Hatcher 1995). However this is more a symbolic relationship than a material or physical one, for as Renold (2005) notes the young people were 'going out', yet rarely went anywhere. Again this links back to the notion of young people's culture as a subset of adulthood. But the proximity of the young people to each other and their own peers' recognition of the relationship creates a space in which gendered and sexualised identities are constructed. However, often researchers such as Hatcher focus upon the transmission of culture to the detriment of young people's own agentic statuses.

Nespor (2000) argues for the need to examine gender as 'trajectories unfolding in time and space' (2000: 28). This connects to my argument that young people subscribe to spatial and temporal dimensions to explore their own (and others' gendered identities. However Nespor, whilst constructing time and space as fluid, fails to incorporate the gendered structures of power. For example he discusses moments when boys and girls are 'on an equal footing' or times when 'women hold the power', suggesting examples of young people 'stepping outside' of gendered interactions.

---

1 The group of two boys and two girls rooted their knowledge within a television programme, which had presented a positive representation of a gay man who had not invested in one-dimensional stereotypes. Although the aim of the programme had been to choose the 'straight man', and therefore perhaps the most hegemonic form, the young people here did not focus upon the man as 'passing as straight' but upon his motivations for taking part, to show he wasn't a stereotype.

In this research, it was this dichotomy of expectation (between the present and the future, young and old, and individual and relationship) that contributed, in part, to girls' early recognition of systematic gender inequalities. They saw themselves as more equal now than in the future. Age intersected their constructions of gender in that the more adult the woman – the more fixed and restrictive her gendered identity became. Their own understandings and expectations of gender were shaped upon their own present lived experiences and their anticipation of their future lives. They saw their own lives now as being a period of freedom, expressed in the fluidity of their gender roles, yet they anticipated adulthood as a time that was constrained and restricted by rigid heterosexual roles – especially girls, as the following quotes illustrate:

> Sarah: I want to be a dancer or a doctor … When I grow up I'll going to have two babies and work part time in the shop down the road.
> (Mary Magdalene School, Group 1)

Over half of the girls anticipated that they would relinquish their own autonomy in adulthood, because their association with 'grown-ups' saw them with fixed gender roles, in a prescribed heterosexual framework. This understanding of the female role also demonstrates the duality between 'them' and 'us'; the girls want to be equal but they do not always see other girls as being so.

For boys, hegemonic masculinity was mobilised around traits that they identified as being encapsulated by grown-up men; marriage, home and children rather than themselves as 11- and 12-year-old boys. Rather than seeing it as an aspiration, they were more likely to view this 'ideal' masculin*ity* as static, fixed and to some extent inevitable, as it was bound up in their futures as men. At this point in their lives (the present), the young people were most likely to view their gendered identities as constantly evolving and more fluid, with a range of identities available to them, rather than being constrained by a singular identity.

O'Donnell and Sharpe (2000) argue that boys have not yet solidified their masculine identity; yet by suggesting this they are defining masculine identity as a fixed and stable concept *at some point*. It is important, therefore, to recognise that the development and application of masculinity for both boys and men is an active and ongoing construction in relation to their embodied selves (young and old), the social definition of their environment (school, work, home) and the shifting social, cultural and historical contexts (Connell 2002). Here I argue that gender identities are fluid and dynamic (regardless of age) and that it is the *perspectives* of the young people that seek to stabilise them.

Yet these identities became more rigid, and less plural, when framed by age, relationships and familial responsibilities. The heterosexual partnership and the gender roles within, become more structured, fixed and rigid and acceptable for the young people (male and female) when aligned with marriage, the private sphere of the home and children. It was through this adherence to heterosexuality, as an ideal to aspire to and a structure to maintain, that framed how young people interpreted men's violence against women within the sphere of relationships.

The Institution of Marriage: Institutionalising Gender

Even when framed by rigidity and inevitability, marriage was still seen as the culmination of the heterosexual ideal. Marriage was a significant milestone in a person's life and one which the majority of girls anticipated for themselves, although marriage was not mentioned by any the boys as being part of their own envisioned 'futures'. In this sense the young people were very conservative in their outlooks for the future, investing within idealised discourses of marriage and children (in that order). Often the maintenance of these frameworks was more important than individual autonomy:

> Stephanie: You want your kids to grow up with a daddy don't you? I would just find another man.
>
> (Mary Magdalene School, Group 2)

For many, there was an understanding that marriage was sacrosanct over and above other forms of relationships. This became obvious when young people relied upon the status of a relationship to determine a woman's actions:

> Nicole: If they lived together and they are not married yet, then she should just leave.
>
> (Mountview School, Group 1)

> Siobhan: [following third vignette] I mean if they had been married or whatever then she should have tried harder, to be with her husband instead of trying to go away. She should have told him.
>
> (Clifton School, Group 4)

In this quote, not only does Siobhan reinforce the importance of marriage and in making a relationship work, she also implicates the woman (in this case Jenny) as being responsible for her own victimisation, thereby justifying Jamie's actions. That is, if Jenny had not had an affair, then Jamie would not have been angry and upset and therefore he would not have hit her. So ultimately, the violence is in response to Jenny's behaviour and is therefore her fault. Whilst this view of marriage was most widely shared in the Catholic school (Mary Magdalene), many of the young people (girls and boys) in the non-denomination schools also held the institution of marriage in the greatest esteem, but in doing so, limited the actions and the choices available to the women in such relationships.

Pupils at Mary Magdalene's were unique in arguing that the worst thing about being violent to your partner was in breaking the vows and going against religious promises:

Stacey:	See if you are married and it's a guy hitting a woman, then that's just abuse. You can get jailed for that.
Lucy:	'Cause he's made a commitment to marry her. He said his vows.

(Mary Magdalene School, Group 1)

For these young people, the societal and community reaction to violence was of greater consequence than the effects upon the partner. It is significant that the young people describe the *responses* as being from the community (in this case the church), but the *reasons* for the violence are not viewed as societal, rather as individual. The implication of marriage being so revered a status was that young people from all schools were less likely to suggest a woman leave following abuse than they were if the couple were dating or cohabiting:

Daisy:	Say you were married to someone and then they started hitting you after a while of having a nice relationship you might want to try and let them do it, or get through it if you are going through a rough patch, you might be thinking that and then after a while, I don't know but it can affect your family.
Nancy:	What about, you said married then, what about people who aren't married?
Daisy:	See but if you had a boyfriend or a girlfriend and you had been going out with them for a short period of time and you would just dump him but when you are married its different.
Nicole:	Yeah, you don't know them as well.
Fatima:	Yeah, your relationship has not gone there.
Daisy:	Like when you've been married a few years, if he hits you and then says sorry, you would forgive him.

(Mountview School, Group 1)

Daisy's understanding of violence in a relationship is almost framed as something that happens, or a 'rough patch' that needs to be worked through. This emphasises the construction of violence as justified within a heterosexual relationship, albeit with varying degrees. The effect upon the genderless adult is almost accepted (and the man's power validated), whereas when the children are seen to be affected then action must be taken. All three of the girls judged a relationship by the length of time it had lasted and saw this as an indicator of how much the couple loved each other and also how willing they were to work on these 'issues'. There is also the anticipation that this is a 'process' all relationships may go through, in terms of Fatima's assumption that the 'unmarried' couple's relationship has just not reached that point yet. This generates the perception that marriages are framed by strict gender roles and expectations, where normative gender roles are anticipated and thereby legitimated. Thus a barrier to leaving a violent relationship was evident in terms of love and a readiness to forgive, rather than envisaged practicalities or sources of support (for example, where would you to and who would help)?

Understanding Heterosexuality: Ownership and Possession

Many of the young people's understandings of heterosexual relationships were based upon issues of owning and belonging, further legitimating a man's entitlement. Marriage was a validation of this belief and created a metaphor for possession:

Stacey: [discussing vignette 1] 'Cause he'd be like, *she's mine* and she's wearing *my ring* and like she's *my wife* and this is *wh*at I married 'cause she's beautiful.

Cheryl: And if people looked at her and came over she'd say look I'm wearing *his ring* and people would be able to see that she's wearing a ring.

(Mary Magdalene School, Group 2, speaker's emphasis)

Boys often saw Claire as an object of sexual desire and felt that having Claire as his possession elevated Lee's masculine identity:

Alfie: He should love it and when they look at her, he should laugh at them and say *you've not got her, I have.*

Ruben: Aye, if the boys looked at her, I'd just go, aye *she's mine.*

(Hardcastle School, Group 3, speaker's emphasis)

In either case, Lee's opinion and feelings were viewed as more valid than Claire's personal choice of clothing. Lee's powerful position was further validated in his 'owning' of Claire:

Lucy: But he's only been seeing her for four months. He's not … like she's not technically his.

Nancy: When will she be technically his?

Stacey: When they are married.

Sarah: When they have children.

Cheryl: When they get engaged.

Stacey: I think when …, it becomes permanent when they move in.
Cheryl: It's when he belongs to her and she belongs to him.
Emma: Just because they are a couple and they'd be closer but it doesn't mean that they belong to each other like you say they are. You belong to me, it's not exactly a case of that.
Stacey: Yes 'cause if a guy came up to you and started flirting and you were in a bar, you'd just put your left hand up and go 'Mmmm?' and show them your ring and make sure he knows you're not available.

(Mary Magdalene School, Group 1)

As highlighted in the quote above, young people often framed relationships in terms of owning or belonging and had specific time scales as to when this came into being. But it is important to note that these beliefs were resisted (see Emma). Commitment was often confused with possession and framed by insecurity. For many of the young people, jealousy was identified as a 'natural' and powerful emotion that could solidify a relationship demonstrating a relationship already based upon inequality and power:

Nancy: So if you go out with someone and they get jealous, how does that make you feel?
Kim: It would be good.
Nancy: Why?
Esme: 'Cause you know he likes you.

(Hardcastle School, Group 4)

Jealousy was more often than not described as a positive emotion, as it proved how much Lee liked Claire and that he was reacting in the way he was, because he loved her so much. The discussions of jealously did not identify it as solely an emotion experienced by Lee, but as an emotion contrived by Claire. Thus, Claire was seen as attempting to construct a powerful position for herself, but one which was determined by a limited heterosexual feminine identity, here in terms of manipulation (to see how much Lee loved her). In this sense, Lee's feelings of jealousy were blamed on Claire's behaviour:

Gayle: You can understand why he doesn't want all these men looking at his girlfriend. Like say you had a boyfriend and there were all these girls that kept looking at him. Obviously you'd get jealous, but you'd also get really annoyed especially if she hadn't done anything to stop it if he knows it annoys you'.

(Baxter Road School, Group 1)

In blaming Claire's behaviour, the young people are further legitimising Lee's behaviour; to regulate and control her clothing, and ultimately her. They are basing this upon a model of heterosexuality that endorses male privilege and entitlement.

Understanding Heterosexuality: Obedience, Regulation and Control

Connell (1987) argues that different organisations and institutions have gender regimes that interact or conflict with each other, generating a 'gender order'. The gender order changes over time, highlighting gender as transient and socially constructed. Therefore the gender order is maintained through both behaviour and practice. Within this order, differing forms of masculinity and femininity are ranked, with the most powerful and dominant at the top.

Young people often framed their understanding of men's violence against women as the result of women's lack of obedience, or not doing what they were told. The theme of obedience aligned women with domestic roles and duties, particularly in discussions of the second vignette. This gender order unequivocally positions men in a position of power, with the focus upon the woman's failing in her expected gender role, rather than the man being wrong. Dave's reaction was justified as being a *result* of Lizzy failing to fulfil the expectations of her role as a woman:

> Shazia: But like what he should have done, what he should do next time is not slap her but say, next time dinner should be ready. I'm giving you your last warning. Because slapping her just makes things worser [*sic*].
>
> (Baxter Road School, Group 2)

Although Shazia maintains Dave should not have slapped Lizzy, she advocates that he uses the threat of violence to force her to obey him. Implicit in the notion of obedience is that of punishment and it is the man who has the power to request obedience and therefore generate the punishment. Some of the groups expressed a belief that Lizzy should apologise for her 'behaviour', as well as Dave for his. The need for both to apologise shows an agreement that firstly Lizzy was wrong to go out without permission and failed in getting tea ready on time and also secondly, it was because she failed and therefore her behaviour was in need of correction that Dave then hit her. So he was not being violent, simply 'correcting' her. Therefore his behaviour, but not hers was legitimated:

Paul: Both of them should say that they are sorry. 'Cause she didn't ask to go out. She went out without his permission and he slapped her.

Iain: Aye she should have told him.

Michael: She should at least contact him when she goes somewhere. He might be worried when she doesn't get back in time because his dinner wasn't ready.

(Mary Magdalene School, Group 4)

This links back to discussions of generational hierarchies between parents and children (with parents having authority in the same way that men were perceived to do), that many of the young people based their expectations of heterosexual relationships upon. Although there were many overt examples of the young people (girls and boys) suggesting that women and girls had to listen to men and do as they were told, there were also less obvious examples, yet ones that nonetheless placed the authority with the man and the need to obey with the woman:

Fatima: But *as long as Claire keeps saying* to Lee that she doesn't care. She's going out with him, it doesn't matter what they think, then maybe he would feel a bit more reassured about it and *he would let her* wear the top.

(Mountview School, Group 1, speaker's emphasis)

In the example above, Fatima places the responsibility upon Claire to firstly accept Lee's controlling behaviour and then to reassure him that she is his. By doing this Claire may be rewarded by being able to wear her top, when Lee said so. Because this example is much less explicit, it is all the more worrying, because the power is not viewed as such, and the control Lee wants is not contested. Therefore his behaviour is legitimated because it is not questioned.

Protection

In many cases the young people sought to justify the control men wanted to have over their partners. Such control was legitimated because it was framed by pre-existing notions of naturalised masculinity, such as protection:

Rosie: But he's thinking he's protecting her.

(Clifton School, Group 2)

This reinforces notions of feminine vulnerability and the need for masculinised protection. This also justifies the belief that abusers are acting in the best interests of their partners, by looking after them and protecting them from things they are deemed as not capable of being able to cope with. There were further inversions of hegemonic masculinity where the young people mistook the men being worried about their partners as being overly protective rather than as a desire to control them (for example Lee not wanting other boys to look at Claire). It could be surmised that this discourse, in highlighting the weakness or the insecurity of the man, places the woman in a position of power. However, this supposition protects Dave and Lee from being viewed as manipulative:

> Christopher: Could [Dave] not say don't do that again 'cause it scared me?
> Nancy: Why would it have scared him?
> Christopher: Well because she has just kind of left him and he doesn't know where she is. She could have run away. Anything could have happened to her.
>
> (Clifton School, Group 1)

Modification of Behaviour

Instead of wholly submissive appeasement, many girls suggested that the women concerned should modify their behaviour, which further legitimated the man's actions. It should be noted that during the fieldwork these suggestions of placation came entirely from girls. Such responses were about placating Lee by suggesting Claire should modify her behaviour to please him, but stopped short of suggesting Claire didn't wear the top:

> Monica: Maybe she could wear something over it. She likes that top.
> Aimee: You could just like put a jumper over it but you could still wear it like when you are out with your girlfriends.
>
> (Clifton School, Group 2)

In the quote above both Monica and Aimee are demonstrating what they believe to be compromise, but is in fact conformity. By suggesting that Claire modifies her outfit and behaviour, they are asserting that Lee is entitled to decide and define what Claire should wear, thereby justifying his request for her to do so. The actual modification of behaviour in response to Lee's demand indicates a greater acceptance of his coercive action. Whilst modifying behaviour (but still choosing to wear the top) can be seen as an act of resistance, particularly when performed by women already in abusive relationships, these girls thought they were empowered by still suggesting that Claire wear the top; but in fact the anticipated behaviour is enacted so as not to anger Lee. Advising that Claire should modify her behaviour demonstrates two things. Firstly, that the relationship is more important than personal choice or individual identity, thereby defining Claire in relation to Lee. And secondly, that Lee has and/or should have the power and authority in this relationship. This positions heterosexuality as a framework of binaries, where men hold the power and women are defined in relation to that.

The group of all girls below struggled with this vignette because most of them recognised that Lee was telling Claire what to wear; but their own sense of style was part of their identity, so they could recognise the importance of choosing their own clothes. However, the real antagonism came when discussing individual choice and maintaining the relationship with your boyfriend:

Karina: I mean like she should be able to wear what she wants.
Monica: Yeah but like she might not want to upset Lee.
Karina: Yeah I know. That's why I really don't know because she should be able … like *I wouldn't like to be told what to wear* but then, I don't know.
Monica: You don't want to upset the person.
Karina: Yeah.

(Clifton School, Group 2, my emphasis)

Karina is struggling with her own belief and recognition of Claire's 'rights' and her own sense of autonomy. There is a discrepancy, evident in many of the discussions, between young people's own 'present' sense of self and the judgements made on 'others' framed by adult heterosexuality.

During the discussion, Monica agrees in part with Karina, but positions Lee's sensibilities above those of Claire's. Therefore, it is often the significance girls placed on Claire's relationship with Lee that led them to suggest she should appease Lee and change her behaviour for the good of the relationship. This illustrates the importance that the girls placed on a relationship in validating a woman's sense of self. Other groups of girls struggled with the same issues but came up with different conclusions:

Farah: It's their own body and they can wear whatever they want. They don't have to wear what that person says. It's about what they like and what they want to wear.
Shazia: But if they do that, they're in danger of missing out on something that they want.
Farah: But then if saying do this, or be like this, he doesn't want to be with her, he just wants to tell her what to do.
Shazia: Yeah, and trying to change her.

(Baxter Road School, Group 2)

Shazia directly ranks the relationship above Claire's autonomy, stressing that if she does not heed Lee's warning then she will lose him. It is significant that it was the girls (and very few boys) who placed restrictions on Claire, regarding her behaviour and clothing. But this does not concur that the girls have the power to define other girls. Rather the girls are not powerful in defining themselves but they appropriate this power, through a possessive masculine gaze to regulate themselves:

Rosie: I would wear the top. But I think that if it was really obvious that people were looking at me then I would wear a wee jumper.

(Clifton School, Group 2)

Although Rosie initially expresses defiance, this is overshadowed by her belief that Lee is 'right' in what he was saying. This demonstrates his control in planting that seed of doubt – boys are looking and you are complicit in that. Not only are the girls regulating themselves, but there is also an expectation that men will also regulate them. Therefore Lee's reaction is anticipated and in some cases necessary:

Nancy: So why do you think Lee said that to her?

Mairi: Because she might not like that top which … that means she wants him to boss her and persuade her not to wear it.

(Baxter Road School, Group 3)

This quote encapsulates an extreme example of this regulation. In the quote, Mairi maintains that Claire cannot make a decision for herself, instead relying upon Lee to take control and define her identity for her. Also, Mairi needs Claire and Lee to take on their 'oppositional' roles, in order that she can make sense of the interaction between a man and a woman.[2] Young people focused upon how other men would judge Lee; his masculinity and his 'ownership' of her would be undermined if Claire did not listen and continued to be on sexual display for other men:

Craig: He's the one who is going to be stood beside her when she's out. And he'll look stupid if he's the one that is going out with her and other boys are looking at her.

(Mary Magdalene School, Group 5)

2 It is important to note that Mairi was the only girl in this discussion group of two boys and a girl. However, rather than aligning herself with their opinions or feeling pressured by them to conform to certain explanations, Mairi put herself out on a limb as the two boys reiterated the choice of clothing was Claire's to make and Lee had no entitlement in defining this choice for her.

Thus a woman's reputation is precariously balanced between sexual morality and male definition. The very limited discussion of Claire's feelings about the other men implies a normalisation of female objectification and an endurance of male regulation and control, thereby further endorsing the naturalised binaries of a heterosexual relationship.

Male Entitlement

As well as discourses of ownership and possession, heterosexual relationships were also constructed with an expectation of a man's sense of entitlement, which was further used to justify men's abusive and violent behaviour. Power was often conceptualised in terms of the rights that were available and that men were entitled to possess. Although at times during the discussion session, various participants had raised the issue of women having rights, this was not constructed in terms of power or their entitlement to such rights. Thus the unequivocal association of men with embodied and ideological power, framed constructions of violence in terms of their levels of entitlement:

> Yolande: He has a *right* to be angry but he doesn't have that much *right* to get angry and hit her.
>
> (Clifton School, Group 4, my emphasis)

Here Yolande identifies men's own sense of entitlement, defining Jamie's violent reactions in terms of the 'rights' he has within his relationship with Jenny. By labelling his sense of entitlement in this way, Yolande is not questioning his right to possess this power, rather she is defining the level of power that Jamie can legitimately have. In the first vignette, the power rested with Lee to decide upon the course of action should Claire not 'do as she was told': Lee could end the relationship:

> Samia: [If you] upset Lee ... it might drive him away from you.
>
> (Baxter Road School, Group 4)

> Daniel: If she wants to be with him then she shouldn't [wear it].
>
> (Mary Magdalene School, Group 5)

> Shaheeda: Because they are a couple, she should do what Lee says if she doesn't want him to leave her.
>
> (Baxter Road School, Group 1)

The extracts above construct a heterosexual relationship based upon the man having the power, and the woman needing to be subordinate to that power (bound by the discourse of knowing one's place), if she wants to remain within the relationship. The emphasis was firmly on Claire losing Lee through her behaviour, rather than Lee losing Claire, because of his demands. This raises questions about a women's own power to end a relationship (or indeed her wish to do so). That more emphasis is placed upon remaining within the relationship than her own position and choices as a woman, shows an acceptance of an unequal heterosexual matrix, where the man is dominant and is able to exert that power without question or recourse to further action. Such discussions were in stark contrast to many of the girls' earlier discussions about themselves and their own empowerment. Girls would talk about the importance of friendship maintenance in their lives:

> Denise: I mean now I have lots of friends, girls and boys. But when I'm older, like when I am married, I'll probably just have one friend and it'll be a woman.
>
> (Hardcastle School, Group 2)

This quote illustrates the discrepancy between the present lived lives of the girls and their anticipations of the future. Their understanding of gender roles and relationships are constructed as much more fluid now, but are anticipated as being limited by both men and heterosexual relationships in the future. Much of this sense of entitlement is constructed around adult men, with girls more likely to resist boys' overt sense of entitlement, but the young women here seem less likely to challenge it when it forms part of an adult relationship.

The vast majority of girls positioned themselves as equal to boys and as able to do whatever they wanted to without restriction, positioning themselves within a discourse of equality, with regard to their own abilities and expectations. Yet when they discussed their future, as women, their expectations of continuing equality narrowed, to the extent that their ambitions and anticipations were limited. In their anticipated futures, they believed in the 'fantasy' of equality, but were reluctant to question the reality of the status quo, believing that it was not equitable that the man should have to change. Therefore the young people's constructions of gender equality are conceived of as women challenging men's privilege but whilst retaining all of their traditional qualities and roles, so as not to destabilise the accepted gender order.[3]

3 For example during the exploratory questionnaire a number of boys and girls said that it was okay for a man to earn more money than a woman, but nobody agreed that it was okay for a woman to earn more money than a man.

Understanding Heterosexuality: Blaming Women for the Violence

Throughout the research process, men were engendered with descriptions such as powerful and strong. For some of the young people, such constructions were undisputed, while others unpicked the discourses that weaved these gender images. Yet within these constructions women were rarely positioned as victims of abuse, because young people did not always label the abusive situations in this way; and instead women were often constructed as weak or manipulative. Such constructions were bound by everyday (mis)understandings of victimised women. The discourse of 'why doesn't she leave?' is perpetuated by many statutory agencies and has filtered down into common currency. By putting the onus on the woman to leave, the emphasis is upon her behaviour, her 'failure' to stop the abuse, rather than focusing upon the abuser and the abuse itself:

> Nicole: It depends on what kind of personality you have. It depends if you are a strong person or not. If someone hits you and says I'm really sorry it won't happen again and then they hit you again, I think if you were strong, you'd leave them.
>
> (Mountview School, Group 1)

Nicole above, talks about if you are a 'strong' person you would leave, implying that those who don't, or can't, are weak. There is also a parallel in what the woman is expected to do. Earlier, this same group talked about how if women were married, they should treat the abuse as a 'rough patch' and work through it. Yet the same group is now condemning the woman for believing her partner was sorry and judging her as a weak person for doing so, and for her failure to leave. Therefore the woman is judged for what the abuser is doing to her. This line of argument was reiterated by boys complaining that girls couldn't take the 'play fighting' in the school yard. In this way, the behaviour of men and boys is justified because they are not even questioned within the equation of blame.

When the positions were reversed, many of the young people framed the roles differently. That is, even though Jamie punched Jenny, the majority of young people saw Jamie as the victim because Jenny had had an affair. Everyone agreed that Jenny was wrong to have an affair. Many more of the young people agreed that Jenny deserved to be punched by Jamie; it was her behaviour that had *provoked* him and therefore he was the victim and was justified in his reaction. Whilst not everybody agreed that Jamie was right to punch Jenny, his behaviour was framed within an empathic understanding of his anger and betrayal. So although Jenny was seen as the 'abuser', it was not a powerful position; instead she was framed as 'manipulative'. Consequently, the aggression demonstrated by Jamie proved that he was not a weak victim:

Craig:	'Cause if they've done something you would hit them rather than doing nothing.

(Mary Magdalene School, Group 5)

This follows on from earlier perceptions by both boys and girls, that boys (rather than girls) are more likely to use violence to save face, and because of pride, linking to constructions of hegemonic masculinity. This can be positioned next to a need to be *seen* to act as well as a desire to act, thereby constructing masculinity as a performance judged in terms of how others viewed it. One group of boys at Mary Magdalene School talked of what they would do if they were in the same situation as Jamie in the third vignette. As highlighted below, several of the boys struggle under the pressure of their peers to agree with them that Jenny deserved to be punched because she had had an affair:

John:	She did deserve it, but she shouldn't have got hit because it's a guy who hit her. If it was a woman then...
Simon:	She did deserve it but she shouldnae of got hit.
Nancy:	So why do you think she deserved it?
Simon:	Don't know.
Jason:	You're daft.
John:	'Cause she went with that other guy.
[Shouting]	
Nancy:	Everyone is entitled to their own opinions, so let's not be calling each other.
Jason:	[to the group] So what would you do if you had a girlfriend who was going out with someone else and you didn't know until she told you?
Simon:	I wouldn't care.
John:	I'd dump her.
Chris:	Pack your bags.
Jason:	Pack her bags you mean [Laughter] You're stupid!

(Mary Magdalene School, Group 4)

The discussions in this group became animated and aggressive because of the opposing ways the boys talked about how they would deal with the situation that Jamie found himself in. There was disagreement between those who felt Jamie had been treated badly, but that violence was the wrong reaction; those who said they felt justified in punching Jenny (as Jamie did) and those who felt it would be more gender-matched (see Chapter 5) to get another girl to hit her for you. Those who hadn't initially agreed with the more aggressive suggestions were called names and it was implied that their beliefs were less valid, or 'softer' options. John became aggressive, raising his voice and getting angry when the others in the group didn't agree with him. John and Jason colluded in their anger and united against the other members of the group. Jason felt so aggrieved that the others did not share his opinion (that Jenny deserved to be punched), that he rephrased the question convinced that it had not been understood. He believed that once he had done this, they would arrive at the selfsame conclusion which indeed they did. The boys, who had previously disagreed with him, succumbed and postured with uncaring, dismissive, hegemonic, masculine reactions giving Jason the approval he was seeking.

For several of the young people, mainly boys, acting tough, popularity, being given respect and displaying violence were viewed as synonymous. Violence was used as a means of conveying a performance of 'toughness', as a way to elicit respect and admiration, thus being cast as a positive attribute. Yet this interpretation of the performance was also dependent upon the victim, thus generating a discourse of 'deserving' and 'undeserving' victims. Even within this binary scale, many of the groups sought to find reasons for the victim being victimised, which began with an analysis of what they had done wrong rather than finding fault with the perpetrator. This resulted in the perpetrators' actions being legitimated and never questioned.

Another example of the process of 'blaming the victim' and thereby justifying violence, had to do with the sexualisation of the female body, limiting girls' choices with moral and sexual responsibilities and the restrictive codes attributed to it. These responsibilities included modestly covering her body (with more clothing) and being aware of the reaction that her (clothed) body may incite. Several of the groups (male and female) invested in this discourse of gendered morality when discussing the first vignette regarding Lee telling Claire not to wear her favourite vest top. Locating the issue with Claire subscribes to the notion that women are defined by how men view them with clothing becoming sexualised and encoded with the means of pleasing or displeasing men. The descriptions used by the young people are all active 'doing' words, suggesting that Claire was inviting male attention through the sexualisation of her clothing, as these heavily sexually connoted examples show:

Stewart: She is *flaunting* herself in front of other people. She could be enjoying that lots of boys are looking at her.
(Clifton School, Group 5, speaker's emphasis)

Shaheeda: She is *revealing* herself to the boys.
(Baxter Road School, Group 1, speaker's emphasis)

David: She wants to wear the pink top to *expose* herself to them.
(Mary Magdalene School, Group 4, speaker's emphasis)

Cheryl: She's got *slutty* clothes.

(Mary Magdalene School, Group 1, speaker's emphasis)

The ultimate responsibility becomes that of the woman to act and change the way men view her. In the vignette, clothing is linked with attractiveness but also compliance in terms of allowing men to define her choices. Yet this did not translate when the situation is reversed, as this one example of many highlights:

Nancy: So what would happen if Lee was wearing a vest top and Claire said she didn't want him to wear it?

Stephanie: She's not the boss of him, she can't tell him what to wear.

(Mary Magdalene School, Group 2)

There were contradictory examples where a young person would argue fervently against the violence perpetrated in one of the vignettes, but then thought it was wholly justified in another. The reason for this change in perspective seems to be dependent upon the actions of the woman (not the male abuser) and feeds again into the discourse of 'deserving' and 'undeserving' victim. For example, in response to the second vignette, Kirsten vehemently rejected Dave's violent actions:

Kirsten: Totally wrong. He has no right to go and slap her.

(Baxter Road School, Group 4)

She frames her argument in terms of a rejection of Dave's entitlement. Yet when responding to the third vignette, Kirsten firmly places the reason for the violence with Jenny:

Kirsten: It serves her right. Jamie must have done lots of things for her and she … she goes with another guy. That's wrong, so she deserves it.

(Baxter Road School, Group 4)

So whereas Kirsten's initial argument was based upon Dave not being entitled to slap Lizzy, we can now analyse it in terms of Kirsten not believing that Dave was justified in doing so. Kirsten sees his anger that tea was not ready, and his expectation that it should be so, as unreasonable, and therefore his actions are wrong. However, in another instance, Kirsten views the fact that Jenny is having an affair with Roddy as wrong, and judges Jamie's violent action as justified, because Jenny has not acted in an acceptable way. Thus, in this sense the violent reactions of both men are viewed as chastisements, as *reactions* to their partners' actions. It is only because Kirsten does not view Lizzy's action as in need of chastisement, that the violence is judged as wrong, not that the violence in itself is wrong. The fact that men themselves are not judged, or their belief in chastisement is not questioned, demonstrates an unequivocal acceptance and normalisation of both their power and their active use of it. Indeed this was clearly demonstrated by Meera, an 11-year-old girl:

> Meera: In order to teach them [Jenny and women in general] a lesson you have to hit them.
>
> (Baxter Road School, Group 2)

Through advocating violence as a means to teach women right from wrong, Meera is colluding with patriarchal authority that deems men have an entitlement to subordinate and abuse women. She is also further implicating herself within this subordinate group, by siding with the oppressor rather than challenging or resisting this violence.

In many instances there was little, or no, discussion of Jamie's violence other than as a reaction to Jenny's infidelity. Thus the violence here was judged in the context of Jenny deserving this 'reaction' and not looking at the violence in terms of Jamie's behaviour:

> Craig: Well she's been cheating on him so she deserves it.
> Daniel: Yeah, she deserves it.
> Nancy: Okay, so what does everyone else think?
> Rachel: He should have pushed her, not hit her.
>
> (Mary Magdalene School, Group 5)

In this group, the young people agree that Jamie punching Jenny was a justified reaction in chastising her for her behaviour, but not all agreed with his methods. Rachel deemed that a push would have been more appropriate, demonstrating that rather than seeing all violent behaviour as destructive, some actions are viewed as less violent and therefore more justifiable than others. But not everybody felt that Jamie was justified:

> Louis: You can't hurt somebody because they might have hurt you, you have to resolve it in another way rather than just hitting them.
>
> (Clifton School, Group 1)

Louis frames his own argument with the futility of retaliation. He views what Jenny did as hurtful, but does not consider violence a desirable or necessary reaction to it. It is significant that because he does not judge Jenny's behaviour in terms of it being an indictment of Jamie's masculine identity, there is no need to react to restore it.

An isolated discussion among one group, subverted hegemonic masculinity and identified Jamie as at fault:

> Ewan: Arrogant fool. He's the one who should be punished for being a lesser husband.
>
> (Clifton School, Group 3)

This argument should be seen in the same way as those blaming Jenny, where the danger of labelling behaviour as someone's fault, simply serves to justify the consequences of their actions. Indeed, it was because of justification being used as an explanation for violence, that some of the young people found it inexplicable when there was not an 'obvious' reason. Many of the young people found fault in women's 'behaviour' and in doing so suggested they appease the man. This constructs women in terms of duty, care and willingness to please, which in turn feeds into discourses that align gender with appeasement:

> Craig: He has asked her politely not to wear it. She needs to listen 'cause she is just upsetting him
>
> (Mary Magdalene School, Group 5)

In saying what he does, Jason (below) implies that if she had have done something 'wrong' Dave would have been justified in his action:

> Jason: 'Cause she doesnae even do anything wrong. She just went to the shops
>
> (Mary Magdalene School, Group 3)

Much of the discussions about Lizzy and Dave focused upon appeasement. Their theory centred upon the belief that if Lizzy changed her behaviour then Dave would not react in this way again. Upon listening again to the tapes, it also became clear that the young people themselves were trying to find ways to appease Dave, through their own 'tiptoeing' around his behaviour. In doing so, and in suggesting Lizzy do the same, the young people are reaffirming Dave's behaviour as a natural expression of masculinity in terms of accepting notions of male privilege. This can be evidenced in their belief that Dave is entitled to react in the way that he does, because Lizzy is not performing (or conforming) to her role as homemaker, and also through their explicit acceptance of the breadwinner role (the young people expect Dave to have been working all day and judge that Lizzy should have made his tea).

Many of the young people expressed the belief that it was up to Lizzy to change, conform or leave. Therefore, the possibility of change was dependent wholly upon her actions. What was significant in discussions of the second vignette was how the young people fervently began their arguments with an anger and disbelief towards Dave. Yet, despite expressing this support of Lizzy in her actions, the argument strayed into them finding ways in which Lizzy could appease Dave through *her* behaviour so that the situation and his violent reaction would not happen again. The following extract is representative of many of the young people's discussions:

Melanie:	She's not a slave, if he wants his dinner he can make it himself.
Aimee:	He's wrong to slap her. That's like really wrong.
Rosie:	Yeah. To slap someone 'cause they didn't make your dinner. He's just really lazy.
Aimee:	Yeah like *it might not be her fault* if she's spent all of her time at the shops. There could have been like really long queues or something.
Melanie:	He's not the boss of her.
Aimee:	She's her own person.
Monica:	Yeah.
Melanie:	Like even if she agreed to make him dinner, he definitely shouldn't, not even if…
Monica:	He didn't even listen to her.
Aimee:	She could have said, I'm sorry I'm late, the queues were long and just explain.
Nancy:	So should Lizzy ask Dave the next time she wants to go to the shops, like he says she should?
Melanie:	She shouldn't say, could I please go to the shops, she should say, I am going to the shops so we can eat today. I'll try and get back in time, and if I'm not back there's something there for your dinner.
Monica:	I don't think she should ask him, she should tell him.
Aimee:	But in a nice way, as in, I'm going out to the shops.

(Clifton School, Group 2, my emphasis)

The young people also related the story relayed in the vignette to their own experiences that reflected similar dynamics and use of justifications. One girl, Lindsay spoke of justifications her dad had used when speaking of violence that he had used against her sister:

Lindsay:	My sister is in a foster home 'cause *she* winds my dad up and *she* takes her anger out on him. But it's her *she* winds him up and he tried to hit her and I tried to stop dad but he pushed me out of the way.

(Clifton School, Group 4, my emphasis)

Here, Lindsay's narrative has become entwined with that of her dad's. The words she uses to justify her dad's actions are those that he has reiterated to her. It is also significant to note that the actions of Lindsay's sister are not described, but the actions of her dad that he uses against both girls are.

When violence was constructed in this way, it was judged as being the fault of the woman and therefore her responsibility – to not provoke, or to manage or prevent the violence. The onus is on the woman to change her behaviour, not to challenge the man. There are again definite links here with adult and child relationships, in terms of those in authority having the power to change what they term as unacceptable behaviour, and being able to chastise when they deemed behaviour unacceptable. This also links to the notion of protection as a further tenet to the justification discourse based upon women's vulnerability.

Rejecting Violence?: Promoting Personal Autonomy in Relationships

Not all of the young people's discussions were framed by an acceptance of institutionalised gender inequity. During discussions of the first vignette, the young people who deemed that it was '*up to her what she wears*' stressed Claire's autonomy and choice. Whilst the focus was on an article of clothing, the responses in favour of Claire asserting her own independence, framed the issue in relation to not being defined or 'controlled' by a partner:

Grace: It's her choice … her options. He can say what he thinks of her but it's up to her to decide on her own whether she like wants to listen to him or she doesn't. If it was me, I'd wear it.

(Baxter Road School, Group 4)

Ewan: It's not his life, it's her life.

(Clifton School, Group 3)

The theme of choice arose regardless of the gender make-up of the discussion groups, with both girls and boys supporting a woman's personal autonomy within a relationship. However, the positioning of boys and girls in the mixed groups was significant in terms of their disagreements about the dynamics of the relationships and their recognition or otherwise of abuse:

Rachel: She should keep on wearing it. Who cares what anybody else thinks? I'd wear the vest.

Craig: But her boyfriend'll be jealous.

Rachel: But it's up to her. Who cares what everyone else thinks?

Daniel: He's the one that's going to be stood beside her when he's out. And he'll look stupid if he's the one that's going out with her and other boys are looking at her.

(Mary Magdalene School, Group 5)

In this discussion, the boys in the group sided with Lee, looking at the situation from his perspective and in terms of pride and ownership. Rachel argued for Claire to have choice and freedom from the (male) gaze. Many of the same-sex groupings had discussions similar to these but it was girls who were generally more likely to suggest that Claire should modify her behaviour. Here the girl was standing up for herself in a situation where boys were attempting to disempower her.

There was an acknowledgement of the role of others in determining Claire and Lee's behaviour; Lee attempted to control what Claire wore by using the anticipated reaction of others to regulate her. Several young people recognised this and felt that this should not deter Claire:

Samia: I think it's her own choice what she wears. I would wear the top. It'd be up to me.

(Baxter Road School, Group 4)

Ewan: He doesn't want her to wear that top because other boys will think she's attractive. So it's about him, not her.

(Clifton School, Group 3)

Significantly more boys than girls stressed that Claire's clothing should be her own choice and not defined by her partner. Yet interestingly, it was also the limits to this choice that were more readily recognised by boys, perhaps because it is anticipated that men set these limits and expect women to conform to them:

Jack: Hmm, well it's not really a good thing for her 'cause *she's not got much choice* and that means *she'll end up* going out with one of the boys that are looking at her.

(Clifton School, Group 3, speaker's emphasis)

Jack is reflecting an underlying expectation, that many girls become resigned to their lack of personal autonomy in future relationships and the confined space in which they have to make these 'choices'. The implication was that Claire would simply be with whoever wanted her, undermining her own strength of choice and self- sufficiency.

Often, the discussions which promoted Claire's autonomy reflected the young people's own sense of independence. When girls discussed what they would 'personally' do, they were more likely to wear the top. More frequently the vignette was discussed in terms of 'others'; adult relationships bound by rigid heterosexual roles, where gender roles were seen as more predetermined and fixed. In these cases it was assumed that it was best to listen to Lee and not question the status quo.

Discussions of the second vignette highlighted that Lizzy's choices were more limited than those afforded to Claire. Although many of the young people saw Lizzy as an independent woman, who could *choose* to go to the shops, as and when she wanted, her life and choices were restricted by her *anticipated* roles and responsibilities. Thus, even though the vignette did not explicitly label Lizzy's role as making tea, the young people expected it to be so. The social practices of making dinner in particular and household chores in general were highly gendered. The vast majority of young people had an unquestioning acceptance, though not necessarily agreeing that it was Lizzy's role to make the dinner. Thus by implication, it was not Dave's reaction that was necessarily wrong, but his *violent* reaction. So whilst all of the young people condemned Dave's slapping of Lizzy, they did not always disagree with his expectation that she should have had his dinner ready. Therefore, Lizzy's 'choices' had to be made in conjunction with her role as a wife (and possibly a mother), who had the responsibility of making dinner and having it ready on time.

The minority of young people, who questioned the expectations of Lizzy's role, did so by positioning their opposition to male entitlement and ownership. The young people identified the limits imposed by Dave and framed his reaction as wrong. They saw him as curtailing Lizzy's freedom and choices because she had not fulfilled an anticipated role of 'woman':

Siobhan: I think that's just pure shocking. It's also sexist saying that the woman has to make the food and because his dinner is not ready he slaps her. That's like really out of order.
Ruth: And the fact that she has to ask him to go out.
Siobhan: It's like he owns her.

(Clifton School, Group 4)

Those young people, who reacted angrily to this vignette, to the violence and the gendered expectations, expected Lizzy to do the same. Therefore, instead of positioning Dave and Lizzy on a binary scale, at opposing ends, the anger and aggression was shared by both people. They saw Lizzy as angry at what was expected of her, at being slapped, and at Dave's sense of entitlement. They did not view this reaction as going against a form of 'femininity', but being constitutive of it:

Emma: Women's [*sic*] got their own life, they don't live for men. They don't sit there and cook all day. They have got their own lives as well.

(Mary Magdalene School, Group 1)

Grace: She's not a slave ... if he wants his dinner he can make it himself

(Baxter Road School, Group 4)

Chrissie: It's sexist saying just because she's a woman she has to make the food

(Clifton School, Group 4)

The minority of young people that agreed that there were choices to be made were the ones who labelled the man's behaviour as wrong and identified that the women need not put up with it. It was those young people who saw prescriptive gender roles as unacceptable, who were more likely to view choice as an option; the choice to defy the expectations of rigid gender identity:

Joe: She shouldn't have asked him, 'cause she doesn't need to

(Clifton School, Group 3)

These challenges to the limits imposed by restrictive gender identities were all the more significant when contextualised alongside others' acceptance of them. That is, many of the young people did not see choice as a viable option within the sphere of male power, and sought to justify it rather than resist it.

Choices were not available in a vacuum, as the young people were aware of the difficulties making choices created. Many of the young people explored the notion of choice when it came to discussing the relationships in the vignettes. Some of them announced that they would leave the violent man immediately. Others mulled over the difficulties that were associated with doing this. A number also suggested small acts of defiance, that when seen individually may not amount to much, but when seen within the context of the relationship, did present small independent challenges:

Nancy: If you were Lizzy what would you do?
Nadia: I wouldn't cook him any dinner.

(Baxter Road, Group 1)

Upon first reading, this could simply be interpreted as Nadia conforming to the gendered role of homemaker and nurturer. Earlier in the sessions however, Nadia had confided that to her, making the marriage work was her priority. So, although initially this could be viewed as accepting a subordinate role, she is using what little power she possesses (in the role of Lizzy) to challenge Dave's power. Other girls suggested that leaving the relationship was a choice, but recognised the difficulty in doing so and the informal support you would rely upon in making this choice:

> Cheryl: I'd try and get out of the relationship before it got any worse.
> Emma: I'd pack my bags and leave. Or I'd tell him to get out of my house.
> Cheryl: You'd just go to your sisters or one of your best friends, even if you've not heard from them for years. You'd still go to them 'cause they were your best friend at primary school, so you'd go to them for help.
>
> (Mary Magdalene School, Group 1)

The theme of choice in this section demonstrates the viability of options. For the few young people above, choice was and must be a feasible option to resist the utilitarian nature of relationships dictated by masculinist principles.

Summary

This chapter has explored how young people justify certain forms of violence, in particular men's violence against women. It is contended that the young people anticipated power in heterosexual relationships and used their acceptance and understanding of it, to justify violence occurring within them. In this chapter it has been shown how young people assess the dynamic processes of age and gender and position them within a static framework of heterosexuality. It is argued that the intersection of these gendered identities, at the point of adulthood, is used as the basis for young people's justifications. That is, violence used by men against women is judged to be an anticipated consequence of gendered inequality, endorsed by expectations of male entitlement, obedience, regulation, control, ownership and possession. It is by understanding heterosexuality in this way that young people go on to blame women for violence perpetrated against them. The dissenting voices were few, but they are critical in recognising that not everyone saw the inequity of adult relationships as inevitable.

Young people's constructed heterosexual identities are relevant to how they construct and understand violence. They are also significant to their present day to day lives and the temporality of childhood (James and Prout 1997; Prout 1990) whilst also creating the basis for their generational life course (Renold 2005). This finding highlights the need to move away from the limitation of heterosexuality, conceptualised as a dualistic phenomenon encased within the dichotomy of male/female and public/private. To do this we need to access the concept of temporality, in terms of age, and look at new ways of conceptualising space, so that it does not limit our ways of interpreting locations and boundaries. This demands a need to create more ways for young girls to understand their own gender identities, as it is demonstrated here that there is an optimum time, before adulthood, when they envisage their gender identities as more fluid and are therefore more receptive to alternative possibilities.

Chapter 8

A Change is Gonna Come?

There have been times that I thought I couldn't last for long
But now I think I'm able to carry on
It's been a long, a long time coming
But I know a change is gonna come, oh yes it will
(Sam Cooke, 'A Change Is Gonna Come', Portrait of a Legend 1951–1964)

Introduction

The research reported in this book presents the first investigation into what younger people, aged 11 and 12 think about men's violence against women. It does this by locating their constructions and understandings within the temporal and spatial location of childhood. Innovative methods were developed so as to prioritise the voices of the young people and encourage their participation. This research represents an original piece of work, while also addressing gaps in the sociological work on childhood, gender and feminism.

In looking at how young people construct and understand men's violence against women, I drew initially upon feminist and childhood theories, in particular the work of Kelly (1988, 1996), looking at how she has attempted to integrate time and space into her theories of men's violence. The influential paradigms of childhood (James and Prout 1997) have been invaluable in constructing the young people in this research, in terms of their own experiential knowledge and position in the lifecourse. Whilst these two theoretical strands have been brought together before, it has tended to be replicated purely in methodological and ethical terms rather than theoretically. To develop a framework in which to theorise how young people understand men's violence against women, I integrated Adam's (1990, 1995, 2000, 2002) theory of 'timescapes'. This enabled the young people's constructions to be theorised as transitory, developed and understood in relation to the intersections of their own temporal, spatial and gendered positions. Indeed, only by constructing violence as temporal and therefore transitory, can we construct it as changeable and preventable.

Feminism has tended to ignore age as a theoretical tool with which to analyse violence (with the exception of older women, see Scott 2004, 2008) but also as a means to analyse difference, between and among women and girls. Young people accessed a discourse of difference when talking about men and women. Much post-structural feminist discussion has looked at the differences between women: sexuality, class, ethnicity, education, religion – yet age has never really been a focus. However, for the young people it was a difference they subscribed to, time and time again. For them it was an explicit indicator of difference, between themselves as girls and an older generation of women. They used age as a signifier in their constructions of gender, judging that the more adult somebody was, the more fixed and restricted their gender identity became. This is an original insight into the gender constructions of young people, as defined in relation to the 'other'. Generally, the 'other' is positioned upon a dichotomous gender scale, with male and female, masculinity and femininity as opposites (Epstein 1997, Frosh et al. 2002; Holland et al. 1994; Mac an Ghaill 1994, 1996; McCarry 2003; Renold 2000, 2005). Little mention is ever made of the dichotomy constructed between young and old, or younger and older with feminism.

Young people's own relationship to patriarchy has only just begun to be explored in its own right (see Holland et al. 2004; McCarry 2003; Renold 2005), rather than as an add-on, an extension of adult's experiences. Such research implicitly acknowledges that men (and boys') power is experienced differently at different times and in different spaces. It not only enables us to envisage social life as a process, but also helps us to apply the referential framework of heterosexuality (heteronormativity) by which gender is understood. The incorporation of time and space is critical to facilitate the moving away from the binary concepts which inform gender. In other words, by enabling all interactions to be framed by temporal and spatial relations – construction is more fluid and it becomes easier to conceptualise gender across time and through the life course. Also, the temporal projections of the young people's own lived and anticipated experiences are intersected with their understandings of space (using the constructs of distance and proximity), which they subscribe to as a means to comprehend violence. The spatial dimension of their accounts incorporates not only physical locality but also their own personal sense of location and self.

Constructing a Typology

A typology can be constructed within which young people's understandings of men's violence against women are classified and explained. The typology varies according to their temporal trajectory, that is, whether the young people are talking about themselves (as young people) or others (as adults). Their accounts also depend upon the spatial location of the violence and their proximity to or distance from that. The social and temporal implications of 'spaces' associated with childhood and adulthood are also significant to young people's constructions. All of these factors are further intersected by gender; the gendering of space, of time (childhood and adulthood) and of the violence itself. The typology is constructed around a sequential model of violence. This model is developed to demonstrate what the young people use to define what is 'real' and 'unreal' violence. Young people understand and make sense of violence in different ways and these centre around three forms of explanation: *naturalising* the violence as an integral part of a man's identity, *normalising* certain forms of violence that takes place among their peers and siblings (thereby not actually labelling it as violence) and then they *justify* male violence using expectations of inequity in gender roles endorsed by heterosexual relationships.[1] The themes of time, space and gender are prominent within these forms of explanation. Young people's understandings draw upon a particular explanation depending upon where they and the violence are, in relation to time and space and how they envisage their own, and others' gender.

Naturalisation describes the process whereby the young people conceived violence as a biological (and therefore natural) difference between men and women. Young people's definitions of 'real violence' were naturalised through temporality (adulthood) and gender (masculinity), both of which were representative of physical strength, prowess and power. This differs from existing research that has located violence within normative gender constructions, but not necessarily adulthood (Burman 2006; McCarry 2003). In this research, young people naturalised violence by explaining it as an aspect of adult male identity and activity, subscribing to both gendered and generational power. Young people looked to the body as providing a representation of the co-existence of power and gender, manifesting itself in physicality.

The associations made by boys and girls, aligning men with strength and power, were done so at an abstract level to represent their constructed anticipation of physical power, which then fed into the ideological paradigm of men as powerful. Rather than violent forms of masculinity being seen as gendered performances (Connell 2000; Frosh Phoenix et al. 2002; Swain 2003, 2004), they were judged by the young people to be biological attributes of adult men (Bowker 1998). By naturalising violence in this way, the actions were not only seen as an inevitable factor of being a man, but also as an inescapable future for the young boys. The instability of this discourse was highlighted when young people then focused upon the social meaning of gender, products of discourses, representations and material practices in order to understand their own lived experiences. For example, their rhetoric did not fit with the lived reality of their experience; most boys aged 11 and 12 were physically smaller than the girls of the same age.

The boys in particular were keen to disassociate themselves from violence, basing their understanding of violence upon abstract examples of adult

1 It is important to note that in these findings, heterosexuality and heteronormativity can be used interchangeably.

men, which meant that they were distancing themselves personally from any relationship with violence. Yet many of their own actions did reflect similar activities to the abstract scenarios they depicted (hitting, punching, kicking), but their desire to detach themselves from the expectations of masculinity, saw many of the boys constructing themselves as physically and temporally distant from this 'real' violence. This created a disjuncture between their reluctance to achieve this adult, violent, masculine identity and their own perpetration of acts that could be construed as such.

Although previous studies have examined young people's constructions of gender they have failed to do so within a framework that allows for both the fluidity of gender and of time. The temporal positioning of the physical body was critical to young people's framing of violent actions. This also demonstrates the further relevance of transitions to their accounts (see Gordon and Lahelma 2004). Existing work on temporality and the body looks to the 'ageing body' (Wainwright and Turner 2004; Tulle 2008), the future body (Ahmed 2004) and the embodied life course (Katz and Monk 1993).

Through the concepts of temporality and spatiality, the body can be theorised as transitional, for example becoming more 'gendered' over time. This is an important theoretical development here, as the young people do not recognise their own bodies as being strong or able to inflict pain, and because of this there is a refusal to acknowledge their own complicity in peer or sibling violence. This anticipation of future physicality, replicates existing research that has found boys looking to adulthood as a time when their physical potential will be achieved (for example, Swain 2003, 2004). It is therefore, necessary to use the concept of temporality to explain how boys in particular, understand power as being not only gendered but generational, and also for them to recognise their present role in perpetuating violence.

Interestingly, this creates a dissonance in how young people construct gender as both fixed (and inevitable) and fluid (and changeable). Many of the young people acknowledged the performative elements of their own gender identities, but also recognised that such performances were strictly regulated. Transgressions of gender were policed closely, with insults of 'being a girl' or 'being gay', regularly heard during the discussion groups as a means of constructing the 'other', or of highlighting failed attempts at masculinity (Chambers et al. 2004; Duncan 1999; Epstein and Johnson 1998; Frosh et al. 2002). This research replicates other research on young boys' constructions of masculinities that identifies the alignment of masculinity with heterosexuality.

Normalisation is the process identified by feminists (see Kelly 1988; Dobash and Dobash 1992), where society endorses abusive actions as part of everyday gendered interactions between men and women. This was demonstrated in two ways; firstly by the symbolism of space afforded by childhood and also by the constructions of gender divisions as normal. What is fundamental to the normalisation thesis is that power and violence are not seen as excessive but as legitimate. The key to this legitimacy is that the violence and victimisation are individualised (viewed as individual incidents) and not framed within the wider structures of male domination (Kelly 1988). The examples here replicated this and were understood as being indicative of the relationships between certain siblings or the actions of individual boys. This research demonstrates that young people learn to accept this behaviour as part of the normalised gender order, which means it is made invisible when they highlight examples of what constitutes 'real' violence.

The closer young people were to the individual and to situations they identified as violent (in terms of age, gender, knowledge of), the less likely they were to identify (or name) actions and behaviour as violent. As such, the normalising of violence required the concepts of space and proximity to be in place. In other words, young people were too near to the 'violence', either physically or because those involved were related or close to them in terms of relationships.

The 'unreal' or dummy fighting at home between brothers and sisters was mentioned by all groups and always normalised as within the parameters of 'normal' sibling behaviour. In this research, the physicality of the violence was highly pertinent, followed by its subsequent normalisation by the young people themselves and often their parents. This was an unexpected finding of the research and one worthy of further investigation.

Kitzinger (1994) questions how the visibility of men's violence against women affects society's understanding of its prevalence. For example, when violence against women was hidden and not talked about, it was not visible and therefore dismissed as a rare occurrence and by implication, not a serious problem. Now, male violence against women is recognised as affecting one in four women in her lifetime (Walby and Allen 2004), its high prevalence succeeds in normalising rather than problematising its existence, leading to acceptance rather than resistance.

As such, it becomes difficult for young girls in particular to explicitly name these actions as violence – especially when it is not validated as such by others and/or adults. Implicit within this is the danger of creating chasms between the locations of such violent behaviour; for example, where one space is deemed okay (the schoolyard) and another (the street) is not. For this reason it is necessary to theorise space (and the meaning of that space) alongside violence. Otherwise girls, as highlighted here, are doubly silenced, by their gender and also by their age.

Divisions of gender were seen as normal and expected within school (separation and division of space at playtime), at home and within friendship groups. As such, the young people were becoming more aware of gender differences and how these were constructed as natural and polemic. As a result girls were finding that they had few means to describe themselves except in relation to boys. This finding endorses previous research as well as highlighting the need for more theoretical and practical focus on alternative ways to conceptualise femininities (Ali 2003; Archer et al. 2007; Chung 2005; Holland 2004; Jones 1996; Kehily et al. 2002; McRobbie 1978, 2000; Renold 2000; Skelton and Hall 2001). As a result, many of the forms of interaction between boys and girls were attributed to difference and were normalised by the beginnings of heterosexual relationships endorsing the old adage of 'if he pulls your pigtails it means he likes you'. The findings of this research show that such behaviour was normalised as it was judged to be how boys and girls interacted. However it is imperative to recognise that such performances are taking part within heteronormative spaces and so are inhibited and regulated by normative gendered expectation (see Bell et al. 1994).

This also highlights the need to explain the social problem of men's violence against women on a societal scale, rather than individualise it (Connell 1995, 2002; Dobash and Dobash 1979, 1998). Young people, girls in particular, were beginning to experience or at least understand aspects of inequality because of their gender. For example, access to playground space, some games and respect from groups of boys, were very much dependent upon their gender. Girls were expressing opinions that demonstrated that being 'a girl' meant they were excluded. There were also countless examples of girls experiencing routine behaviour that they and their friends described as abusive or harassment but failed to be recognised as such by teachers, resulting in an invalidation of their experiences. This leads to their minimisation of such actions and an acceptance that it formed part of their everyday lives (Dobash and Dobash 1992). This finding endorses the earlier work of Renold (2005: 115), who found that the girls she asked about this daily experience of sexual harassment from their male peers, concluded, 'we are used to it'. A positive aspect of the discussions, for girls in single sex groups, was their sharing of their individualised incidents, and this recognition of the collectivistic nature of their experiences was empowering.

Boys were not unaware of girls' reactions, but their silence colluded in this inequity by distancing themselves from their own actions, or in maintaining that part of being a girl was to 'react' against this injustice (exclusion and abuse). As such, it was seen by many of the boys, that the solution lay in girls fighting against the injustice, rather than the injustice itself being prevented. This replicates Connell's (1995, 2000) own theorisation of the patriarchal dividend and men (and boys') own vested interest in the gender regime staying the same.

Time, Space and Gender: Violence as Justified

The previous example of normalisation, illustrates how boys' and girls' actions are based upon constructed differences of their gender and in turn, these are perceived to be normal. For the young people, adulthood generated a more rigid framework of heterosexuality, where these gender differences begin to exemplify inequality upon which justifications can be based. Violence is justified because inequality is not questioned – it is endorsed and taken for granted as being part of an adult heterosexual relationship.

The framework of heterosexuality (described as seemingly invisible by Smart 1996) was highly visible to the young people when looking through the lens of anticipated adulthood. Heterosexuality was seen synonymous with adulthood in terms of sexual practice, marriage and children. They also saw it as located in places they associated with adulthood, school, home and work – even though these were also places that they themselves inhabited (highlighting here the inequity of space and how definitions of the same place can vary (see Bowlby et al. 2010).

Gilfoyle et al. (1993), looks at how women talk about heterosexuality using a pseudo-reciprocal gift discourse. Whereas they talk in terms of women giving themselves to men and men giving women orgasms, many of the girls in this research framed the anticipation of heterosexuality as providing the security of having a relationship, being given children and being provided with a validation of self. Many of the young people have already internalised this idea and are understanding their own gender (rather than it being a continuous negotiated process), more as a fixed, essential product that is in the process of stabilising itself. In envisaging gender in this way, the young people are aware of there being room for deviation, because they do not yet see themselves as 'real' men and women, so they position themselves as not yet restricted by adult defined and expected heterosexual frameworks. However, because they see themselves as enroute, they are beginning to anticipate the restriction of gendered adulthood. In this sense, girls see themselves as possessing more freedom to define their fluid and present opportunities, but they still position themselves in relation to men when they become older. It is this anticipation of institutionalised heterosexuality that may impact or restrict the construction of their present own gendered identity.

Much research in this area of young people and gender identity has found that many young people already identify the benefits of being a boy (see Reay 2001: 153, 158) over and above those of being a girl. These are seen physically, in terms of being more able to 'do more' and in terms of anticipations for the future. Young people in this study also shared these views – not currently in terms of the benefits now, although the young people all gave definitive examples of how being a boy had more benefits – but rather in terms of what the future had to offer – girls saw their futures as limited and both boys and girls identified adult men as being the most powerful and having the most options e.g. in terms of careers and personal freedoms.

It is these constructions and understandings of heterosexuality that underlie young people's justifications of violence. Restrictive normative gender roles that endorse dichotomous masculine and feminine identities are framed by rigid expectations of heterosexuality. This view promotes a hegemonic form of masculinity supported by notions of male dominance that include power, entitlement, control, physicality and regulation of women's behaviour. Women are positioned in opposition to this, in terms of weakness, submission and obedience. This is further endorsed by the construction of 'deserving' and 'undeserving' victims, where women are placed upon a scale depending upon how well they conform to their normative gender roles. Such a position also informed young people's 'gender codes' of violence, which were structured upon dichotomous ideas of women's weakness and men's strength. Violence needed to be 'gender-matched' to be 'fair'. This perception, however, held a caveat that men should not hit women – unless they had to.

The restrictions young people attributed to heterosexuality manifested themselves within adulthood but particularly within their constructed understandings of marriage. Relationships were based upon love, jealousy, ownership and highly gendered dichotomous roles, where a woman's failure to achieve this normative status could result in 'justified' chastisement. This understanding replicated relationships based upon generational power. For many of the young people, there was an expectation that an adult could chastise a child because a child had less power and was therefore not equal to an adult. Young people often framed adult gender relationships in this way substituting the adult role for 'men' and the 'child' for 'women'. By placing people within existing roles of powerful and powerless, the person with control becomes justified in their controlling actions.

The concept of heterosexuality was framed and understood differently by boys and girls. Girls saw it as inevitable, restrictive and a compromise. Boys rarely considered it, although when they did, they judged heterosexual relationships in terms of men having power. What is significant is that although aspects of the young people's lives were defined (and recognised as such) by heterosexuality, their own lived experiences of gender were blurred. Justification comes into existence with adulthood – young people contest the inequality when it impacts upon their *own* lived lives now. This study also found that young people were actively constructing their own (and others) gendered identities but that there was a real dissonance between their present fluid identities and the rigid, heterosexually defined, stable identities that they associated with adulthood.

This dissonance was reflected in the young people's construction of other people's gender identities. They saw these as also having to be fixed and located within rigidly defined boundaries of what they deemed acceptable. For example, if a woman, or another girl is failing to conform to an accepted version of femininity, violent 'reactions' are justifiable; 'it was women who had to change their behaviour in order to bring the problem under control' (Gillan and Samson 2000: 342). The disjuncture between the 'temporal' and generalised 'other' in relation to their own construction of gendered self is striking. It was only when young people looked to the future, that they defined these boundaries as fixed, stable and as entwined with power. Thus the power the young people associated with normative heterosexuality was only made visible when they are discussing men and women.

Temporal and Spatial Transitions: Being not Becoming

The framework of spatial and temporal transitions developed in this research has overcome the limitation of the 'becoming' thesis. It has demonstrated the limitations of conceiving of childhood as a singular, linear progression to adulthood. Young people see childhood as a time of opportunity and endless possibilities but see these as narrowing with adulthood. It is these limits to adulthood, confined within restrictive gendered expectations that influences how young people understand men's violence against women and persuades them of situations whereby they naturalise, normalise and justify certain acts of violence. Young people judge gender as more 'fixed' in adulthood. Therefore, those in positions of care and authority need to educate young people as to the possibilities and choices of adulthood rather than its gendered limitations. In achieving this, young people can be encouraged to hold onto the optimistic adage 'I can do anything' that they associated with childhood.

Implications for Policy and Future Research

This research offered a valuable input to methodology in terms of demonstrating that research with young people on a sensitive subject can be successfully done. It illustrated that feminism and the sociology of childhood are compatible and complementary philosophies where empowerment and policy change are key objectives. The main contribution to methodology was in highlighting how one piece of research can use differing, complementary methods, with each method creatively informing the next one using the input of the young people themselves.

This research was unique in enabling young people (under 12) to express their understandings and conceptualisations of men's violence against women and girls, within a framework that highlighted their own constructions of gender. The impact of gender and age in framing certain actions as violent and the role of gendered expectations in naturalising, normalising and justifying men's violence against women are the key findings in this research.

By examining what younger people think about violence and gender, it is illustrated that the conceptual frameworks for understanding these phenomena need to be broadened. This research reveals that young people rarely locate or name violence that occurs in their own lives, only that which is framed by characteristics of adulthood, unknown men, excessive violence, distant spaces and subject to official consequence and sanction. For example, the theorisations of violence and the conceptual framework of space, has significance in terms of the invalidation of women's experiences (Radford and Kelly 1996). Although here some girls questioned the 'violent' actions of boys towards them, others did not judge their experiences as 'real' examples of abuse, as they did not fit the preconceived frameworks they held. Thus, as a result the girls had few discourses to draw upon to encapsulate or explain their own experiences and did not officially label them as abusive. It was this lack of validation that enabled young people (girls and boys) to seek justification in the actions of the victims leading to the regulation and control of women's (and girls') actions, behaviours and identities. This demonstrates the need to give a voice to young people and listen to what they say in relation to understanding the gendered dynamic in reporting and naming abuse. This research highlights to policy makers that such invalidation begins at an early age and that these behaviours need to be labelled as wrong early on. This also has implications for boys' use of violence and expectations of gendered privilege.

Such a finding highlights the need for continued provision of equality themed work in schools and youth projects as well as women's organisations. There needs to be engagement with all primary school children at a national level. Teachers can encourage the promotion of positive, respectful relationships and the prevention of violence through engaging with the new Curriculum for Excellence (Scotland), in particular the elements which draw upon healthy relationships, issues of control and sex education. The findings are also adaptable to personal and social education classes, anti-bullying strategies, and equality and citizenship classes.

The findings highlighted that where gender divisions and stereotypes were perpetuated, the young people were less likely to challenge men's violence against women. Therefore, the promotion of gender equality and the reduction of gender segregation is key. Related to this is the inconsistencies between young people's reproduction and endorsement of a discourse of gender difference at the level of abstraction (where they would reiterate conventional cultural stereotypes) and their fluid constructions of gender where they based their discussions upon their own personal grounded knowledge demonstrated in their resistance of dominant stereotypes. This created a disjuncture between their own lived experiences of gender as fluid and (at times) radical, and their limiting trajectories with implications for their own futures of (in)equality.

On a positive note, this provides evidence of how some changes regarding gender attitudes have been successful and are making a distinct difference to the lives of young people. Yet it also highlights how the potential futures of many young girls are narrowed by gendered expectation and daily realities. Policy initiatives need to focus upon possibilities for change and on how young people's personal narratives can challenge restrictive forms of gender. Awareness raising material should highlight the need for access to multiple positive gender identities and encourage the development of strategies with which to experience and realise them.

Also relevant for teachers and head teachers are the implications of the themes of the research including space, gender and power and how the views of the young people can directly engender change within the school environments. Teachers need to be constantly aware, and act upon, the use of (and exclusion from) space in the playground and suppressing gender division by discouraging separate activities for boys and girls, (for example, lining up together, widening expectations and means of attainment for careers, including the promotion of role models for all).[2]

The impact which teachers and other authority figures have is critical, particularly in relation to their role in constructing a gendered framework of 'real' violence when dealing with complaints of violence and injury. Young people legitimate violence and violent behaviour by accessing powerful cultural discourses, which enable them to do so. When violence fails to conform to these preconceived frameworks (of adult men in public spaces resulting in authoritative consequence) young people have access to fewer means with which to make sense or understand it and so do not label the behaviour as violence but normalise it. Their position then becomes one that legitimises violence by seeking to make sense of it, or in failing to recognise violence at all. It then occurs that young people are only likely to demonise acts of violence that to them appear illegitimate; for example ones that use excessive force, are without (gendered) justification or cause great injury.

How teachers chastise some behaviour and minimise others needs to be examined in relation to their role in perpetuating gendered stereotypes. This would in part involve teachers looking at their own expectations of gender and how this influences their treatment of boys and girls. As such, teachers, youth workers and others working in this field can question/challenge/debate what constitutes as violence for young people. In doing so the tenuous nature of the typology begins to be unravelled and the aspects that do not 'fit' can be brought to the fore: young people's own experiences; the silencing of girls and women; emotional and psychological abuses. Again, education and awareness raising is

2 Such themes currently form the basis of gender equality work I have developed and am currently delivering to educational practitioners.

necessary to promote wider understanding of the prevalence, causes and effects of violence and violent behaviour so they can recognise it, challenge, resist and validate their own experiences of it.

Indeed, for third sector organisations (such as Women's Aid and Rape Crisis) the findings provide further credence for their arguments about the necessity of awareness raising materials and prevention work particularly in relation to young people's gendered identities and their reluctance or inability to 'name' violence unless it conforms to a set of pre-existing criteria. Such agencies will also benefit in terms of using the findings from academic based research as the basis for justification for funding resources.

A significant finding of this research was the extent of violence between siblings and in particular the normalisation of it by the young people themselves. This is an issue that needs to be explored and researched further. While there is much focus upon the effects of domestic abuse and child abuse we continue to normalise and therefore endorse the extent of physical and emotional violence between siblings. To rectify this disparity violence between siblings needs to be brought onto the public agenda and critiqued in the same way that domestic abuse was in the 1970s.

Summary

The typology presented here is valuable in explaining how young people's position in childhood impacts upon how they construct, understand, explain and experience men's violence against women. The typology helps to illustrate what conforms to their linear model of 'real' violence and also to understand what doesn't ('unreal') and why. This is not achieved simply by highlighting some behaviours and not others. Rather the significance of 'timescapes' (Adam 2002) – the intersection of the past, present and future – is highlighted, which in turn impacts upon how violence is understood and experienced now, in the present, by the young people. It also illustrates the significance of spaces, in terms of proximity and distance and the abstract spaces occupied by childhood and adulthood. For example, when gender is constructed in adulthood as 'fixed', the young people go on to generate more justifications for the violence.

The young people see the violence (in its less extreme forms that does not require intervention or have physical injury) as a prerequisite of many adult relationships, based upon heteronormativity, inequality, entitlement and expectations of control. Although they react against many of these constructions now, many of their anticipated ideas of adulthood support them. For example, the inevitability of (fixed) adulthood results in the separation of their friendship groups, endorsement of gender divisions and the further division of space by gender. In this way the 'timescape' of childhood is significant to how young people both understand and construct men's violence against women. The transition has begun and the young people anticipate it as inevitable.

As we have seen here young people's own understandings are not always informed by direct experience but developed and consolidated through complex and multifarious interactions. Such interactions take place within the context of home, school, family, the media, politics, the criminal justice system, everywhere. Gender inequality underpins both men's violence and young people's understandings and constructions of it – so whilst we can work to prevent violence we cannot do so within current restrictive gender regimes that naturalise, normalise and justify men's violence. I join a long line of academics, policy makers, activists and members of society who claim the only answer is long lasting transformative change. The time to change is now.

Bibliography

Acker, J., Barry, K. and Esseveld, J. (1983) 'Objectivity and Truth: Problems in Doing Feminist Research'. *Women's Studies International Forum*, 6(4), pp. 423–35.

Adam, B. (1990) *Time and Social Theory*. Cambridge: Polity; Philadelphia: Temple UP.

——— (1995) *Timewatch: The Social Analysis of Time*. Cambridge: Polity Press.

——— (2000) 'The Temporal Gaze: Challenge for Social Theory in the Context of GM Food'. *The British Journal of Sociology*, 51(1), pp. 125–42.

——— (2002) 'The Gendered Time Politics of Globalisation: Of Shadowlands and Elusive Justice'. *Feminist Review*, 70, 3–29.

Ahmed, S. (2006) *Queer Phenomenology: Orientations, Objects, Others*. Durham: Duke University Press.

Alderson, P. (1995) *Listening to Children: Children, Ethics and Social Research*. Barkingside: Barnardo's.

——— (2000) 'Children as Researchers: The Effects of Participation Rights in Research Methodology'. In: P. Christensen and A. James (eds). *Research with Children: Perspectives and Practices*. London: Falmer Press, pp. 241–57.

——— (2002) 'Ethics, the Rights of the Child, and Legal Considerations in Paediatric Clinical Research'. *European Forum for Good Clinical Practice*, Spring, 10–12.

——— (2008) *Young Children's Rights: Exploring Beliefs, Principles and Practice*. Second edition. London: Jessica Kingsley.

Ali, S. (2003) '"To Be a Girl": Culture and Class in Schools'. *Gender and Education*, 15(3), pp. 269–83.

Allen, L. (2003) 'Power Talk: Young People Negotiating (hetero)Sex'. *Women's Studies International Forum*, 26(3) pp. 235–44.

Amnesty International (2004) 'Stop Violence Against Women: It's in our Hands'. Oxford: Amnesty International Publications [Online]. Available at: http://www.amnesty.org/en/library/asset/ACT77/001/2004/en/d711a5d1-f7a7–11dd-8fd7-f57af21896e1/act770012004en.pdf. http://www.amnesty.org/en/library/asset/ACT77/003/2004/en/822dd390-d64d-11dd-ab95-a13b602c0642/act770032004en.html (Accessed 3 February 2015).

Amnesty International, http://web.amnesty.org/actforwomen/domestic-index-eng.

Annan, K. (2005) 'Atrocious manifestation of continued systematic discrimination, inequality', Press release, United Nations, http://www.un.org/press/en/2005/sgsm10225.doc.htm (Accessed 2 February 2015).

Archer, L., Halsall, A. and Hollingworth, S. (2007) 'Class, Gender, (hetero) Sexuality and Schooling: Paradoxes within Working-Class Girls' Engagement with Education and Post-16 Aspirations'. *British Journal of Sociology of Education*, 28(2) pp. 165–80.

Bacchi, C. (1999) *Women, Policy and Politics: The Construction of Policy Problems.* London: Sage Publications.

Backett-Milburn, K. (2004) Learning material. *Listening to Children Course.* Edinburgh.

Backett-Milburn, K. and McKie, L. (1999) 'A Critical Appraisal of the Draw and Write Technique'. *Health Education Research*, 14(3), pp. 387–98.

Barbour, R.S., and Kitzinger, J. (1999) *Developing Focus Group Research: Politics, Theory, and Practice.* London: Sage Publications.

Barker, J., Weller, S. (2003) '"Is it fun?" Developing Children Centred Research methods'. *International Journal of Sociology and Social Policy*, 23(1/2), pp. 33–58.

Barker, M. (2001) 'The Newson Report. A Case Study in "common sense"'. In: M. Barker and J. Petley (eds). *Ill Effects. The Media/Violence Debate.* London: Routledge, pp. 27–46.

Barnard, M.A. and Barlow, J. (2003) 'Discovering Parental Drug Dependence: Silence and Disclosure'. *Children & Society*, 17(1), pp. 45–56.

Barron, J. (1990) *Not Worth the Paper…? The Effectiveness of Legal protection for Women and Children experiencing domestic violence.* Bristol: Women's Aid Federation England.

Barter, C. and Renold, E. (1999) 'The Use of Vignettes in Qualitative Research'. *Social Research Update*, 25, Summer [Online]. Available at: http://sru.soc.surrey.ac.uk/SRU25.html (Accessed 3 February 2015).

Barter, C., Renold, E., Berridge, D. and Cawson, P. (2004) *Peer Violence in Children's Residential Care.* Buckingham: Palgrave.

Barter, C. and McCarry, M. (2011) 'Love, Power and Control: Girls' Experiences of Partner Violence and Exploitation'. In: N. Lombard and L. McMillan (eds). *Violence Against Women: Current Theory and Practice in Domestic Abuse, Sexual Violence and Exploitation.* London: Jessica Kingsley Publishers.

Batchelor, S. (2007) '"Getting Mad Wi' It": Risk-Seeking by Young Women'. In: K. Hannah-Moffat and P. O'Malley (eds). *Gendered Risks.* Abingdon: Routledge-Cavendish.

Bateson, M. (1990) *Composing a Life.* New York: Plume.

Bell, D., Binnie, J. Cream, J. and Valentine, G. (1994) 'All Hyped Up and No Place to Go'. *Gender Place and Culture*, 1(1), pp. 31–47.

Bergin, C., Talley, S., and Hamer, L. (2003) 'Prosocial Behaviors of Young Adolescents: A Focus Group Study'. *Journal of Adolescence*, 26, pp. 13–22.

Bhatti-Sinclair, K. (1994) 'Asian Women and Violence from Male Partners'. In: C. Lupton and T. Gillespie (eds). *Working With Violence.* Basingstoke: Macmillan.

Bloor, M., Frankland, J., Thomas, M. and Robson, K. (2001). *Focus Groups in Social Research*. London: Sage Publications.

Bograd, M. (1988) 'Feminist Perspectives on Wife Abuse: An Introduction'. In: K. Yllo and M. Bograd (eds). *Feminist Perspectives on Wife Abuse*. London: Sage Publications, pp. 11–26.

Bond, J, and Phillips R. (2000) 'Violence Against Women as a Human Rights Abuse'. In: C. Renzetti, J. Edleson and R. Bergen. *Sourcebook on Violence Against Women*. London: Sage Publications.

Boneparth, E. and Stoper, E. (eds) (1988) *Women, Power and Policy*. Oxford: Pergamon Press.

Borland, M., Hill, M., Laybourn, A. and Stafford, A. (2001) 'Improving Consultation with Children and Young people in Relevant Aspects of Policy Making and Legislation in Scotland'. Executive Summary of report commissioned for the Scottish Parliament Education, Culture and Sport Committee. Scottish Parliament Information Centre [Online]. Available at: http://archive.scottish.parliament.uk/business/committees/historic/education/reports-01/edconsultrep.htm (Accessed 3 February 2015).

Bowker, L.H. (ed.) (1998) *Masculinities and Violence*. London: Sage Publications.

Bowlby, S., McKie, L., Gregory, S. and MacPherson, I. (2010) *Interdependency and Care Over the Lifecourse*. London: Routledge.

Boyden J. and Ennew, J. (1997) *Children in Focus: A Manual for Participatory Research with Children*. Stockholm: Radda Barnen.

Brah, A. and Phoenix, A. (2004). 'Ain't I A Woman? Revisiting Intersectionality'. *Journal of International Women's Studies*, 5(3), pp. 75–86.

Brannen, J. (2005) 'Time and the Negotiation of Work-Family Boundaries: Autonomy or Illusion?' *Time and Society*, 14(1) pp. 113–31.

Brannen, J. and Nilsen, A. (2002) 'Young people's time perspectives: from youth to adulthood'. *Sociology*, 36(3), pp. 513–37.

Brannen, J. and O'Brien, M. (eds) (1996) *Children in Families: Research and Policy*. London: Falmer Press.

British Sociological Association (BSA) [Online]. Available at: http://www.britsoc.co.uk/media/27107/StatementofEthicalPractice.pdf.

Brown, J. (2007) 'Gender, Time and Space: Understanding Problem Behaviour in Young Children'. *Children & Society*, 21(2), pp 98–110.

Brownmiller, S. (2013) *Against our Will: Men, Women and Rape*. Open Road Media.

Bryman, A. (2008) *Social Research Methods*. Third edition Oxford: Oxford University Press.

Burke, R.J. and Weir, T. (1978) 'Sex Differences in Adolescent Life Stress, Social Support, and Well-Being'. *The Journal of Psychology*, 98, pp. 277–88.

Burman, M., Batchelor, S. and Brown, J. (2001) 'Researching Girls and Violence: Facing the Dilemmas of Fieldwork'. *British Journal of Criminology*, 41, pp. 443–56.

Burman, M., Brown, J. and Batchelor, S. (2003) '"Taking it to Heart": Girls and the Meanings of Violence'. In: E.A. Stanko (ed.). *The Meaning of Violence*. London: Routledge.

Burman, M. and Cartmel, F. (2006) *Young People's Attitudes Towards Gendered Violence*. Edinburgh: NHS Health Scotland.

Burton, S. and Kitzinger, J. with Kelly, L. and Regan, L. (1998) *Young People's Attitudes Towards Violence, Sex and Relationships: A Survey and Focus Group Study*. Glasgow: Zero Tolerance Trust.

Butler, I. and Williamson, H. (1994). *Children Speak: Trauma and Social Work*. Essex: Longman.

Butler, J. (1990) *Gender Trouble: Feminism and the Subversion of Identity*. London: Routledge.

Buzawa, E.S. and Buzawa, C.J. (1996) *Domestic Violence: The Criminal Justice Response*. London: Sage Publications.

Chambers, D., Tincknell, E. and Van Loon, J. (2004) 'Peer Regulation of Teenage Sexual Identities'. *Gender and Education*, 16(3), pp. 397–415.

Charles, N. (1995) 'Feminist Politics, Domestic Violence and the State'. *Sociological Review*. 43(4), pp. 617–40.

Children's Act (Scotland) 1995: Part 1.6.b, http://www.legislation.gov.uk/ukpga/1995/36/section/6 (Accessed 2 February 2015).

Christensen, P.M. and James, A. (2000) *Research with Children: Perspectives and Practices London*. New York: Falmer Press.

Chung, D. (2005) 'Violence, Control, Romance and Gender Equality: Young Women and Heterosexual Relationships'. *Women's Studies International Forum*, 28(6), pp. 445–55.

Clark, A. (1992) 'Humanity or Justice: Wifebeating and the Law in the Eighteenth and Nineteenth Centuries'. In: C. Smart (ed.). *Regulating Womanhood Historical Essays on Marriage, Motherhood and Sexuality*. London: Routledge, pp. 187–206.

Clark, A. and Moss, P. (2001) *Listening to Young Children: The Mosaic Approach*. London: National Children's Bureau for the Joseph Rowntree Foundation.

Coffey, A. and Atkinson, P. (1996) *Making Sense of Qualitative Data*. London: Sage Publications.

Cohen, S. (1972) *Folk Devils and Moral Panics*. St Albans: Paladin.

Connell, R.W. (1987) *Gender and Power*. Stanford: Stanford University Press.

——— (2001) [2000] *The Men and The Boys*. Cambridge: Polity Press.

——— (2002) *Gender*. Cambridge: Polity Press.

——— (2005) [1995] *Masculinities*. Cambridge: Polity Press.

Cooke, S. 'A Change Is Gonna Come' Portrait of a Legend 1951–1964, ABKCO Records.

Cree, V.E. (2003), 'Worries and Problems of Young Carers. Issues for Mental Health'. *Child & Family Social Work*, 8(4), pp. 301–309.

Cree, V.F., Kay, H., Tisdall, K. and Wallace, J. (2002) 'Research with Children: Sharing the Dilemmas'. *Child & Family Social Work*, 7(1) pp.47–56.

Davies, K. (1989) *Women and Time. Weaving the Strands of Everyday Life*. Lund: University of Lund Press.

De Block, L., and Buckingham, D. (2010) *Global Children, Global Media: Migration, Media and Childhood.* Basingstoke: Palgrave Macmillan.

Department of Health (2000) *Responding to Domestic Abuse: A Handbook for Health Professionals* [Online]. Available at: http://webarchive.nationalarchives.gov.uk/20130107105354/http://www.dh.gov.uk/prod_consum_dh/groups/dh_digitalassets/@dh/@en/documents/digitalasset/dh_4065379.pdf (Accessed 2 February 2015.

de Vylder, S. (2004) 'Costs of Male Violence'. In: Ferguson, H., Hearn, J., Øystein Gullvåg, H., Jalmert, L., Kimmel, M., Lang, J., Morrell., R. *Ending Gender Based Violence: A Call for Global Action to Involve Men*. Stockholm: Swedish International Development Agency.

Dicker, R. and Piepmeier. A. (eds) (2003) *Catching a Wave: Reclaiming Feminism for the 21st Century*. Boston: Northeastern University Press.

Dobash, R.E. and Dobash, R.P. (1979) *Women, Violence and Social Change* London: Routledge

——— (1992) *Women, Violence and Social Change*. London: Routledge.

——— (1998) 'Violent Men and Violent Contexts' In: R. Dobash and R.E. Dobash. *Rethinking Violence against Women*. London: Sage Publications.

Dublin Women's Aid (1999) *Teenage Tolerance: The Hidden Lives of Young Irish People: A Study of Young People's Experiences and Responses to Violence and Abuse.* Dublin: Women's Aid.

Duncan, N. (1999) *Sexual Bullying*. London: Routledge.

Dunhill, C. (ed.) (1989) *The Boys in Blue: Women's Challenge to the Police*. London: Virago.

Economic and Social Research Council (ESRC) [Onine]. Available at: www.esrc.ac.uk/esrccontent/researchfunding/sec22.asp.

Edleson, J. (1999) 'Children's Witnessing of Adult Domestic Violence'. *Journal of Interpersonal Violence*, 14, pp. 839–70.

Edwards, R. and Mauthner, M. (2002) 'Ethics and Feminist research: Theory and practice'. In: M. Mauthner, M. Birch, J. Jessop and T. Miller (eds). *Ethics in Qualitative Research*. London: Sage Publications.

Edwards, S. (1981) *Female Sexuality and the Law*. Oxford: Martin Robertson.

——— (1986) *Women on Trial: A Study of the Female Suspect, Defender and Offender in the Criminal Law and the Criminal Justice System*. Manchester: Manchester University Press.

——— (1991) *Policing Domestic Violence: Women, the Law and the State*. London: Sage Publications.

Eldridge, J., MacInnes, J., Scott, S., Warhurst, C. and Witz, A. (2000) *For Sociology: Legacies and Prospects*. York: Sociology Press, pp. 145–59.

Epstein, D. (1997) '"Boyz" Own Stories: masculinities and sexualities in schools'. *Gender and Education*, 9(1), pp. 105–15.

Epstein, D. and Johnson, R. (1998) *Schooling Sexualities*. Buckingham: Open University Press.

Equal Opportunities Commission (2001) *Young People and Sex Stereotyping – Research Findings*. London: EOC.

Farquar, C. (1990) *What do Primary School Children Know About Aids? A Report of a Feasibility Study Exploring Children's Knowledge and Belief About Aids*. London: Thomas Coram Research Unit.

Fergusson, D., Horwood, J. and Ridder, E. (2005) 'Partner Violence and Mental Health Outcomes in a New Zealand Birth Cohort'. *Journal of Marriage and Family*, 67(5), pp. 1,103–19.

Finch, J. (1987) 'The Vignette Technique in Survey Research'. *Sociology*, 21, pp.105–14.

Flood, M. (1997) 'Responding to Men' [Online]. Available at: http://www.xyonline.net/content/responding-mens-rights-groups (Accessed 10 February 2015).

Flood, M. and Pease, B. (2009a) 'Factors Influencing Attitudes to Violence Against Women'. *Trauma Violence Abuse*, 10(2), 125–42.

Flood, M., Pease, B., Taylor, N. and Webster, K. (2009b) 'Reshaping Attitudes to Violence Against Women'. In: E. Stark and E. Buzawa (eds). *Violence Against Women in Families and Relationships Volume 4: The Media and Cultural Attitudes*. California: Praeger.

Flood-Page, C. and Taylor, J. (eds) (2003). *Crime in England and Wales 2001/2002*. Supplementary volume. London: Home Office.

Forsberg, G. (2005) 'The Gendered City'. In: T. Friberg, C. Listerborn, B. Andersson and C. Scholten (eds). *Reflections of Rooms: Codes of Gender, Places and Contexts*. Stockholm: Symposion Förlag, pp. 10–19.

Foucault, M. (1980) '"Body/Power" and "Truth and Power"'. In: C. Gordon (ed.). *Michel Foucault: Power/Knowledge*. Hemel Hempstead: Harvester.

Fraser, S. and Robinson, C. (2004) 'Paradigms and Philosophy'. In: Fraser, S., Lewis, V., Ding, S., Kellet, M. and Robinson, C. (eds). *Doing Research with Children and Young People*. London: Sage Publications.

Frosh, S., Phoenix, A. and Pattman, R. (2002) *Young Masculinities: Understanding Boys in Contemporary Society London*. Basingstoke: Palgrave.

Gadd, D. (2014) 'Evaluating the Effectiveness of Domestic Abuse Prevention Education'. *Legal and Criminological Psychology*.

Gadd, D, Corr, M-L., Fox, C.L. and Butler, I. (2014) 'This is Abuse or Is it? Domestic Abuse Perpetrators' Responses to Anti-Domestic Violence Publicity'. *Crime Media Culture*, 10(1), pp. 3–32.

Gadd, D., Farrell, S., Lombard, N. and Dallimore, D. (2002) *Domestic Abuse Against Men in Scotland.* Edinburgh: Scottish Executive Central Research Unit.

García-Moreno, C. (2002) 'Dilemmas and Opportunities for an Appropriate Health-Service Response to Violence Against Women'. *The Lancet*, 359 (9,316), pp.1,509–14.

Gelles, R. J. (1983) 'An Exchange/Social Control Theory'. In: D. Finkelhor, R.J Gelles, G.T Hotaling and M.A. Straus (eds). *The Dark Side of Families: Current Family Violence Research.* London: Sage Publications, pp. 151–65.

——— (1987) *Family Violence Research.* London: Sage Publications.

——— (1993) 'Through a Sociological Lens: Social Structure and Family Violence'. In: R.J. Gelles and D.R. Loseke (eds). *Current Controversies on Family Violence.* London: Sage Publications.

——— (1997) *Intimate Violence in Families.* London: Sage Publications.

Ghate, D. and Hazel, N. (2002) *Parenting in Poor Environments: Stress, Support and Coping.* London: Jessica Kingsley Publishers.

Giddens, A (1979) *Central Problems in Social Theory* London: Macmillan.

——— (1984) *The Constitution of Society: Outline of the Theory of Structuration.* Cambridge: Polity Press.

——— (1994) 'Living in a Post Traditional Society'. In: U. Beck, A. Giddens and S. Lash (eds). *Reflexive Modernisation.* Cambridge: Polity Press, pp. 56–109.

Gilfoyle, J., Wilson, J. and Own, B. (1993) 'Sex, Organs and Audiotape: A Discourse Analytic Approach to Talking about Heterosexual Sex and Relationships'. In S. Wilkinson and C. Kitzinger (eds). *Heterosexuality: A Feminism and Psychology Reader.* London: Sage Publications, pp. 181–202.

Gill, A. (2013) 'Intersecting Inequalities: Implications for Addressing Forced Marriage and 'Honour' Based Violence for Those Working in Social Work and Related Professions'. In: L. McMillan, and N. Lombard (eds). *Current Theory and Practice in Domestic Abuse, Sexual Violence and Exploitation.* London: Jessica Kingsley Publishers.

Gillan, E. and Samson, E. (2000) 'The Zero Tolerance Campaigns'. In: J. Hamner and C. Itzin with S. Quaid and D. Wigglesworth (eds) *Home Truths About Domestic Violence: Feminist Influences on Policy and Practice: A Reader.* London: Routledge, pp. 340–56.

Glucksman, M. (1994) 'The Work of Knowledge and the Knowledge of Women's Work'. In: M. Maynard and J. Purvis (eds). *Researching Women's Lives from a Feminist Perspective.* London: Taylor & Francis.

Gordon, T. and Lahelma, E. (2004) 'Who Wants to Be a Woman? Young Women's Reflections on Transitions to Adulthood'. *Feminist Review*, 78, pp. 80–98.

Grace, S. (1995) *Policing Domestic Violence in the 1990s.* Home Office Research Study No. 139. London: HMSO.

Greenan, L. (2004) *Violence Against Women: A Literature Review.* Scottish Executive.

Grieve, R. and Hughes, M. (1990) 'An Introduction to Understanding Children'. In: R. Grieve and M. Hughes (eds). *Understanding Children: Essays in Honour of Maragret Donaldson*. Oxford: Blackwell Publishers Ltd, pp. 1–11.

Griffin, C. (1993) *Representations of Youth*. Cambridge: Polity Press.

Groves, L. (2003) 'A Case Study from Central America'. Listening to Children course material. Edinburgh: University of Edinburgh.

Guba, E.G. and Lincoln,Y.S.(1994) 'Competing Paradigms in Qualitative Research'. In: N.K. Denzin and Y.S. Lincoln (eds). *Handbook of Qualitative Research*. Thousand Oaks, CA: Sage Publications, pp. 105–17.

Hague, G. (1999) 'Domestic Violence Policy in the 1990s'. In: S. Watson and L. Doyal (eds). *Engendering Social Policy*. Buckingham: Open University Press.

Hague, G. and Malos, E. (1998) *Domestic Violence: Action for Change*. Cheltenham: New Clarion Press.

Halberstam, J. (1998) *Female Masculinity*. Durham, NC: Duke University Press.

Hammersley, M. (1992) 'On Feminist Methodology'. *Sociology*, 26(2), pp. 187–206.

Hanmer, J. and Saunders, S. (1984) *Well-Founded Fear: A Community Study of Violence Against Women*. London: Hutchinson.

Harden, J., Scott, S., Backett-Milburn, K. and Jackson, S. (2000) 'Can't Talk, Won't Talk?: Methodological Issues in Researching Children'. *Sociological Research Online*, 5(2) [Online]. Available at: http://socresonline.org.uk/5/2/harden.html.

Harding, S. (1987) 'Introduction: Is There A Feminist Method?' In S. Harding (ed.). *Feminism and Methodology*. Milton Keynes: Open University Press, pp. 1–14.

Harvey, D (1993) 'Class Relations, Social Justice and the Politics of Difference'. In: S. Pile and M. Keith (eds). *Place and the Politics of Identity*. London: Routledge, pp. 41–66.

Hatcher, R. (1995) 'Boyfriends, Girlfriends: Gender and Race in Children's Cultures'. *International Play Journal*, 3, pp.187–97.

Hatty, S.E. (2000) *Masculinities, Violence and Culture*. London: Sage Publications.

Hazel, N. (1995a) 'Elicitation Techniques with Young People'. *Social Research Update*, 12, Winter [Online]. Available at: http://www.soc.surrey.ac.uk/sru/SRU12.html.

——— (1995b*) 'Seen and Heard?': An Examination of Methods for Collecting Data from Young People*. Unpublished Master's thesis, University of Stirling.

——— (1999) *'A Helping Hand?' Young People's Perceptions of Adults' use of Physical Force in Disciplinary Relationships with Children*. Unpublished PhD thesis, University of Stirling.

Hearn, J. (1998) *The Violences of Men: How Men Talk and How Agencies Respond to Men's Violences Against Women*. London: Sage Publications.

——— (1999) 'A Crisis in Masculinity or New Agendas for Men?' In: S. Walby (ed.). *New Agendas for Women*. London: Macmillan, pp. 148–68.

Hearn, J. and McKie, L. (2009) 'Gendered and Social Hierarchies in Problem Representation and Policy Processes: "Domestic Violence" in Finland and Scotland'. *Violence Against Women*, 16(2), pp. 136–58.

Hendrick, H. (1990) 'Constructions and Reconstructions of British Childhood: An Interpretative Survey, 1800 to the Present'. In: A. James and A. Prout (eds). *Constructing and Reconstructing Childhood: Contemporary Issues in the Sociological Study of Childhood London*. London: Falmer Press, pp. 34–63.

Hendry, J. (1996) *Primary School Children's Perception and Consumption of Fruit and Vegetables*. Interim Report to the Chief Scientist Office. Edinburgh: Scottish Office.

Hester, M. (2006) 'Making it Through the Criminal Justice System: Attrition and Domestic Violence'. *Social Policy and Society*, 5(1), pp.79–90.

——— (2009) *Who Does What to Whom? Gender and Domestic Violence Perpetrators*. Bristol: University of Bristol and the Northern Rock Foundation.

Hester, M., Pearson, C. and Harwin, N. (2000) *Making an Impact – Children and Domestic Violence. A Reader*. London: Jessica Kingsley Publishers.

Hester, M. and Westmarland, N. (2004) *Tackling Street Prostitution – Towards a Holistic Approach*. Home Office Research Study 279. London: Home Office Research, Development and Statistics Directorate.

——— (2005) *Tackling Domestic Violence: Effective Interventions and Approaches*. Home Office Research Study 290. London: Home Office Research, Development and Statistics Directorate.

Heywood, L. and Drake, J. (1997) *Third Wave Agenda: Being Feminist, Doing Feminism*. Minneapolis, MN: University of Minnesota Press.

Highet, G. (2003) 'Cannabis and Smoking Research: Interviewing Young People in Self Selected Friendship Pairs'. *Health Education Research: Theory and Practice*, 18(1), 108–18.

Hill Collins, P. (2000) *Black Feminist Thought: Knowledge, Consciousness, and the Politics of Empowerment*. Second edition. New York: Routledge.

Holland, J. and Ramazanoglu, C. (1994) 'Coming to Conclusions: Power and Interpretation in Researching Young Women's Sexuality'. In: M. Maynard and J. Purvis (eds). *Researching Women's Lives from a Feminist Perspective*. London: Taylor & Francis.

Holland, J., Ramazanoglu, C., Sharpe, S. and Thomson, R. (2004) *The Male in the Head: Young People Heterosexuality and Power*. Second edition. London: The Tufnel Press.

Holliday, A. (2002) *Doing and Writing Qualitative Research*. London: Sage Publications.

Holloway, S.L. and Valentine, G. (2000) 'Spatiality and the New Social Studies of Childhood'. *Sociology*, 34, 763–83.

Hollway, W. and Jefferson, T. (2000) *Doing Qualitative Research Differently: Free Association, Narrative and the Interview Method*. London: Sage Publications.

Holstein-Beck, S. (1995) 'Consistency and Change in the Lifeworld of Young Women'. In: J. Fornas and G. Bolin (eds). *Youth Culture in Late Modernity.* London: Sage Publications

Home Office (2013) New definition of domestic violence. News stories: Inside Government GOV.UK. Available at: https://www.gov.uk/government/news/new-definition-of-domestic-violence (Accessed 2 February 2015).

Hood, S., Kelley, P. and Mayall, B. (1996) 'Children as Research Subjects: A Risky Enterprise'. *Children & Society*, 10(2), pp. 117–28.

Hornsby-Smith, M.P. (1993) 'Gaining Access'. In: G.N. Gilbert (ed.) *Researching Social Life.* London: Sage Publications, pp. 52–67.

Hughes, A. and Witz, A. (1997). 'Feminism and the matter of bodies: from de Beauvoir to Butler'. *Body & Society*, 3(1), pp. 47–60.

Humphreys, C. (2000) *Social Work, Domestic Violence and Child Protection: Challenging Practice.* Bristol: Policy Press.

Humphreys, C., Hester, M., Hague, G., Mullender, A., Abrahams, H. and Lowe, P. (2000) *From Good Intentions to Good Practice: Mapping Services Working with Families Where There is Domestic Violence.* Bristol: Policy Press.

Itzin, C. (2000) 'Gendering Domestic Violence: The Influence of Feminism on Policy and Practice'. In: J. Hamner and C. Itzin with S. Quaid and D. Wigglesworth (eds). *Home Truths About Domestic Violence: Feminist Influences on Policy and Practice: A Reader.* London: Routledge pp. 356–80.

Jackson, S. (1999) *Heterosexuality in Question.* London: Sage Publications.

James, A. (2005) 'Life Times: Children's Perspectives on Age, Agency and Memory Across the Life Course'. In: J. Qvortrup (ed.). *Studies in Modern Childhood: Society, Agency and Culture.* London: Palgrave.

James, A., Jenks, C. and Prout, A. (1998) *Theorising Childhood.* Cambridge: Polity Press.

James, A. and Prout, A. (1997) [1990] 'Re-presenting Childhood: Time and Transition in the Study of Childhood'. In: A. James and A. Prout (eds). *Constructing and Reconstructing Childhood. Contemporary Issues in the Sociological Study of Childhood.* Basingstoke: Falmer Press.

Jenks, C. (1996) *Childhood.* London: Routledge.

Johnson, M. (1995). 'Patriarchal Terrorism and Common Couple Violence: Two Forms of Violence Against Women'. *Journal of Marriage and Family*, 57, pp. 283–94.

——— (2005) 'Domestic Violence: It's not about gender – Or is it?' *Journal of Marriage and Family*, 67(5), pp. 1,126–30.

Jones, L. (1996) 'Young Girls' Notions of "Femininity"'. *Gender and Education*, 8(3), pp. 311–32.

Katz, C. and Monk, J. (1993) 'Making Connections: Space, Place and the Lifecourse'. In: C. Katz and J. Monk (eds). *Full Circles: Geographies of Women over the Life Course.* London: Routledge, pp. 264–79.

Kaufman, M. (1999) 'Men, Feminism, and Men's Contradictory Experiences of Power' in J.A. Kuypers (ed.). *Men and Power.* Halifax: Fernwood Books, pp. 59–83. http://www.feminish.com/wp-content/uploads/2012/08/men_feminism.pdf (Accessed 8 February 2015).

Kehily, M.J., Mac an Ghaill, M., Epstein, D. and Redman, P. (2002) 'Private Girls and Public Worlds: Producing Femininities in the Primary School'. *Discourse Studies in the Cultural Politics of Education,* 23(2), pp. 167–77.

Kehily, M.J. and Nayak, A. (1997) '"Lads and Laughter": Humour and the Production of Heterosexual Hierarchies'. *Gender and Education,* 9(1), pp. 69–87.

Kelly, L. (1988) *Surviving Sexual Violence.* Cambridge: Polity Press; Oxford: Blackwell.

——— (1999) 'Violence Against Women: A Policy of Neglect or a Neglect of Policy?' In: S. Walby (ed.). *New Agendas for Women.* London: Macmillan.

——— (2000) 'Joined Up Responses to Complicated Lives: Making Connections Across Recently Constructed Boundaries'. Speech at Domestic Violence – Enough is Enough conference, London.

——— (2005) 'A Gap or a Chasm? Attrition in Reported Rape Cases'. Home Office Research Study 293. London: Home Office Research, Development and Statistics Directorate.

Kelly, L. Regan, L. and Burton, S. (1991) *An Exploratory Study of the Prevalence of Sexual Abuse in a Sample of 16–21 Year Olds.* London: Child Abuse Studies Unit, University of North London.

——— (1994) 'Researching Women's Lives or Studying Women's Oppression? Reflections on What Constitutes Feminist Research'. In: M. Maynard and J. Purvis (eds). *Researching Women's Lives from a Feminist Perspective.* London: Taylor & Francis.

Kenway, J. and Fitzclarence L. (1997) 'Masculinity, Violence and Schooling: Challenging Poisonous Pedagogies'. *Gender and Education,* 9, pp. 117–34.

Kimmel, M. (1987) 'Rethinking Masculinity: New Directions in Research'. In: M.S. Kimmel (ed.). *Changing Men: New Directions in Research on Men and Masculinity.* London: Sage Publications, pp. 9–24.

——— (1994) 'Masculinity as Homophobia: Fear Shame and Silence in the Construction of Gender Identity'. In: H. Brod and M. Kaufman (eds). *Theorizing Masculinities.* London: Sage Publications, pp. 119–41.

Kintrea, K., Bannister, J., Pickering, J., Suzuki, N. and Reid, M. (2008) *Young People and Territoriality in British Cities.* York: Joseph Rowntree Foundation [Online]. Available at: http://www.jrf.org.uk/bookshop/eBooks/2278-young-people-territoriality.pdf.

Kirk, J. and Miller, M.L. (1986) *Reliability and Validity in Qualitative Research.* Qualitative Research Methods series, volume 1. Thousand Oaks, CA: Sage Publications.

Kitzinger, J. (1994) 'Challenging Sexual Violence Against Girls: A Public Awareness Approach'. *Child Abuse Review*, 3(4), pp. 246–8.

——— (2002) 'The Ultimate Neighbour from Hell? Stranger Danger and the Media Framing of Paedophiles'. In: Y. Jewkes and G. Letherby (eds). *Criminology: A Reader.* London: Sage Publications, pp. 145–59.

Kitzinger, J. and Barbour, R.S. (1999) 'Introduction: The Challenge and Promise of Focus Groups'. In: R.S. Barbour and J. Kitzinger (eds). *Developing Focus Group Research: Politics, Theory and Practice.* London: Sage Publications.

Krahe, B. and Temkin, J. (2009) 'Addressing the Attitude Problem in Rape Trials: Some Proposals and Methodological Considerations'. In: M.A.H. Horvath and J.M. Brown (eds). *Rape: Challenging Contemporary Thinking.* Devon: Willan Publishing.

Lacasse, A. and Mendelson, M.J. (2007) 'Sexual Coercion Among Adolescents: Victims and Perpetrators'. *Journal of Interpersonal Violence*, 22, pp.424–37.

Langsted, O. (1994) 'Looking at Quality from the Child's Perspective'. In: P. Moss and A. Pence (eds). *Valuing Quality in Early Childhood Services: New Approaches to Defining Quality.* London: Paul Chapman Publishing.

Lauwers, H., Meire J., Vanderstede, W. and Van Gils, J. (2005) *Methods in the Making. Some Methodological Implications of Considering Children as Actors.* Paper presented at the Childhoods 2005 conference, Oslo, 30 June.

Layland, J. (1990) 'On the Conflicts of Doing Feminist Research into Masculinity'. In: L. Stanley (ed.). *Feminist Praxis: Research, Theory and Epistemology in Feminist Sociology.* London: Routledge, pp. 125–33.

Leach, F. and Humphreys, S. (2007) 'Gender Violence in Schools: Taking the "Girls as Victims" Discourse Forward'. *Gender and Development*, 15(1), pp. 51–65.

LeCompte, M.D., and Goetz, J.P. (1982). 'Ethnographic Data Collection and Analysis in Evaluation Research'. *Educational Evaluation and Policy Analysis*, pp. 387–400.

Lees, S. (1993) *Sugar and Spice: Sexuality and Adolescent Girls.* Harmondsworth: Penguin Books.

——— (2002) *Carnal Knowledge: Rape on Trial.* The Women's Press: London.

Lentz, S.A. (1999). Revisiting the Rule of Thumb: An Overview of the History of Wife Abuse. *Women & Criminal Justice*, 10(2), pp. 9–27.

Letherby, G. (2002) 'Claims and Disclaimers: Knowledge, Reflexivity and Representation in Feminist Research'. *Sociological Research Online* 6(4).

——— (2004) 'Quoting and Counting: An Autobiographical Response to Oakley'. *Sociology*. 38(1). pp. 175–89.

Liebling, A. and Stanko, E.A. (2001) 'Allegiance and Ambivalence: Dome Dilemmas in Researching Disorder and Violence'. *British Journal of Criminology*, 41(3), pp. 421–30.

Lincoln, Y.S. and Guba, E. (1985) *Naturalistic Enquiry*. Thousand Oaks, CA: Sage Publications.

Livingstone, S. (2002) *Young People and New Media: Childhood and the Changing Media Environment*. London: Sage Publications.

——— (2008) 'Taking Risky Opportunities in Youthful Content Creation: Teenagers' use of Social Networking Sites for Intimacy, Privacy and Self-Expression'. *New Media & Society*, 10(3), pp. 393–411.

Livingstone, S., Haddon, L., Görzig, A., and Ólafsson, K. (2010) Risks and Safety for Children on the Internet: The UK Report. *Politics*, 6.

Local Government Act 1988 (c. 9), section 28, http://www.legislation.gov.uk/ukpga/1988/9/contents (Accessed 2 February 2015).

Lombard, N. (2013a) 'But What About the Men?' In: N. Lombard and L. McMillan (eds). *Violence Against Women: Current Theory and Practice in Domestic Abuse, Sexual Violence & Exploitation*. Research Highlights in Social Work series. London: Jessica Kingsley Publications.

——— (2013b) 'Young People's Temporal and Spatial Accounts of Gendered Violence'. *Sociology*, 47(6), 1,136–51.

——— (2014) 'Because They're a Couple She Should do What He Says': Justifications of Violence: Heterosexuality, Gender and Adulthood'. *Journal of Gender Studies*.

Lombard, N. and Scott, M. (2013) 'Older Women and Domestic Abuse: Where Sexism and Ageism Intersect'. In: N. Lombard and L. McMillan (eds). *Violence Against Women: Current Theory and Practice in Domestic Abuse, Sexual Violence & Exploitation*. Research Highlights in Social Work series. London: Jessica Kingsley Publications.

Lombard, N. and Whiting, N. (forthcoming 2015) 'The unique case of Scotland'. In: L. Goodmark and R. Goel (eds). *Comparative Perspectives on Domestic Violence: Lessons from Efforts Worldwide*. Oxford: Oxford University Press.

Lovenduski, J. and Randall, V. (1993) *Contemporary Feminist Politics: Women and Power in Britain*. Oxford: Oxford University Press.

Mac an Ghaill, M. (1994) *The Making of Men*. Buckingham: Open University Press.

——— (1996) 'Deconstructing Heterosexualities within School Arenas'. *Curriculum Studies*, 4(2), pp.191–209.

Mac an Ghaill, M. and Heywood, C. (2007) 'Masculinity, Homophobia, and Teaching'. In: B.B. Banks (ed.). *Gender and Education: An Encyclopaedia*. New York: Greenwood Press.

MacKinnon, C.A. (1989) *Toward a Feminist Theory of the State*. Cambridge, MA: Harvard University Press.

Madriz, E. (1997) 'Images of Criminals and Victims: A Study on Women's Fear and Social Control'. *Gender and Society*, 11(3), pp. 342–65.

Mahon, A., Glendinning, C., Clarke, K. and Craig, G. (1996) 'Researching Children: Methods and Ethics'. *Children & Society*, 10, pp. 145–54.

Mandell, N. (1991) 'The Least Adult Role in Studying Children'. In: F.C. Waksler (ed.). *Studying the Social Worlds of Children.* Basingstoke: Falmer.

Marshall, B. and Witz, A. (2004) *Engendering the Social. Feminist Encounters with Sociological Theory.* Maidenhead: Open University Press.

Mason, J. (2004) [2002] *Qualitative Researching.* London: Sage Publications.

Mauthner, M. (1997) 'Methodological Aspects of Collecting Data from Children: Lessons from Three Research Projects'. *Children & Society*, 11, pp. 16–28.

Mauthner, N. and Doucet, A. (1998) 'Reflections on a Voice Centred Relational Method Analysing Maternal and Domestic Voices'. In: J. Ribbens and R. Edwards (eds). *Feminist Dilemmas in Qualitative Research – Public Knowledge and Private Lives.* London: Sage Publications, pp. 119–46.

Mayall, B. (1994) *Children's Childhoods: Observed and Experienced.* London: Falmer Press.

——— (2000) 'Conversations with Children: Working with Genderational Issues'. In: P. Christensen and A. James (eds). *Research with Children: Perspectives and Practices.* London: Falmer Press, pp. 120–35.

Maynard, M. (1990) 'The Re-Shaping of Sociology? Trends in the Study of Gender'. *Sociology*, 24, pp. 269–90.

Maynard M. and Purvis, J. (1994) 'Doing Feminist Research'. In: M. Maynard and J. Purvis (eds). *Researching Women's Lives from a Feminist Perspective.* London: Taylor & Francis, pp. 1–27.

McCall, Leslie (2005). 'The Complexity of Intersectionality'. *Signs: Journal of Women in Culture and Society*, 30(3), pp. 1,771–800.

McCarry, M. (2003) *The Connection between Masculinity and Domestic Violence: What Young People Think.* Unpublished PhD thesis, University of Bristol.

——— (2009) 'Justifications and Contradictions: Understanding Young People's Views of Domestic Abuse'. *Men and Masculinities*, 11(3), pp.325–45.

——— (2010) 'Becoming a "Proper Man": Young People's Attitudes about interpersonal Violence and Perceptions of Gender'. *Gender and Education*, 22(1), pp. 17–30.

McFeely, C., Whiting, N., Lombard, N., Brooks, O., Burman, M. and McGowan, M. (2013) 'Domestic Abuse and Gender Inequality: An Overview of the Current Debate'. Centre for Families and Relationships, University of Edinburgh Briefing 69. http://www.crfr.ac.uk/assets/briefing-69.pdf.

McKie, L. and Hearn, J. (2004) 'Gender-Neutrality and Gender Equality: Comparing and Contrasting Policy Responses to "Domestic Violence"'. *Scottish Affairs*, 48, Summer, pp. 85–107.

McKie, L. and Lombard, N. (2005) 'Violence and Families: Boundaries, Memories and Identities'. In: S. Cunningham-Burley and L. McKie (eds). *Families in Society: Boundaries and Relationships.* Bristol: Policy Press.

McMahon, A. (1993) 'Male Readings of Feminist Theory: The Psychoanalyzation of Sexual Politics in the Masculinity Literature'. *Theory and Society*, 212(22/5), pp. 675–95.

McMillan, L. (2013) 'Sexual Victimisation: Disclosure, Responses and Impact'. In: N. Lombard and L. McMillan (eds). *Violence Against Women: Current Theory and Practice in Domestic Abuse, Sexual Violence and Exploitation*. London: Jessica Kingsley Publishers, pp. 71–86.

McMillan, L. and Thomas, M. (2009) 'Police Interviews of Rape Victims: Tensions and Contradictions'. In: M. Horvath and J. Bron (eds). *Rape: Challenging Contemporary Thinking*. Devon: Willan publishing, pp. 255–80.

McNay, L. (1999) 'Gender, Habitus and the Field: Pierre Bourdieu and the Limits of Reflexivity'. *Theory, Culture & Society*, 16(1), pp. 95–117.

McRobbie, A. (1978) 'Working Class Girls and the Culture of Femininity'. In: Women's Study Group (eds). *Women Take Issue*. London: Hutchinson.

——— (2000) *Feminism and Youth Culture*. Basingstoke: Macmillan.

Merton, R.K. (1968) *Social Theory and Social Structure*. New York: The Free Press.

Messerschmidt, J.W. 2000. 'Becoming "Real Men": Adolescent Masculinity Challenges and Sexual Violence'. *Men and Masculinities*, 2, pp. 286–307.

Mildorf, J. (2007) *Storying Domestic Violence: Constructions and Stereotypes of Abuse in the Discourse of General Practitioners*. Lincoln: University of Nebraska Press.

Miller, T. and Bell, L. (2002) 'Consenting to What! Issues of Access, Gate-Keeping and 'Informed' Consent'. In: M. Mauthner, M. Birch, J. Jessop and T. Miller (eds). *Ethics in Qualitative Research*. London: Sage Publications, pp. 53–70.

Mills, C. Wright (1959) *The Sociological Imagination*. Oxford: Oxford University Press.

Mitchell, J. (2003) *Siblings: Sex and Violence*. Cambridge: Polity Press.

Montgomery, H. (2005) 'Gendered Childhoods: A Cross Disciplinary Overview'. *Gender and Education*, 17(5), pp. 471–82.

Moran, C. (2011) *How To Be a Woman*. London: Edbury Publishing.

Morgan, D.H.J. (1992) *Discovering Men*. London: Routledge.

Morley, R. and Mullender, A. (1994) *Home Affairs Committee on Domestic Violence: Preventing Domestic violence*. Police Research Group Crime Prevention Unit Series. Paper 48. London: HMSO.

Morrow, V. (2001) '"It's Cool … 'Cos You Can't Give Us Detention and Things, Can You?!": Reflections on research with Children'. In: B. Carolin and P. Milner (eds). *Time to Listen to Children: A Handbook for Students, Professionals and Parents*. London: Routledge.

Morrow, V. and Richards, M. (1996) 'The Ethics of Social Research with Children: An Overview'. *Children & Society*, 10, pp. 90–105.

Mullender, A. (2004) *Tackling Domestic Violence: Providing Support to Children who have Witnessed Domestic Violence*. Home Office Development and Practice Report No. 33. London: Home Office.

Mullender, A., Hague, G., Imam, U., Kelly, L., Malos, E. and Regan, L. (2002) *Children's Perspectives on Domestic Violence*. London: Sage Publications.

Nayak, A. and Kehily, M. (1996) 'Playing it Straight: Masculinities Homophobia and Schooling'. *Journal of Gender Studies*, 5(2), pp. 211–30.

Nespor, J. (2000) 'Topologies of Masculinity: Gendered Spatialities of Preadolescent Boys', in N. Lesko (ed.), *Masculinity at School: Research on Men and Masculinity Series* V11. California: Sage Publications.

Newell, P. (1989) *Children are People Too*. London: Bedford Square Press.

Nowotny, H. (1994) *Time. The Modern and Postmodern Experience*. Cambridge: Polity Press.

Oakley, A. (1994) 'Women and Children First and Last: Parallels and Differences between Children's and Women's Studies'. In: B. Mayall (ed.). *Children's Childhoods: Observed and Experienced*. London: Falmer Press, pp. 13–32.

——— (1998) 'Gender, Methodology and People's Ways of Knowing: Some Problems with Feminism and the Paradigm Debate in Social Science'. *Sociology*, 32(4), pp.707–31.

——— (2004) 'Response to Quoting and counting: An Autobiographical Response to Oakley'. *Sociology*, 38(1), 191–2.

O'Donnell, M. and Sharpe, S. (2000) *Uncertain Masculinities: Youth, Ethnicity and Class in Contemporary Britain*. London: Routledge.

O'Kane, C. (2000) 'The Development of Participatory Techniques: Facilitating Children's Views about Decisions which Affect Them'. In: P. Christensen and A. James (eds). *Research with Children: Perspectives and Practices*. London: Falmer Press.

Opie, A. (1992) 'Qualitative Research, Appropriation of the "Other" and "Empowerment"'. *Feminist Review*, 40, pp. 52–69.

Paechter, C. (2006) 'Masculine femininities/feminine masculinities: Power, identities and gender'. *Gender and Education*, 18(3), pp. 253–63.

Parker, A. (1996) 'The Construction of Masculinity within Boys' Physical Education'. *Gender and Education*, 8(2), pp.141–57.

Parsons, T. (1959) 'The Social Structure of the Family'. In: R.N. Anshen (ed.). *The Family: Its Functions and Destiny*. New York: Harper & Row.

Piaget, J. (1953) *Logic and Psychology*. Manchester: Manchester University Press.

——— (1955) *The Child's Construction of Reality*. London: Routledge and Kegan Paul.

——— (1977) *The Grasp of Consciousness: Action and Concept in the Young Child*. London: Routledge and Kegan Paul.

Pleck, E. (1987) *Domestic Tyranny: The Making of Social Policy against Family Violence from Colonial Times to Present*. New York: Oxford University Press.

Prout, A. (1990) 'Re-presenting Childhood: Time and Transitions in the Study of Childhood'. In: A. James and A. Prout (eds). *Constructing and Reconstructing Childhood: Contemporary Issues in the Sociological Study of Childhood.* London: Falmer Press.

——— (2001) 'Researching Children as Social Actors: An Introduction to the Children 5–16 Research Programme'. *Children & Society*, 16(2), pp. 67–76.

Prout, A. and James, A. (1997) 'A New Paradigm for the Sociology of Childhood? Provenance, Promise and Problems'. In: A. James and A. Prout (eds). *Constructing and Reconstructing Childhood: Contemporary Issues in the Sociological Study of Childhood.* London: Falmer Press, pp. 7–34.

Punch, S. (2002) 'Youth Transitions and Interdependent Adult-child Relations in Rural Bolivia'. *Journal of Rural Studies*, 18(2), 123–33.

——— (2007) 'Negotiating Migrant Identities: Young People in Bolivia and Argentina'. *Children's Geographies*, 5(1), 95–112.

——— (2008) 'Researching Childhoods in Rural Bolivia'. In: E.K.M. Tisdall, J.M. Davis and M. Gallagher (eds). *Research with Children and Young People: Research Design, Methods and Analysis.* London: Sage Publications.

Qvortrop, J. (1994) 'Childhood Matters: An Introduction'. In: J. Qvortrup, M. Bardy, G. Sgritta and H. Wintersberger (eds). *Childhood Matters: Social Theory, Practice and Politics.* Aldershot: Avebury.

Raab, G. (2007) *Development of Instruments and Procedures for a Randomized Controlled Trial to Evaluate the Zero Tolerance Respect Package in Midlothian Primary Schools.* Edinburgh: Chief Scientist Office.

Radford, J. (1987) 'Policing Male Violence – Policing Women'. In: J. Hanmer and M. Maynard (eds). *Women, Violence and Social Control.* New Jersey: Humanities Press International.

Radford, J. and Kelly, L. (1996a) '"Nothing Really Happened": The invalidation of women's experiences of sexual violence'. In: M. Hester, L. Kelly and J. Radford (eds). *Women, Violence and Male Power.* Buckingham: Open University Press.

Radford, J. and Stanko, E. (1996b) 'Violence Against Women and Children: The Contradictions of Crime Control Under Patriarchy'. In: J. Radford, L. Kelly and M. Hester (eds). *Women, Violence and Male Power.* Buckingham: Open University Press.

Radford, L. and Hester, M. (2006) *Mothering Through Domestic Violence.* London: Jessica Kingsley.

Rae, W.A. and Fournier, C.J. (1986) 'Ethical Issues in Pediatric Research: Preserving Psychosocial Care in Scientific Inquiry'. *Children's Health Care*, 14(4), pp. 242–8.

Ray, L. (2000) 'Memory, Violence and Identity'. In: J. Eldridge, J. MacInnes, S. Scott, C. Warhurst, and A. Witz. *For Sociology: Legacies and Prospects.* York: Sociology Press.

Reay, D. (2001) '"Spice Girls", "Nice Girls", "Girlies" and "Tomboys": Gender Discourses, Girls' Cultures and Femininities in the Primary Classroom'. *Gender and Education*, 13(2), pp. 153–66.

Renold, E. (2000) '"Coming out": Gender, (hetero)Sexuality and the Primary School'. *Gender and Education*, 12(3), pp. 309–26.

——— (2005) 'Girls, Boys and Junior Sexualities: Exploring Childrens' Gender and Sexual Relations in the Primary School'. London: Routledge.

Rich, A. (1980) 'Compulsory Heterosexuality and Lesbian Existence'. *Signs*, 5, pp. 631–60.

Ringrose, J. and Renold, E. (2012) 'Teen girls, working class femininity and resistance: retheorising fantasy and desire in educational contexts of hetero-sexualised violence'. *International Journal of Inclusive Education*, 16(4), pp. 461–77.

Rix, J. (2004). 'Building on Similarity – A Whole Class Use for Simplified Language Materials'. *Westminster Studies in Education*, 27(1), pp. 57–68.

Roberts, J. and Taylor, C. (1993) 'Sexually Abused Children and Young People Speak Out'. In: L. Waterhouse (ed.) *Child Abuse and Child Abusers*. London: Jessica Kingsley.

Robinson, C. and Kellett, M. (2004) 'Power'. In: S. Fraser, V. Lewis, S. Ding, M. Kellett and C. Robinson (eds). *Doing Research with Children and Young People*. London: Sage Publications, pp. 81–96.

Robson, C. (2002). *Real World Research*. Oxford: Blackwell Publishers.

Rose, G. (1993) *Feminism and Geography*. Cambridge: Polity Press.

Rowland, R and Klein, R.D. (1990) 'Radical Feminism: Critique and Construct?' In: S. Gunew (ed.). *Feminist Knowledge: Critique and Construct*. London: Routledge, pp. 271–303.

Russell, D.E.H. (1990) *Rape in Marriage*. Bloomington: Indiana University Press.

Russell, R. and Tyler, M. (2005) 'Branding and Bricolage: Gender, Consumption and Transition'. *Childhood*, 12(2), pp. 221–37.

Schep, D. (2012). The Limits of Performativity: A Critique of Hegemony in Gender Theory. *Hypatia*, 27(4), pp. 864–80.

Schoon, I., McCulloch, A., Joshi, H., Wiggins, R.D. and Bynner, J. (2001) 'Transitions From School to Work in a Changing Social Context'. *Young*, 9, pp. 4–23.

Scott, H. (2003) 'Stranger Danger: Explaining Women's Fear of Crime'. *Western Criminology Review*, 4(3), pp. 203–14.

Scott, J. (2000) 'Children as Respondents: The Challenge for Quantitative Methods'. P. Christensen and A. James (eds). *Research with Children: Perspectives and Practices*. London: Falmer Press.

Scott, M. (2008) *Older Women and Domestic Violence: Update 2008*. Edinburgh: Centre for Research on Families and Relationships.

Scott, M., McKie, L., Morton, S., Seddon, E. and Wasoff, F. (2004) *Older Women and Domestic Violence in Scotland*. Edinburgh: Health Scotland.

Scottish Executive (2000) *National Strategy to Address Domestic Abuse in Scotland.* Edinburgh: Stationary Office.

——— (2001) *Preventing Violence Against Women: Action Across the Scottish Executive.* Edinburgh: Stationary Office.

Scottish Government Statistical Bulletin Crime and Justice Series (2013) 'Recorded crime in Scotland, 2012–13'. http://www.scotland.gov.uk/Resource/0042/00427834.pdf (Accessed 2 February 2015).

Segal. L. (ed.) (1997) *New Sexual Agendas.* London: Macmillan.

——— (2007) [1990]. *Slow motion: Changing masculinities, changing men.* London: Virago; New Brunswick, NJ: Rutgers University Press.

Sharpe, S. (1994) *Just Like A Girl, How Girls Learn To Be Women.* London: Penguin.

Sieber, J. (1993). 'The Ethics and Politics of Sensitive Research'. In: C. Renzetti and R.M. Lee. (eds). *Researching Sensitive Topics.* London: Sage Publications.

Silverman, D. (2000) [1998] *Doing Qualitative Research.* London: Sage Publications.

Skeggs, B. (1991) 'Challenging Masculinity and Using Sexuality'. *British Journal of Sociology of Education,* 12(2), pp. 127–39.

——— (1994) 'Situating the Production of Feminist Ethnography'. In: M. Maynard and J. Purvis (eds). *Researching Women's Lives.* Basingstoke: Taylor & Francis, pp.72–93.

Skelton, C. (1997) 'Primary Boys and Hegemonic Masculinities'. *British Journal of Sociology of Education,* 18(3), pp. 349–69.

Skelton, T. and Hall, E. (2001) *The Development of Gender Roles in Young Children: A Review of Policy and Literature.* Manchester: Equal Opportunities Commission.

Skinner, T., Hester, M., and Malos, E. (eds) (2005) *Researching Gender Violence: Feminist Methodology in Action.* Devon: Willan Publications.

Smart, C. (1996) 'Collusion, Collaboration and Confession: On Moving Beyond the Heterosexuality Debate'. In: D. Richardson (ed.). *Theorising Heterosexuality.* Buckingham: Open University Press.

SRA Guidelines (2003) [Online]. Available at: http://the-sra.org.uk/wp-content/uploads/ethics03.pdf (Accessed 3 February 2015).

Stainton Rogers, R. and Stainton Rogers, W. (1992) *Stories of Childhood: Shifting Agendas of Child Concern.* Hemel Hempstead: Harvester Wheatsheaf.

Stanko, E.A (1985) *Intimate Intrusions: Women's Experience of Male Violence.* London: Routledge and Kegan Paul.

——— (1990) 'When Precaution is Normal: A Feminist Critique of Crime Prevention'. In: L. Gelsthorpe and A. Morris (eds). *Feminist Perspectives in Criminology.* Buckingham: Open University Press, pp.173–83.

——— (1992) 'The Case of Fearful Women: Gender, Personal Safety and Fear of Crime'. *Women and Criminal Justice,* 4, pp. 117–35.

——— (2003) 'Conceptualising the Meaning of Violence'. In: E.A. Stanko (ed.). *The Meaning of Violence.* London: Routledge.

——— (2006) 'Theorizing About Violence Observations From the Economic and Social Research Council's Violence Research Program'. *Violence Against Women*, 12(6), pp. 543–55.

Stanley, L. and Wise, S. (1993) [1983] *Breaking Out: Feminist Consciousness and Feminist Research*. London: Routledge and Kegan Paul.

Stark, E. (2007) *Coercive Control: How Men Entrap Women in Personal Life*. Oxford: Oxford University Press.

Statistical Bulletin Crime and Justice Series: Domestic Abuse [Online]. Available at: http://www.scotland.gov.uk/Publications/2008/11/21110133/0.

Steinmetz, S.K. (1977–1978) 'The Battered Husband Syndrome'. *Journal of Interpersonal Violence*, 18, pp.1,247–70.

Stoudt, B.G. (2006) 'You're Either In or You're Out': School Violence, Peer Discipline, and the (re)Production of Hegemonic Masculinity. *Men and Masculinities*, 8, pp. 273–87.

Straus, M., Gelles, R. and Steinmetz, R. (1980) *Behind Closed Doors: Violence in the American Family*. New York: Double Day/Anchor.

Swain, J. (2003) 'How Young Schoolboys Become Somebody: The role of the Body in the Construction of Masculinity'. *British Journal of Sociology of Education*, 24(3), pp. 299–314.

——— (2004). 'The Resources and Strategies that 10-11 Year-Old Boys use to Construct Masculinities in the School Setting'. *British Educational Research Journal*, 30(1), pp. 167–85.

Sweeting H. and West P. (2003) 'Sex Differences in Health at Ages 11, 13 and 15'. *Social Science & Medicine*, 56, pp. 31–9.

Thomas, C., Beckford, V., Lowe, N. and Murch, M. (1999). *Adopted Children Speaking*. London: BAAF.

Thomas, N. and O'Kane, C. (1998) 'The Ethics of Participatory Research with Children'. *Children & Society*, 12, pp. 336–48.

——— (2000) 'Discovering what Children Think. Connections between Research and Practice'. *British Journal of Social Work*, 30(6), pp. 819–36.

Thomson, R., Henderson, S. and Holland, J. (2003) 'Making the Most of What You've Got? Resources, Values and Inequalities in Young Women's Transitions to Adulthood'. *Educational Review*, 55(1), pp. 33–46.

Thorne, B. (1987) 'Re-visioning Women and Social Change: Where Are the Children?' *Gender and Society*, 1(1), pp. 85–109.

——— (1993) *Gender Play: Boys and Girls in School*. Buckingham: Open University Press.

Thrift N.J. (1983) 'On the Determination of Social Action in Space and Time' *Environment and Planning D: Society and Space*, 1(1), pp. 23–57.

Thrift N.J. and May J. (eds) (2001) *Timespace: Geographies of Temporality*. London: Routledge.

Tisdall, K., Davis, J. and Gallagher, M. (2009) *Researching with Children and Young People: Research Design, Methods and Analysis*. London: Sage Publications.

Totten, M. (2003) 'Girlfriend Abuse as a Form of Masculinity Construction Among Violent, Marginal Male Youth'. *Men and Masculinities*, 6, pp. 70–92.

Treacher, A. (2006) 'Children's Imaginings and Narratives: Inhabiting Complexity'. *Feminist Review*, 82, pp. 96–113.

Tulle, E. (2008) *Ageing, the Body and Social Change: Running in Later Life*. Basingstoke: Hampshire: Palgrave Macmillan.

UNICEF (1997) The Progress of Nations [Online]. Available at: http://www.unicef.org/pon97/le4to48.htm.

United Nations (2006) 'Ending Violence Against Women: from words to action – Study of the Secretary-General'. http://www.un.org/womenwatch/daw/vaw/launch/english/v.a.w-exeE-use.pdf (Accessed on 2 February 2015).

Urry, J. (1996) *Consuming Places*. London: Routledge.

Valentine, G. (1992) 'Images of Danger: Women's Sources of Information About the Spatial Distribution of Male Violence'. *Area*, 24(1), pp. 22–9.

——— (2007) 'Theorising and Researching Intersectionality: A Challenge for Feminist Geography'. *Professional Geographer*, 59, pp. 10–21.

Wainwright, S. and Turner, B. (2004) 'Epiphanies of Embodiment: Injury, Identity and the Balletic Body'. *Qualitative Research*, 4, pp. 311–37.

Walby, S. (2013). 'Violence and Society: Introduction to an Emerging Field of Sociology'. *Current Sociology*, 61(2), pp. 95–111.

Walby, S. and Allen, J. (2004) 'Domestic Violence, Sexual Assault and Stalking: Findings from the British Crime Survey'. Home Office Research Study No. 276. London: Home Office.

Walby, S. and Myhill, A. (2001) 'New Survey Methodologies in Researching Violence Against Women'. *British Journal of Criminology*, 41, pp. 502–22.

Ward, L. (1997) *Seen and Heard: Involving Disabled Children and Young People in Research and Development Projects*. York: Joseph Rowntree Foundation.

Warner, M. (1991) 'Introduction: Fear of a Queer Planet'. *Social Text*, 29(4), pp. 3–17.

Watts, C. and Zimmerman, C. (2002). 'Violence against women: global scope and magnitude'. *The Lancet*, 359(9,313), 1,232–7.

Websdale, N. and Chesney-Lind, M. (1998) 'Doing Violence to Women: Research Synthesis on the Victimisation of Women', in Bowker, L.H. (ed.), *Masculinities and Violence*. Thousand Oaks/London: Sage Publications.

Williamson, E., Goodenough, T.A., Kent, J. and Ashcroft, R. (2005) 'Conducting Research with Children: The Limits of Confidentiality and Child Protection Protocols'. *Children & Society*, 19(5), pp. 397–409.

Willis, P. (1977) *Learning to Labour*. New York: Columbia University Press.

Wittig, M. (1991) *The Straight Mind and Other Essays*. New York: Harvester Wheatsheaf.

Wolfner, G.D. and Gelles, R.J. (1993) 'A Profile of Violence Toward Children: A National Study'. *Child Abuse & Neglect*, 17(2), pp. 197–212.

Women's Aid's Consultation Response (2003) *Safety and Justice, the Government Consultation Paper on Domestic Violence*. 16 July 2003 [Online]. Available at: http://www.womensaid.org.uk/domestic-violence-articles.asp?section=000 10001002200070001&itemid=1186 [Accessed 11 December 2014].

World Health Organization (2005) WHO Multi-Country Study on Women's Health and Domestic Violence Against Women: Summary Report of Initial Results on Prevalence, Health Outcomes and Women's Responses. Geneva: World Health Organization. http://www.who.int/gender/violence/who_multicountry_study/summary_report/summary_report_English2.pdf (Accessed 2 February 2015).

Yardley, L. (2000) 'Dilemmas in Qualitative Health Research'. *Psychology and Health*, 15, pp. 215–28.

Yllo, K. (1983) 'Using a Feminist Approach in Quantitative Research: A Case Study'. In: D. Finkelhor, R.J. Gelles, G.T. Hotaling, and M.A. Straus (eds). *The Dark Side of Families: Current Family Violence Research*. London: Sage Publications.

——— (1993) 'Through a Feminist Lens: Gender, Power, and Violence'. In: R.J. Gelles and D.R. Loseke (eds). *Current Controversies on Family Violence*. London: Sage Publications.

Young, I.M. (1990) *Throwing Like a Girl and other Essays in Feminist Philosophy and Social Theory*. Bloomington: Indiana University Press.

Index